BATTLE FOR
THE ENVIRONMENT

TONY ALDOUS

# Battle for the Environment

Foreword by
Dr Kenneth Mellanby

FONTANA/COLLINS

First published in Fontana 1972
Copyright © Tony Aldous 1972

Printed in Great Britain
by William Collins Sons and Co Ltd, Glasgow

# CONTENTS

## PART V. INDUSTRIAL POLLUTION
## AND OTHER KEY BATTLES

## PART VI. PLANNING AND THE PUBLIC

# ABBREVIATIONS USED IN TEXT

| | |
|---|---|
| AA | Automobile Association |
| CBA | Council for British Archaeology |
| CPRE | Council for the Protection of Rural England |
| CPRW | Council for the Protection of Rural Wales |
| dBA | decibel, Scale A |
| DIA | Design and Industries Association |
| DOE | Department of the Environment |
| GLC | Greater London Council |
| GLDP | Greater London Development Plan |
| ILA | Institute of Landscape Architects |
| ILEA | Inner London Education Authority |
| kV | kilovolt |
| LATA | London Amenity and Transport Association |
| LBA | London Boroughs Association |
| LCC | London County Council |
| LPA | local planning authority |
| MHLG | Ministry of Housing and Local Government* |
| MOT | Ministry of Transport* |
| MPBW | Ministry of Public Building and Works* |
| (*now all three merged in the DOE) | |
| PLA | Port of London Authority |
| RAC | Royal Automobile Club |
| RIBA | Royal Institute of British Architects |
| RTPI | Royal Town Planning Institute |
| TCPA | Town and Country Planning Association |
| TPI | Town Planning Institute (now RTPI) |
| SST | supersonic travel/supersonic passenger aircraft |

TO VIVIAN

# FOREWORD

*Dr Kenneth Mellanby*

The first thing that needs to be said about Tony Aldous'
book is that it is unlike any of the other volumes about
'The Environment' which have appeared in such profusion
in the last two or three years. It is positive and practical,
giving facts about our surroundings. It describes things
that have actually happened—not fantasies about the eco-
catastrophes that may possibly lie in wait for mankind. It
contains accounts of many unfortunate happenings and mistakes, but it is also refreshing to find an author willing to
give credit to the authorities when they have taken wise
and longsighted decisions.

The battle for the environment is a political battle, and
Tony Aldous deals with the politics of conservation. The
new Department of the Environment is a major ecological
factor with which we have all to deal. Its genesis is ex-
plained, and the qualities of the Secretary of State and of
his henchmen are discussed critically and sympathetically.
They are not described as crooks or as saints, but as human
beings who, so far, are given the benefit of the doubt. Mr
Peter Walker's statement that the acronym for his department, D O E, is appropriate as it is 'where the buck stops',
is not actually quoted, but it does sum up the general impression.

Many of us are still unaware of the new ministerial and
governmental set-up, and of the different responsibilities of
the various ministers and of their organisations. The clear
picture given here should prove very useful. The many case-
histories of inquiries and planning procedures as they have
affected particular localities will also prove illuminating to
students in all branches of environmental studies. I therefore warmly recommend *Battle for the Environment* as a
text to those introducing new courses, at all levels from the
sixth form even up to the post-graduate, as well as to all
those interested in practical conservation.

The vast majority of the population of Britain today lives

in our cities and towns and in their suburban surroundings. This environment has, previously, received far less attention than has the wilderness in our depopulated mountains and moorlands. Tony Aldous does much to redress the balance. His battle is, in the main, for the environment in which man actually lives.

The arch-villain is here shown to be the motor car, not so much because it fouls the air by its exhaust gases—a form of pollution often exaggerated by modern environmentalists—but because it exists in such numbers. Cars crowd our existing streets and make the journey from Downing Street to Kings Cross railway station by Mr Heath's fast limousine considerably slower than by Mr Gladstone's horse-drawn carriage. Most attempts to improve the situation by building urban motorways destroy many people's surroundings and, in the end, produce even worse traffic chaos nearer the centre of the city. The loss of fine buildings from ringroads and by-passes is irremediable. Mr Aldous supports the idea of the 'black box', which would price all but really essential traffic from city centres, and which will almost certainly be forced on us in the end— perhaps this book will help to persuade 'them' to come to this decision before it is too late.

Conservation is often seen as a device by the prosperous to maintain their privileged environment, and to prevent improvement for the mass of the population. Tony Aldous does not give any support to this view. He believes in change where it can be shown to be progress not retrogression. His attitude is summed up in the motto of the Faversham Civic Society :

> 'Cherish the past, adorn the present,
> and create for the future.'

But if we only cherish and adorn, the battle will be lost. We must create—new roads, new towns, a new countryside. But the quality of our creation is all important. I believe this book will help those who are engaged in the task of trying to create something worth cherishing by future generations.

# INTRODUCTION

In the last two or three years there has been a great explosion of popular concern about 'environment'. This in turn has spawned a huge literature about the subject. It seemed to me, however, when I considered whether to add to these outpourings, that there was a gap to be filled. Most of the books published in Britain up to that time (and since) dealt either in some detail with particular bits of 'The Environment', like marine pollution or urban conservation; or else they claimed to take a global look, but did so in such a way—for instance, by importing American examples and American assumptions—that they lacked the immediacy and immediate relevance demanded by the British reader.

Some of them seemed to me to have another failing. Because their authors or editors were committed believers in the imminence of ecological dooms of one kind or another —sometimes apparently all kinds—, they had a stridency of tone which persisted from first chapter to last, with decreasing effect. The danger here is environmental overkill: despite the truth and urgency of the message, if its expression is all 'Gloom and Doom', readers may become bored and discount it. I may believe that man is in danger of killing marine life in considerable sections of our oceans, but that should not blind me, as a professional writer, to the likelihood that calm but pointed understatement stands more chance of getting my message home than the sort of high-pitched monotone which the great, sluggish-to-rouse British public can mistake for crankishness or panic-mongering.

This book is mainly about battles for the British environment. That does not mean I am unaware of the ecological and sociological interdependence of the cabins aboard 'spaceship earth'. Rather that *Battle for the Environment* starts with the work I did in the first eighteen months in which I wrote about this subject for *The Times*. It is meant to be more than that: the specific case studies illustrate general arguments and principles, and have also suggested a number of—I hope, constructive—criticisms, and some positive suggestions for change.

It is about Britain, because I have preferred to write on what I could examine at first hand. It had a bias towards conservation and improvement of the urban environment because my work and inclinations bore it that way. The motor car, which in synopsis was to have taken one chapter, voraciously ate its way into the whole or parts of several others. But that is the nature of the beast: it takes just as much space as we give it.

Those to whom I owe thanks for material, ideas and help that have made the book what it is are too numerous to mention, even were my memory less faulty than it is. Those I must mention include, first, *The Times* (and especially Mr Michael Cudlipp and my News Editor, Mr Colin Webb) for their understanding, encouragement and support; the staff of *The Times* cuttings library, who have helped me more often than they knew; Pearce Wright, *The Times* Science Correspondent; the Civic Trust (and especially Arthur Percival); G L C and D O E press officers for their cheerfulness under a barrage of obscure queries; Michael Ellison for sight of his paper on London parks; Miss Pamela Payne for permission to quote from her Haldane Prize essay on planning inquiries and for the illumination it brought; and Colin Bonsey and Edward Holdaway for their knowledge and ideas on countryside management. Warmest thanks, too, to Francis Bennett of Fontana for his enthusiasm for and confidence in the idea of this book, and to both him and Lydia Greeves for their patience in the face of deadlines missed and papers mislaid; and to Mrs Joan Butcher who produced a fair and accurate manuscript from my original mistyped abortions. Finally, with love, gratitude and regret, to my wife Vivian, and to Simon, Kate, and Jessica, from whom work on this book stole one whole precious summer, I mean to make it up to them.

*Blackheath, September 1971.*

# PART I

# The Department of the Environment

---

*Chapter One*

## THE NEW DEPARTMENT

Britain's Environment Minister arrived on the political scene suddenly on October 27, 1970, brought into being by Mr Heath's White Paper on the Machinery of Government. The Department of the Environment over which the Secretary of State was to preside followed on November 12. In Peter Walker it had a new, young, ambitious minister whose star was clearly in the ascendant. Mr Walker, commentators remarked, came from the same kind of suburbanish, self-made middle-class background as Mr Heath. Since the politics of pollution had been looming large of late, what mainly caught their attention was the opportunity the new department gave for political advancement and headline catching. As Press and public stood blinded by this éclat, and by the arrival of the other new superminister John Davies, the real nature and significance of the ministry were to some extent overlooked.

The Department of the Environment was, in fact, a very novel creation. For the first time in England it concentrated under one minister as well as in one ministry all the statutory powers, patronage, budgetary control and political decision-making which had previously belonged to three separate and influential ministers and ministries: Transport, Public Building and Works, and Housing and Local Government. One only need look at the careers and influence of such former holders of these offices as Barbara Castle (Transport), or Robert Mellish, George Brown and Geoffrey Rippon (Works or Public Building and Works) to understand how fundamental a change this was.

*Ministers and powers*

With the creation of the D O E, came an interesting alteration in other ministers' titles. Mr John Peyton, recently appointed Minister of Transport, became Minister *for* Transport Industries; Mr Julian Amery Minister *for* Housing and Construction; and Mr Graham Page, until then Peter Walker's Minister of State, Minister *for* Local Government and Development. The significance of the 'for' in these titles was, however, to become fully apparent only with Mr Walker's own statement later that month as to how his new empire would operate.

In this statement he made clear that not only were all the statutory and financial powers, and powers of appointment to public posts, formerly enjoyed by the separate ministers now the prerogative of the Secretary of State. He also made it plain that a substantial reallocation had taken place of day-to-day responsibilities among the members of his ministerial team—which now, including parliamentary secretaries, numbered eight. The new set-up, which Mr Walker expected to need some later modification in detail, can be best shown diagramatically (Figure 1).

Thus, though John Peyton in theory ranked higher and drew a higher salary (£8,500) than the newly promoted Graham Page (only £7,625), the responsibilities of the Minister for Local Government and Development included virtually all those Mr Walker had exercised as Housing Minister plus the key sector of road planning and construction. This Mr Peyton had taken from him, with only the bizarre addition of Sport (in practice handled by a junior minister, Eldon Griffiths) to his Road Industries portfolio as consolation prize. He had had half his empire taken from him—and—some would say, the more important half.

Yet in a curious way the change failed to impinge on the public consciousness. It happened—and yet appeared not to have happened. Within the department it was the political reality. On the other hand, civil servants responsible for road planning and building continued for the most part to work south of the river at St Christopher House in Southwark, and—from a public relations point of view important—press notices about roads though now bearing a

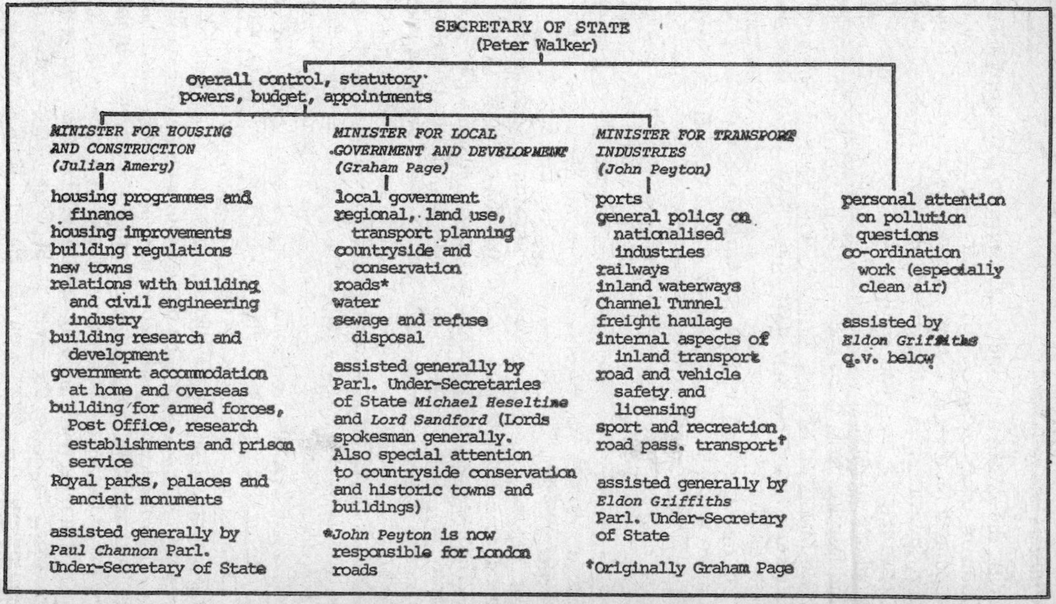

**SECRETARY OF STATE**
(Peter Walker)

overall control, statutory
powers, budget, appointments

---

*MINISTER FOR HOUSING AND CONSTRUCTION*
(Julian Amery)

housing programmes and
finance
housing improvements
building regulations
new towns
relations with building
and civil engineering
industry
building research and
development
government accommodation
at home and overseas
building for armed forces,
Post Office, research
establishments and prison
service
Royal parks, palaces and
ancient monuments

assisted generally by
*Paul Channon* Parl.
Under-Secretary of State

---

*MINISTER FOR LOCAL GOVERNMENT AND DEVELOPMENT*
(Graham Page)

local government
regional, land use,
transport planning
countryside and
conservation
roads*
water
sewage and refuse
disposal

assisted generally by
Parl. Under-Secretaries
of State *Michael Heseltine*
and *Lord Sandford* (Lords
spokesman generally).
Also special attention
to countryside conservation
and historic towns and
buildings)

*John Peyton is now
responsible for London
roads

---

*MINISTER FOR TRANSPORT INDUSTRIES*
(John Peyton)

ports
general policy on
nationalised
industries
railways
inland waterways
Channel Tunnel
freight haulage
internal aspects of
inland transport
road and vehicle
safety and
licensing
sport and recreation
road pass. transport†

assisted generally by
*Eldon Griffiths*
Parl. Under-Secretary
of State

†Originally Graham Page

---

personal attention
on pollution
questions
co-ordination
work (especially
clean air)

assisted by
*Eldon Griffiths*
g.v. below

---

FIGURE 1. Responsibilities in the D O E.

DOE heading, continued to carry the old MOT phone number.

Moreover a large part of both Press and public continued to regard Mr Peyton as Minister of Transport and to associate him with a now non-existent body, the Ministry of Transport. The DOE was sufficiently worried about its message not getting through to send out a memorandum to news editors explaining that there was no mystical trinity of ministries, only the one department. Motoring correspondents, however, in many cases continued to regard Mr Peyton as 'their minister', with Mr Page nowhere in the picture. And as late as February 1971—three months after the change—the city surveyor of one important provincial city, responsible for its roads and for close liaison with the DOE, was quite flabbergasted to be told that Mr Peyton was not the man who would decide the fate of a local trunk road proposal: it would either be Mr Page or if the particular case warranted it, Mr Walker.

## International comparisons

Nor was it readily appreciated how different the DOE set-up was from other 'Environment Ministries' abroad. The Swedish ministry, which was established rather earlier, and the French, which M Pompidou created some months later, were both very different in concept and function. The DOE is probably armed with as wide a range of powers over the environment as it is politically acceptable for a single ministry to have within a democratic, Prime-Ministerial-type parliamentary system. Neither the French Environment minister, M Robert Poujade nor, to a lesser degree, Mr Ingemund Bengtsson of Sweden (primarily an agriculture minister) enjoyed anything like this amount of actual administrative and budgetary control.

There are two views on this. Some observers have argued that the French concept of a minister who is guardian angel for environment and whose chief function is to fight for it against other cabinet ministers concerned with harmful development of one kind or another, is likely to be a more effective protection. If he dirties his hands in development, this argument seems to run, he will inevitably become tainted with it and less able to see clearly when to say no.

This view would seek to arm the minister well with powers to say 'Stop' but leave his colleagues with spending departments to say 'Go'.

And this, I think, is its weakness. Influential politicians like M Poujade and Mr Bengtsson may, where the climate is right and colleagues by inclination or from political necessity sympathetic, be able to exercise a very benevolent influence on what is and is not done, and to carry out much in the field of control and positive amelioration of certain sectors of the environment. But in the last resort, if they are not to interfere in the day-to-day running of colleagues' departments, there will be collisions at cabinet level. And by that time much work will have been done, expectations aroused, and committed positions have been taken up.

## Reasons for integration

To my mind, one of the great virtues of the D O E structure is that it seeks to synthesise the developmental and the regulatory functions of government over a wide area. The conflicts are to be resolved inside the department at an earlier stage, rather than outside it and, if need be, by political determination in the cabinet. And this arrangement is surely both more efficient and likelier to deliver the goods. A cabinet is after all less likely to give such questions adequate time and study, and more likely to consist of men who have either made up their minds or are not particularly interested and don't particularly care, than ministers within the Department of the Environment.

The taking of so many decisions within a single department, and the synthesis of developmental and regulatory functions does, however, it must be admitted, threaten to make the constitutional difficulties of a minister as judge and jury in his own cause more acute. It also places a heavier responsibility on voluntary bodies and individuals as objectors in cases where the ministry, having 'done its thing' inside, still appears to the informed or involved public to have got the answer wrong. Chapter 14 on public participation will suggest some possible means of dealing with this. In spite of such difficulties and democratic perils, however, I have become convinced that the single ministry both guiding and proposing development, and arbitrating on it, offers the best means of protecting the environment. Conservation broadly construed is, after all, not just a matter of saying no. It is at least as much a matter of saying what, where and how.

While making international comparisons, one cannot ignore government arrangements for environmental protection in the United States. There, broadly, the picture is of high-powered advisers to the President influencing government decisions and powerfully moulding public opinion. The arrangement is nearer the French model than the British D O E. In the American federal system and with the public attitude to government which exists there, there is no place for a D O E or a Peter Walker type operation.

Though many people did not appreciate how the new department would function, there was little difficulty in grasping the central fact: that planning—that is, what used to be called 'town and country planning'—had at last come under the same ultimate control as two of the activities that affected it most: roads and motor vehicles, and public building. And this delighted the conservationists. Motorways, by-passes and other trunk road building have an arguably bigger impact on both town and country, both cumulatively and in particular places, than any other activity of government. The impact of the public building agency, the old M P B W, is perhaps less obvious. For the moment suffice it to say that this agency has been responsible for the development or redevelopment of many key or sensitive town centre sites for government offices or post office buildings, and because of a hangover of the doctrine of Crown privilege they are not subject to local planning authority control in the same way as private developers. The results of their work have in some cases been regarded by local amenity groups as disastrous. So broadly the conservation lobby was pleased with the new structure, though perhaps reserving judgement on the man picked to run it.

As Mr Walker put it with considerable frankness in an open lecture at Cambridge three months after the creation of the new department, before the D O E's advent 'the administrative machinery for dealing with our environmental problems was fragmented and, due to that fragmentation, was far less effective than was necessary. There were then three separate government departments where now there is one. The Ministry of Transport was frequently in conflict with the Ministry of Housing and Local Government, and the Ministry of Public Building and Works had a certain contempt for both.'

## Politicians and conservationists

The conservation groups, hopeful that a government which bothered to give a minister the title 'environment' would also really act to protect it, were quicker than that city surveyor mentioned earlier to seize the central fact about the DOE: that all the real, ultimate power was vested in the Secretary of State. They may not have appreciated the niceties of vesting of statutory powers, but they took the main point and began to address their round robins and cris de coeur not to Messrs Amery, Page or Peyton, but to the man at the top. They were often at first extremely sceptical of the new minister's motives—'Is his concern for the environment more than political fashion?' was a question often asked, especially in Mr Walker's first months as Environment Minister—but they appreciated where the power lay.

And this basic fact is, of course, the crucial difference between the new department and the loose overlordship exercised by Anthony Crosland in the later stages of the Wilson government. It often seemed to close observers during the Crosland period that the Secretary of State did not always know what was happening in the departments over which he nominally held sway.

Fred Mulley (Transport) in many ways went on acting as an independent departmental minister, and John Silkin (MPBW) was not under his overlordship. Though Mr Crosland sought to establish an early warning system of possible environmental conflicts posed by proposed departmental action, sometimes the warning seemed to come, and come tardily, only when conservationist bodies learned what was happening and started protesting. Mr Mulley's much criticised line for the M40 motorway across the Chilterns escarpment was a case in point. The merits of the case apart, it is clear that under an integrated department the matter could and would have been handled from the start more sensitively and with more attention to the weight of conservationist opinion.

How then did a skilful and ambitious politician like Mr Crosland come to accept this ineffectual overlordship and Peter Walker to avoid it? There were, after all, enough precedents even in post-war political history as to the emptiness of such overlordships, even when their holders were influential in the Cabinet, as compared with the real political power and initiative of an important spending and executive ministry.

In fact, though this largely escaped notice as Defender of the Environment Peter Walker arrived in a flash of Heath-powered lightning, clothed in his new and shining armour, the D O E was not wholly a product of original Conservative thinking. Something very like it had been fashioned for Mr Crosland and was about to be revealed in the last days of the Labour government. But for the Conservative election victory—indeed, but for the accident of a postponed press release—Mr Crosland would have been seen wearing shining armour curiously similar to that donned by Mr Walker. What happened between June 1970 and October was that the new Prime Minister took it out, dusted it, and finally decided that, with modifications of style and build, it would fit a Conservative Walker as well as the Labour Crosland who had never got round to wearing it.

The only important respect in which the Labour plans differed from the Conservative reality was that road planning and construction would have been left as a responsibility of the minister dealing with transport industries rather than transferred to the planning minister. In this respect the advice tendered to the Tories by a high-powered working party of ex-Whitehall knights and dames, among them Sir Eric Roll and Dame Evelyn Sharp, was a better recipe for effective government than that given to Mr Wilson.

### Overall planning, overall control

One long-standing criticism of the old pre-D O E set-up—and it came not only from environment and conservationist interests, but from many professional planners—was that the planning process was split in two. Different ministers, as well as different teams of civil servants, dealt with physical planning as a whole and with what is arguably its most important single ingredient—roads. The MOT, they complained, went its own sweet way, planning and costing roads on a narrowly economic basis with too little regard paid too late to the very great impact they could have on the planning functions supervised by the Ministry of Housing and Local Government. A four-lane dual carriageway fitted into very nearly any landscape has a bigger effect in separating or severing as well as linking communities than any other common planning development. Of course MOT planners always took some account of 'environmental' factors, but generally (or so it seemed from results) in too negative a way. Their guiding principle seemed to be, 'We will avoid a solution which inflicts damage too great to be tolerated,' rather than, 'We will look for the best route environmentally considered which serves our purpose and is not excessively expensive or difficult.'

Relations between Peter Walker and the two senior ministers he 'took over' could have been more of a problem than to date they appear to have been. Both John Peyton and Julian Amery were, after all, faced with a considerable curtailment of the powers and freedom of manoeuvre they had enjoyed as departmental ministers. On the face of it, though they continued to exercise day-to-day control in their special fields, all the crucial decisions, all the potentially controversial ones, were likely to be looked after by their new master. True, the new department had a glamour, a breadth of scope, an aggregation of power and a possibility for initiative that made it a vastly more exciting place for a politician to work in. But a cynic in *realpolitik* might well have concluded that Messrs Amery and Peyton had exchanged real power for the role of advisers and administrators.

This view seems to me both jaundiced and unfair to the ministers concerned, and in any case overlooks the reality of political decision-taking before the DOE existed. Inter-departmental consultations generally ensured, for example, that the Ministry of Housing and Local Government's views were known on MOT trunk road proposals, even if those views were not often enough acted upon.

Moreover, in cases where ministers felt strongly enough, or could be persuaded by top officials who felt strongly enough, pressure could be brought to a ministerial level, and even taken to the Cabinet. The case of the Levens Park trees is one where, aided by public opinion, these processes were evidently at work. So to this extent Messrs Amery and Peyton were not, in pre-D O E days, completely masters in their own houses. What the D O E set-up does, however, is to substitute for inter-departmental consultation and occasional trials of strength a continuous process of regulation, adjustment and ministerial arbitration within a single department.

It would probably be idealistic to suppose that enthusiasm for such an improved decision-making machine alone led ministers to serve with a fair display of willingness in the Walker team. Several factors are likely to have reconciled them to their changed roles. The Prime-Ministerial art of *fait accompli*, with the more or less explicit message 'Take it or leave it' has, of course, a wonderful way of persuading ministers to accept unlikely roles. A conviction that Peter Walker's reputation was a rising one to which wagons could with advantage be hitched may also have been a factor. Moreover, the Secretary of State certainly showed considerable skill in his handling of his two colleagues. The diplomacy of takeover bids was not, after all, an entirely strange field for him.

Thus one well-tried gambit is to talk vigorously in terms which imply a collective leadership much less firmly controlled by the real master than is in reality the case. Another favourite device, both in business and politics, is to allocate glamorous, crusade-like activities with little power but plenty of opportunity for publicity.

## Relations between ministers

In one sense John Peyton lost most in the changes. Control over roads and road planning had been taken away from him and awarded to Graham Page, and he had gained a theoretical supervision over sport through the parliamentary secretary attached to him, Mr Eldon Griffiths. He therefore might have been thought most likely to display discontent with the new set-up. But Mr Peyton as an independent

Minister of Transport had not made much public impact, and had not struck political observers as one of the heavyweights in the administration created by Mr Heath in June 1970.

Julian Amery, on the other hand, had he felt ill-disposed to his new master, could have been a considerable thorn in the D O E's flesh. With a long political career, with powerful connections, including a brother-in-law, Maurice Macmillan, as chief secretary to the Treasury, and undoubted drive and ambition, Mr Amery had he felt frustrated could have presented Peter Walker with considerable problems.

Such evidence as there is suggests Mr Walker never allowed this to happen. Mr Amery quickly adopted the notion of a department run by a team, using in one of his earliest public appearances as Minister for Housing and Construction the formula 'Peter Walker and I are determined . . .' Housing, since Harold Macmillan's target-tackling spell with that portfolio in the fifties, has always had a strange attraction for would-be crusading politicians. The signs suggested that Mr Walker was letting his colleague make the running in this area for the moment, with rents policy, squatters and action on bad housing conditions as the current equivalent of Macmillan's quick-build new council homes.

### Three ministries into one

One of the difficulties of the D O E from the outset was that its staff remained of necessity scattered in three main and numerous subsidiary buildings on both sides of the river. The prospect of settling staff from all the old ministries into 2 Marsham Street, the giant block in Horseferry Road designed by the Ministry of Public Buildings and Works and long delayed by labour troubles, receded as 1971 arrived and the move was not finally completed until the late summer of that year. If ministers had continued to sit in the old buildings listening to inevitably rather sectional advice from officials still not quite attuned to the implications of integration, the hiatus could have been damaging.

A key corrective was inaugurated right from the start in the form of the Secretary of State's 9.30 a.m. ministerial meetings, for which all eight ministers including parliamentary secretaries gathered daily in Mr Walker's room at the old Ministry of Housing and Local Government in Whitehall. Apart from being valuable in their own right as an efficient device for keeping policy and its implementations unified and constantly under review, they served two further purposes. They gave substance to the notion of collective decision-taking, forming in effect Walker's mini-cabinet. And as crack-of-dawn confrontations with the reality of centralised control, they were shrewdly calculated to stiffen ministers' resistance to any narrowly departmental arguments to which they might listen on returning to their desks at St Christopher House, Southwark (the old M O T headquarters) and Lambeth Bridge House, the old Ministry of Public Building and Works' headquarters on Albert Embankment.

This is not to suggest that Graham Page was subject to no special pleading at the Ministry of Housing and Local Government. His case was, however, different in three respects. He had not tasted the joys of being master in his own house (his previous post was Minister of State to Peter Walker); he was in the same building and just along the corridor from his master; and the civil servants under his wing in that building were more apt to appear in the role of regulators or controllers of development than 'developers'.

Another corrective to any centrifugal tendency was the recruitment of a small group of officials from all three former ministries called the Project Team. Only ten in all, including typists as well as the three assistant secretaries who provided the brainpower and expertise, their job was to make the new department begin in terms of practical detail to work as one. Starting with such formal but pressing preoccupations as how many copies of the Secretary of State's official seal were needed—one for each of the three main buildings in which a sealing might have to take place—they went on to mechanics of the merger like a unified office directory and a single set of statistics and reference system.

Then came meatier matters like setting in motion preparations for a single finance and accounting system and the unified research operation. It was also judged good sense economically and administratively to have one personnel management and establishment set-up and one management services organisation; and finally a unified economic and statistical service. The project team was never concerned with policy—only with the mechanics of carrying out what was already policy. Nonetheless, without it the merger would have been slower and less thorough. And, in a way that would gladden the heart of disciples of Northcote Parkinson, after exactly five months, on March 15, 1971, having fulfilled its function, it ceased to be, its members going back—or on—to other things.

## Chapter Two

# DOE: MEN AND AIMS

*Peter Walker*

The personalities and backgrounds of Mr Walker and his ministerial team make a fascinating political study. Peter Walker, as we have seen, was a product of suburban meritocracy. Younger son of an engineering worker turned retail grocer, he grew up in a Harrow semi, as a schoolboy founded Walker's Anti-Labour league and spoke precociously from a Hyde Park Corner soap-box. He also spoke at the 1946 Conservative Party conference—he was fourteen at the time—and so impressed that respected Tory figure L. S. Amery that he was invited back to a very different family house in Eaton Square. Julian Amery by that time had already fought his first election and seemed a grown-up and glamorous figure. Now he is Walker's lieutenant.

It was on Amery senior's advice, however, that the young Walker set about, as a deliberate prelude to his political career, making himself a fortune. His parents had by this time moved to Gloucester, and his first job—in an insurance office—paid him just £1.50 a week. Perhaps even then he had an eye to the quick percentage. The story has it that, as the lad whose job it was to make tea—and buy the ingredients—he switched business to the Co-op and pocketed the 2d a week 'divi'. Be that as it may, by twenty-two he was a company director and by thirty-two had made a million or pretty near it.

His independent business career was a real rags-to-riches affair calculated to gladden all who preach the doctrine of initiative and self-help. It started with one room, a table, four chairs and borrowed capital of £200—and he chose insurance, he has said, because at the time the only man in his road with a car was an insurance man. He ended up as Jim Slater's partner and deputy chairman in the Slater Walker property and investment empire, worth when he quit it to become a minister something like £90 million.

'A hard worker, and extremely competent,' they said of him in both politics and business. But at the same time he was working hard in the political world, becoming known as a willing speaker in distant, empty provincial halls and an efficient office-holder in the Young Conservative organisation.

Yet just as that reputation for managerial 'competence' and tremendous financial success endeared him to his party, it made the conservationists highly suspicious of him when he came to ministerial office in June 1970. How could a man so dedicated to the business ethic that he had made a million possibly be in sympathy with the defence of beauty, history, tranquillity, against more materialistic forces? There was something indecent, they felt instinctively, about making that kind of money. And they waited warily for a move from Walker that would condemn him for what they already half knew him to be—a philistine.

He made the move they were waiting for when, as Minister of Housing and Local Government, he gave Whitbread permission, against the advice of his inspector, to build a brewery at Samlesbury in Lancashire: in open countryside (though not, as has often been claimed, Green Belt land) between Preston and Blackburn. There was a near-universal howl of rage from conservationists and, as far as many of them were concerned, that might have been the end of Peter Walker as a defender of environment had not the October cabinet reshuffle transformed him into something new and strange. It can be convincingly argued that they were wrong about Samlesbury from the overall planning and environment point of view, and that the only mistake Mr Walker made was in announcing the decision when he did—as a first tell-tale indication of character on which the conservationists were poised to pounce.

In any case, they had got their man wrong. There was more to him than commercial 'competence'. He had all through the years of his rapid business rise not only worked hard in party politics, but read widely and sought in other ways, as L. S. Amery had advised him, to make good the years at university which circumstances had denied him.

So while critics may be right when they complain that he

does not care too deeply about certain aspects of conservation, or is opportunist and wears his environmental heart sometimes on his sleeve, that does not make him necessarily a less effective minister or even less effective as a defender of overall environmental standards. Besides, both marriage and ministerial power have been good for him, and he has grown rapidly in stature, particularly since the D O E began. There is also the fact that Peter Walker sets out to master thoroughly and successfully whatever brief he is set, whether unit trusts or pollution control. He does so the more gladly if he thinks he is on to a winner—and in the battle for the environment, he has detected a winner.

## The other ministers

Julian Amery, as we have seen, was already established in politics while Peter Walker was still at school. The glamour of an established political name together with a certain abrasive combativeness were characteristics that early moulded his political style. The high point of his career was probably his appointment as Minister of Aviation in 1962, and though subsequent events there, including escalation of project costs and the Ferranti profits scandal, marred his two-year tenure, he seems to look back on that period with nostalgia. Mr Heath made him Minister of Public Building and Works in June 1970, only to take away his independence abruptly with the transfer of plenary powers in that and the other two D O E ministries to Mr Walker. Yet though his real political and administrative powers were in that moment much curtailed, Amery seemed to go on enjoying his new role in a characteristically swashbuckling way. It was almost as if his new master had given him tacit licence to go up and down the country making crusading speeches about homelessness while making lightning appearances among squatters and slum dwellers, or the fashionable noise about standing on one's own feet without governments bailing one out to local federations of worried or Micawberish master builders.

John Peyton, the sturdy, independently-minded M P for Yeovil, whom few outside the Commons had ever heard of when Mr Heath made him Minister of Transport in June, in truth lost far more power in the October changes than

Mr Amery. If as fully-fledged Transport minister he made little enough impact, as Minister for Transport Industries he made even less. One opinion—probably accurate enough —among civil servants in the D O E estimated that what real power was exercised under the Secretary of State by the three middle-rank ministers, was shared between Peyton, Amery and Page in the ratio 1:2:5. Page, Walker's Minister of State at Housing and Local Government, though in theory bottom in the pecking order, had the lion's share of real responsibility.

All this of course prompts the question: is there room for three ministers of cabinet rank (though not in the Cabinet) even in a super-ministry? To answer this, one has only to ask another question: had Walker become Minister of the Environment with the same responsibilities straight away after the general election, would he have had this heavy second tier? There can be little doubt he would not, for there would have been no obligation to accommodate Messrs Amery and Peyton. He would have probably coped happily with Mr Page and possibly one other as Ministers of State, with four or more parliamentary secretaries to do the political donkey work.

But in the event he did not, to borrow the jargon of the planners, start with 'a green field site'. He had to accept for the time being a couple of historical fixtures already on it.

And Graham Page—the man he would probably have had there anyway? What kind of a minister was he? At fifty-nine a relative latecomer to ministerial office, he was by training a solicitor who entered politics because, he said, it gave him more opportunity to 'get things done'—practical reforms like the Cheques Act (which abolished unnecessary endorsements and other banking rituals): the getting rid of obstructive nonsenses. And this is very much the tone he likes to convey: that of the reasonable, practical man who likes to make things work better. An obvious target was the planning system—admirable in principle, but clogged with a backlog of detail it could not cope with. He took pride in telling the Royal Town Planning Institute's 1971 conference in Edinburgh that the new system of 'structure plans' introduced in 1968 had been pushed forward so vigorously in place of old development plans that this logjam would disappear within months.

But under this rather bland, play-it-cool exterior, not-so-still waters ran rather deeper. When a local councillor from Wales at that same R T P I conference somewhat too facilely attacked planning and planners as not being concerned with people, Mr Page showed himself unexpectedly roused. Planning was nothing if not concerned with people, he retorted with anger in his voice. Its whole purpose was to serve the sum of their needs. In personal contacts, he gives the impression of being not unduly concerned with theoretical niceties, but very much concerned in his *de facto* role as *the* planning minister with catching and stamping on the odd really outrageous proposal. 'We couldn't let them get away with that,' he said of one plan, backed by an extremely powerful local authority, which would have wrecked a famous, historic vista. In that case he had got Peter Walker to use his power to 'call in' the application for public inquiry, the inspector had thoroughly damned it, and the ministers had agreed with him and turned it down. Graham Page may prefer modest but solid achievement more than grand designs which founder for want of resources or practicality; but he cares about some environmental issues more deeply than he usually chooses to reveal.

In some ways the most interesting of the four junior ministers—and the one most closely concerned with aspects of environment like urban and rural conservation, on which he reported direct to Peter Walker—was the Rev Lord Sandford. A former sailor and a great enthusiast for voluntary effort, John Sandford did not go down well with the conservation lobby after his Labour predecessor, Lord Kennet, who had been a very effective fighter of conservationist causes in Whitehall. In the urban field, Sandford lost a lot of sympathy early on because of the new government's decision not to implement the 50 per cent matching grants for restoration in historic towns which the official Preservation Policy Group under Kennet's chairmanship had recommended and Anthony Crosland as departmental minister had accepted. That decision—which I still think both a bad and a sad one—was more comprehensible in terms of Mr Walker's overall priorities, but it lost Sandford a lot of sympathy. 'He's a nice guy,' people said, 'but he can't deliver the goods as Wayland [i.e. Lord Kennet] used to.' A year later, however, one detected a change of attitude in many quarters. Sandford's sincerity, enthusiasm and hard work were more appreciated, and he did gradually seem to be 'getting some results'. Kennet, whose political aspirations had originally lain in other directions than environment, seemed in opposition to have got hooked on the subject. Within a year of the election he had accepted the chairmanships of both the Council for the Protection of Rural England and the militantly anti-motorway London Amenity and Transport Association.

## The Department's aims

The public goals which the D O E set itself were very explicitly put in the open lecture by Peter Walker at Cambridge on February 24, 1971, from which I have already quoted. He pointed out that there was a positive as well as negative, defensive side to the battle for the environment—improvement and renewal as well as preservation—and went on to list as the first priority of the new department 'the improvement of the environment for that rather large proportion of our population who suffer a bad environment at the present time. Not only is this socially and morally the correct policy for us to pursue, but it is also perhaps the most rewarding investment we can make.'

After dwelling for some time on the huge social and economic costs of having people living in slums—high sickness rate, high crime rate, loss of efficiency by the people concerned as employees and so on—the minister then went on to speak of the further problem of 'the dead hand of uniformity and monotony that weighs so heavily on large areas, particularly in the north.' He quoted the vivid description of this subtopia by Keith Waterhouse writing in the *Daily Mirror* of the 'identical High Streets, the thickets of concrete lamp-posts and sad plains of tarmac, the bowling alleys, supermarkets, car parks, Wimpy bars, Launderettes and council houses, the sports fields and oblong, single-storey factories' which followed each other in inevitable sequence, town after town.

Peter Walker wanted, he said, to counteract the spread of this 'depressing grey environment' by giving full rein, in the planning and building of new towns, to the most imaginative work of architects and town planners. 'Indeed,' he added, 'what my department is aiming for is to create a new age of elegance for the mass of the people whose surroundings have been anything but elegant during the whole of their lifetime.' That is what he regarded as the first great offensive needed under that No 1 priority of improving the environment of those with a substandard one. Offensive No 2 for the achievement of this aim was the attack on pollution. But it is interesting to note in passing that he mentioned this second, although in terms of newspaper headlines and TV coverage it had been leading the field, probably over housing conditions and certainly over the 'grey environment' syndrome. The explanation is, of course, that pollution, like squatters and evictions, is dramatic and threatening—easily focused by newspapers and television. The greyness of shabby urban and suburban living is not, though in terms of cumulative misery and of its erosive effect on the stuff of our society, its effect may well be greater. Hence the emphasis on providing a stimulating, 'elegant' environment from the start in new towns and cities.

As for the attack on a poor material environment in the towns and cities, it had early become clear that the main instrument of policy here was to be the controversial application to public sector housing of Labour's 'fair rent system', originally attacked by many Conservatives as unworkable because it depended upon an artificial concept: the assumption, never true in reality in the places where it needed to apply, that there was no imbalance of supply and demand. Peter Walker now stated that he intended to apply it to council and other public housing, the purpose clearly being a twin one: to cut the Gordian knot of conflicting rent policies and council tenants' entrenched vested interests, and to limit the rise in government subsidy to this mass tenantry, attaching the subsidy on the basis of personal need rather than to a particular unit of bricks and mortar (or, more probably, pre-cast concrete). This would simultaneously free funds for a wider assault on poor physical environment—a prime example of the D O E's wider outlook. The Labour opposition distrusted this, but more it seems because they feared the detailed application would be harsh than out of opposition to subsidies attachable to the person on the principle of 'fair rents'. Their apprehension was that, at least where both the local council and the central government were Tory, the 'fair' of fair rents would need to be very much in inverted commas.

In reality, this kindling of traditional party warfare on housing disguised a remarkable narrowing of the gap in political thinking on this issue. Robert Mellish, in his few days back in the saddle as Housing Minister before the 1970 general election ousted him, gave promise of a complete reshaping of Labour policy, with economic rents and subsidies tailored to personal need as its keynotes. On the other hand, Peter Walker showed the measure of his own thinking, if not that of all Tories, on this subject when he boldly stated in a BBC TV Panorama interview in January 1970: 'I have always felt that to talk about a free market in housing when there is any indication of a housing shortage —which there certainly is in many of the towns and cities of this country—is a policy which you can't defend.' Market rents were only meaningful when there was a power of eviction, he argued, adding: 'I have always been opposed to having the power of eviction because I think the social consequences of turning families out of their homes on to the streets so demonstrably wrong if there is no alternative for them to go to.'

In this respect, as in others, Walker the self-made man of the insurance and unit trust world was no proponent of *laisser-faire* policies in government. He said as much in a radio interview in Nicholas Taylor's *This Island Now* series later that month. Priding himself in already taking a number of decisions which had been highly unpopular with commercial and industrial interests because he felt they were right from a national point of view, he added: 'I certainly don't look on the Conservative Party as being the *laisser-faire*, free enterprise party; I look on it as a responsible party, trying to hold the balance between various interests.' A familiar enough stance, but already a number of the minister's decisions on planning and pollution points suggested that he meant to apply it pretty forcefully in practice.

Returning to his Cambridge open lecture, we find him spelling out in rather more detail his 'second great offensive' in the assault on bad environment—tackling pollution.

More of that later. But worth noting here are his references to planning control as an instrument for checking pollution, and to the Stockholm Conference of summer 1972 for which he was already making preparations.

## Making polluters pay

'The planning instrument is a very effective one in preventing pollution,' he told his Cambridge audience, and gave as an example his decision of earlier that month on effluent from a potash mine in North Yorkshire which did appear to display a new toughness towards potential industrial polluters. In effect what the minister had told the company concerned, Cleveland Potash (a joint subsidiary of ICI and the mining giant, Charter Consolidated), was: 'You say you are sure a pipeline stretching one mile out to sea will handle your effluent so that it does not make a mess of this stretch of coast. I'm not altogether sure you're right, but the only way of finding out is to test it. However, if I let you try it out, you must not regard that as meaning you can go on using it if it turns out that it doesn't work. You say you're sure it will. All right, you must be prepared to risk your money on it.' The planning permission was given for a trial period of five years on condition that if the minister decided in that period to order a stop to its use, the company could not claim compensation. This was the first substantial case in which such a condition had attached to this kind of consent. The company's undertaking not to claim compensation if ordered to cease using the effluent system was stated to be 'voluntary', but since they would not otherwise have been given permission, this voluntary character must be regarded as to some extent a technicality. They were asked to back their faith in the effluent control system working satisfactorily by shouldering the risk, and they did so reasonably cheerfully.

In that decision one detects several intertwined developments. First there is the reaction of large public companies with effluent disposal problems to the remarkable change in public expectations and standards with regard to pollution control, and the political fact that any minister was now obliged to take account of that change. Another was the arrival in a position of unprecedented political and

34

administrative power of a minister specifically charged
with the job of controlling pollution and with the weapons
to do so directly in his own hands; one, moreover, who believed that the international tide of opinion against pollution could only grow stronger and higher and therefore
concluded it was better to push British industry along faster
in this respect than they conceded was reasonable, and
that pushing them hard would prove a wise course economically in the long run. Right from the start he went
about uttering deliberately tough noises on 'Making the
polluter pay'. His decision not to sanction heavier lorries
(which he said himself under the old Ministry of Transport would probably have gone the other way) was seen as
a straw in the wind, and this early show of determination
by a minister at the beginning of a government's life must
have had a considerable psychological impact on industry's
willingness to respond.

This different international horizon has been an important factor in Peter Walker's attitude to environment
problems. Though it is unfair to compare the pre-D O E Crosland with the post-D O E Walker, there is a remarkable contrast between the Labour Government's line on car engine
pollution, which saw no good reason why we should
adopt the same stringent standards designed by the Americans to cope with Los Angeles smog, and the new government's line, which was essentially: It will pay before long
in terms of international markets to set higher standards
earlier. Perhaps Crosland found himself obliged to take this
line as part of the political horse-trading between ministers
on an environment-versus-economics basis. Certainly in
retrospect it looks an odd stance for a notably international-
ist politician to adopt. But there was a strong lobby in the
later days of the Wilson government which said: 'We
cannot allow the frills of environmental improvement, such
as relatively harmless car fumes and unspoiled national
parks, to stand too much in the way of a healthy balance
of trade.' It was on that basis that Mr Wilson's ministers
sanctioned mining in the North Yorks Moors national park.

## Preparing for the Stockholm Conference

And then there was Mr Walker's approach to the United

Nations conference on 'Problems of the Environment' in Stockholm in June 1972. While he was simply saying the nice acceptable things about the conference not being a talking shop but a spur to action, observers tended, with a cynicism born of experience, to reserve judgement. But his establishment of four working parties to prepare for the conference in February 1971 was reassuring—not so much the fact of their establishment, but its manner and the role he allocated to them. The fields covered by three of them were predictable, but the fourth, and the manner of choosing their membership, showed that the Secretary of State, even if—as some of his opponents alleged—he wore his principles on his sleeve, had a refreshingly open mind. The first three working parties were concerned with pollution, the human habitat, and natural resources, and the choice of chairmen was extremely sound: Sir Eric Ashby, already heading the Royal Commission on the subject, for pollution; Lady Dartmouth, who had succeeded as chairman of the G L C's historic buildings board in making old buildings sound more exciting to a wider public than they had been before for human habitat; and for natural resources, Ralph Verney, member of the historically famous family of Buckinghamshire Tory landowners, but a far-sighted and imaginative planner whose enthusiasm for the notion of a North Bucks city in the early sixties was a major factor in the later establishment of the new city of Milton Keynes.

The fourth chairman was in some ways the most interesting, and he reflects Walker's oft-expressed determination that, in exercising the immense powers of public appointment provided by the D O E, he wanted people— often, but not necessarily, young people—with new and valuable contributions to make in terms of ideas and sound and systematic knowledge of their fields. These he would search out, he said, rather than have officials take down, dust, and update lists of worthy county aldermen in their eighties whose contributions by way of original thinking, if any, had long since been given. The fourth working party was to be concerned with the contribution young people could make towards environmental improvement, and its chairman was a twenty-five-year-old market researcher whom Walker had met for the first time only a fortnight before. Dennis Stevenson had carried out research on such eminently qualifying subjects as the problems of old-age pensioners, living in high-rise flats and the reactions of West Indians to police. He had done community work among West Indians and lived in the West Indian area of Brixton. Like the other three chairmen he was to be completely free to pick the membership of his working party without any pressure from the minister, though like Sir Eric, Lady Dartmouth and Mr Verney he appreciated the minister's sensible suggestion that the four chairmen should leave room to add any promising men and women they discovered in the authors of memoranda submitted to them.

The minister also showed a refreshingly open attitude on the manner in which the results of his four working parties' labours were to find their way into the policy making of the department. No monumental, formal reports for him, but a continuing informal dialogue, with chairmen free to come and tell him when they thought they had anything valuable to pass on. He was, of course, careful to avoid any commitment to act on their advice—ministers always and necessarily are. But his attitude on publication of results was disarmingly permissive—they could make known particular points of current interest as they went along, and would, he hoped, have published an overall but informal report on reports at the end of the day—and this attitude suggested that he was prepared to justify himself publicly if in the end he declined to act on any substantial piece of advice given. To say that this is no more than any minister setting up such committees ought to do is quite different from saying that they always, or even usually, so cheerfully and straightforwardly accept the implications of such a course. Mr Walker added that he hoped one or more of his four chairmen would go to Stockholm with the British delegation, which he intended to lead.

All that, refreshing though it might be, may be thought of as a reflection of no more than the Walker style of doing things. What was perhaps more significant about these four Stockholm working parties was his declared reason for setting them up. He could, he told the Press in announcing his Stockholm preparations in February 1970, have simply asked for a departmental brief—dependable and predictable. But he wanted fresh thought, fresh approaches, and the involvement of outside men and women. There was an echo here of one of the questions he had been asking non-Whitehall lunch guests at informal little four-somes at his home off Smith Square, Westminster, in the weeks following the creation of the D O E. 'How and where do I find new men with fresh ideas and solutions to man bodies like new town development corporations?'*

## Walker on conservation

So much, for the moment, for Stockholm and the war on pollution. Mr Walker made that, in his Cambridge lecture, his second front or offensive in the improvement of existing bad environments. Priority No 2, he went on to say, must be 'to conserve the good and beautiful which exists within our country'. And the converse of the renewal problems of Britain's old industrial towns was, he said, that of conservation in historic towns. He then adopted a distinction culled, he said from the *Architectural Review*: 'Preservation is about buildings, conservation is about places.' It is a distinction, which, as we shall see later, has all too often been missed or lost sight of; and the result can be (and has too frequently been) that though individual buildings of great worth were saved, the character of the 'place' of which they formed the visual keys was nonetheless destroyed.

Mr Walker then went on to speak of one very common element in the destruction of 'places': traffic and the roads it runs on. Preserving historic buildings themselves by spending money on their structures was, he pointed out, only one part of conservation. You needed to safeguard their whole 'environment'. This meant, he told his approving Cambridge audience, 'not only preventing them from being knocked down for redevelopment or road widening. It means taking traffic, vibration and congestion out of narrow streets, which were never intended for it. A sound road scheme which takes the heavy traffic out of a historic high street is as much a contribution to conservation as money spent on repairing the buildings in it: indeed it may be an even better investment.' He might have taken this

* In January 1972 he appointed Dennis Stevenson Chairman of Aycliffe and Peterlee Development Corporations.

further and added that it is little use carrying out careful restoration and repair work on, say, a timbered Tudor house in a high street if heavy lorries continue to rumble past and shake it to bits again. His broad argument is hard to fault, though he had been quite heavily, and with some justice, criticised for not confirming the previous government's commitment to higher state expenditure on *preservation* grants; and sensitiveness on this point may have been one reason why he only gave the preservation side of his conservation strategy a passing mention.

In truth, of course, the two are complementary. It is not much use propping up individual buildings if their surroundings and the sense of place decay; nor, conversely, does it make sense to remove through traffic and restore a civilised, tranquil environment if insufficient funds are to hand to care for and restore the architectural set pieces or decaying townscape which is the most important ingredient of a place's character. What the minister was stressing, however, was that his new, integrated department provided for the first time an effective instrument for dealing with the problems of historic towns and villages as one. 'We can coordinate building preservation, road building, traffic management with a single aim. And the amounts of money that are being spent on the improvement of traffic conditions in historic towns are far greater than the sums ever likely to be available for preservation more narrowly construed.' So the message here was that a humane and comprehensively 'environmental' approach to the work of what had been the Ministry of Transport could do more to help old buildings and treasured places than any amount of restoration grants, and that the effect of a concerted programme of the two—even though many would say more money ought to be given in grants—had to be seen to be believed.

The second front of Mr Walker's priority No 2 was rural conservation, and this he dealt with quite briefly and in a tone which was nothing if not optimistic. He saw no unmanageable threat to the countryside from development, in the sense of building. Careful planning could take care of this, he said—a bold statement calculated to draw low whistles of incredulity both from those rural conservationists so upset by his planning consent, given while still plain Minister of Housing, to a new Whitbread brewery at Samlesbury; and from the anti-planning wing of his own party.

But of course the word planning becomes more acceptable in such circles if it is dubbed management—and it was of 'planning and management' that the minister went on to talk. Our approach to countryside problems, he said, must be 'less towards preservation in a narrow sense and more towards proper planning and management of rural resources.' This planning implied a comprehensive approach, with use of the scarce resource the countryside was now becoming written into the new local structure plans and regional planning studies. Management meant catering positively for the growth of recreational demand, often by using a 'rural resource' like a forest or a reservoir for more than one purpose, i.e. multiple recreational uses as well as the primary one of wood production or water supply. But in this lecture he showed no keen appreciation of the direness of the threats—ecological or recreational—which many people believe face the countryside, at all comparable in keenness to his concern about pollution or poor urban environment. Maybe Cambridge was simply not the right place or occasion to plunge into that particular quagmire. Perhaps simply he was anxious to press on to his peroration and the pleasures of answering questions from so unwontedly intellectual an audience. His final words to them were full of optimism and hope. Given the reformed local government system he expected to have working by 1974 to complement the reformed Whitehall structure, he saw Britain better equipped to wage an all-out offensive on pollution that would give the British cleaner air and water than any other industrial nation, and producing 'planning strategies' that could conserve our most beautiful countryside while coping with the problems of housing need and industrial growth.

And his ambition for the better Britain that would emerge: 'If in the first few years of the new department we can protect far more effectively the good that currently exists and we can remove far more speedily the squalor and the slums, the derelict land and the pollution in our rivers; if we can harness public opinion so that the demand of the manufacturer is for goods that are both clean and quiet; *if we can create a society in which the landscape architect is of as great an influence as the accountant—* then the creation of the new Department of the Environment will have been more than worthwhile.' That last 'if' is perhaps the biggest. It is certainly the most remarkable from a man who made a million, or nearly a million, in unit trusts and insurance. But just to state it is to lay an indictment against our present society, and to perceive how far short we fall of truly civilised standards.

# PART II

# Pollution by Motor Car

---

## Chapter Three

# ROADS AND TRAFFIC

*Cars pollute by mere presence*

When people talk of 'pollution' by motor vehicles, they generally think, first and foremost, of the effect of petrol and diesel fumes in the atmosphere. They may, often as an afterthought, also be concerned about noise and vibration. If they live close to an elevated motorway like London's Westway, or on a narrow stretch of high street that doubles as access road and main trunk lorry route, they are likely to be at least as concerned about these effects as about atmospheric pollution.

There is, however, a sense in which the presence of motor vehicles, by their numbers, penetration and voracious demand for space, itself constitutes a form of pollution. One of the main arguments put forward in this chapter is that this is by far the most threatening form of pollution generated by the internal combustion engine—and that it would remain so even if some quieter, non-fume-producing form of power were substituted for petrol or diesel oil.

The main reason for this belief is that pollution by motor engine is basically a technological problem. Though formidable, it is relatively specific. Public awareness of it, and agreement that it should be dealt with, already exist. Public opinion is even beginning to accept that we should be prepared to pay for it—at least in principle, if not at the petrol pump or in the higher prices for goods resulting from dearer transport.

The same changing public attitude is beginning to be true,

rather more slowly, of noise and vibration. Here however there is a great gulf between those directly affected and the mass of the public who, unless they have experienced the hell created by, for instance, heavy goods vehicles changing gear at close range, day and night, fail to appreciate what is involved. They very often, as in other areas of public concern or lack of it, protect themselves unconsciously by a cocoon of suspended belief. They fail to appreciate actively what conditions their fellow citizens are subjected to, because if they did they would either feel moved to do something about it or feel guilty because they could or would not do anything.

For that reason, paradoxically, the community owes a great debt to the G L C engineers and politicians who pushed on with building Westway, the £33 million elevated motorway, even though it was a stretch of road outdated in terms of changing road strategy and environmental standards. The row that followed its opening—when the residents of Acklam Road, only twenty or thirty feet away from this expensive new piece of urban motorway were subjected to a constant bludgeoning by traffic noise—focused public attention by T V camera, microphone and press photo on the real social cost and barbaric nature of such schemes. It did more, arguably, than seven years' reflection on Professor Colin Buchanan's epoch-making *Traffic in Towns* report to ensure that politicians would not in future be allowed so flagrantly to ignore environmental impact, and that traffic engineers would not be so blinkered by a peculiar professional 'tunnel vision' which takes account of traffic flows, construction costs and mechanics and road safety, but discourages them from thinking of the devastating social impact of their work.

This is not to argue that motorways, or even urban motorways, are always unnecessary or undesirable, but there is a strong and possibly increasing body of conservationist opinion which does hold this view, and would say of them all: 'Over my dead body.'

## The rising tide of motorisation

I think this view comes twenty years, probably fifty years, too late. The central, inescapable fact is that the motor vehicle is the most flexible, universal means of transport we have, have ever had, or are likely to have for at least some decades. It is not the most lovable, nor the most civilised. One suspects that in the twenty-first century people will look on concertina crashes on motorways, the crude juxtaposition of cars and pedestrians at zebra crossings and the subjection of road users to the vagaries of individual motorists' lapses and risk-taking as unthinkable barbarities in much the same way as our age regards the torture chamber and burning at the stake, or the black hole of Calcutta.

But, in Britain certainly, we cannot now do without this wonderful, deplorable machine. Its numbers have grown from 650,000 in 1920 to 15 million in 1970, while the numbers of private cars have risen from 187,000 to 12 million. As Table 1 shows, the growth has been most rapid in the last decade, and the greatest growth is not surprisingly in cars rather than other vehicles.

*Table 1. Increase in number of motor vehicles in Britain*

| Year | All motor vehicles | Cars |
|------|--------------------|------|
| 1920 | 650,000 | 187,000 |
| 1930 | 2,200,000 | 1,000,000 |
| 1939 | 3,100,000 | 2,000,000 |
| 1950 | 4,400,000 | 2,300,000 |
| 1960 | 9,400,000 | 5,500,000 |
| 1970 | 15,200,000 | 12,000,000 |

This growth in numbers itself, then, constitutes a gross form of pollution because we have not been able to guide and control it. Nor do you need to look to extreme cases of attempts to drive huge six-lane elevated highways through the tight-packed urban fabric of inner London to discover the damage the motor vehicles' appetite for space causes. If cars and lorries could get into towns only along expensively constructed tracks, it would be far easier, politically, to limit and control them. But their power of penetration is at once their asset and their potential for damage. In default of the Westway, they destroyed the Shepherds Bush Greens. Before the M1, they shook the hell out of Fenny

Stratford. Let us look at one or two examples of our failure to guide and control this population explosion of the internal combustion engine.

## Odiham: victim of bureaucracy

Odiham is an attractive little town in north Hampshire, with some fine Georgian and older buildings in its stylish, well-proportioned high street. But that high street is also the A287 road (see Figure 2) which is a natural route from Farnham and Aldershot toward Reading and Oxford—indeed, the natural route from south-east England to Oxford and the Midlands for the motorist who wants to avoid London's southern suburbia. Just west of the high street proper, but still very much in Odiham's built up area, the A287 meets the A32. When traffic is heavy that junction is not an easy or pleasant place, whether you are driving or going on foot.

For more than twenty years now Odiham has been asking for a by-pass. When I went there just over a year ago it had just reached the top of the Department of the Environment's priority list for by-passes in Hampshire, but this meant work starting, if they were lucky, in about 1975 with completion by perhaps 1978. All too common an experience, the cynical reader may say. But what made Odiham's case different was that it could have had its by-pass but for what one can only regard as blinkered, compartmental thinking in the then Ministry of Transport and a stubborn adherence to red tape.

For Odiham had had for some years a perfect route for that by-pass, owned by the county council, alongside the Basingstoke Canal. The building of the road there involved very little disturbance to property, and the canal route was 1½ miles long—half the length of the route through the town which it would replace. Those are rare virtues in a by-pass route.

The town's by-pass committee, started by Mr Michael Conville who lives in an attractive seventeenth-century house in the high street, was nothing if not farsighted. It knew of plans to build the M3 motorway west of the town with an interchange at Bartley Heath, little more than a

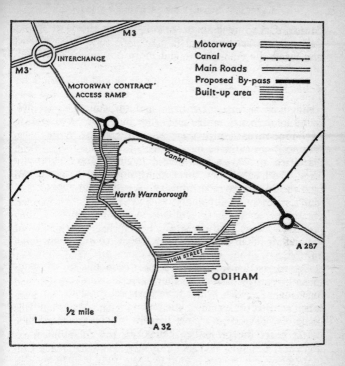

FIGURE 2. Proposed Odiham by-pass.

mile away. Traffic counts in Odiham high street showed
1,000 cars and 200 lorries an hour, and the committee feared
that Odiham would become in effect the slip road for that
interchange. So they lobbied hard, arguing that, while the
contractors had their plant and machinery a mile away
working on a £9.2 million motorway contract, they should
be hired also to use it for the £500,000 by-pass that would
take most of that traffic north of the town. They argued
this early and energetically because they had already seen
£600,000 spent at the other, eastern end of the town on a

county council road improvement whose effect, as far as Odiham was concerned, was simply to funnel lorries and cars from the A287 faster and more noisomely than ever into their beautiful and historic high street.

The county highways authority, it should in fairness be added, took their point. It wanted that by-pass. But by-passes were a ministry matter, and the county could not spend its £500,000 on one even though it was convinced of its importance. Clearly there was little point in their refraining from carrying out another improvement they *were* permitted to do even if they thought it less important. They could only lobby for a high priority to be given the by-pass in the particular ministry list which did apply.

Aware of such administrative niceties, then, the by-pass committee exerted themselves to their utmost. They preached reason to their M PS, successively Sir Eric Errington and Mr Julian Critchley. They lobbied county councillors and officials. They even got the contractor, W. C. French & Co., to say that it would be a most economic use of plant to build that by-pass while they were at work on the M3. (Of course French's would have been delighted to add 5 or 6 per cent to the value of their motorway contract, but it could also have been a good bargain for the ministry.) But no. It upset the prescribed categories and priorities. M PS argued, the county surveyor cajoled—in vain.

So cars and lorries continued to rumble bumper to bumper through Odiham, designated a conservation area by Hampshire county council; continued to shake its fine old buildings, get caught on the tight double bend at Prior's Corner, and make life difficult and dangerous for the 2,600 townsfolk and the 3,000 staff and service families at nearby R A F Odiham.

And then, in early 1971, that sixteen-mile section of the M3 did open, and Mr Conville and his friends' fears proved only too well justified. Traffic volume, noise levels and stagnation all increased even more than they had expected.

### Welshpool: a destructive 'by-pass'

Another rural case study, Welshpool on the A5 in Montgomeryshire, is described in detail in Chapter 12 for its canal and recreational implications, but is worth mentioning here for other reasons. First, it provides depressing evidence that merely to have roads and planning under a single minister and department of state (in this case, the Welsh Office) does not of itself mean avoiding thinking of projects in separate parcels—traffic solution, town development, recreational use—rather than as an integrated environmental package. Second, it teaches us to beware of the label 'by-pass' and to look at what it means in detail. In Welshpool, the Welsh Office's 'by-pass' was a road which unnecessarily cut an unoffending small town in two with a four-lane dual carriageway road. And third, it shows that the readiness of the government to sanction by-pass proposals depends on locality, and a rather artificial view of the relative importance of traffic routes.

Welshpool's need for traffic relief of its high street was certainly much less than Odiham's but, had there been no objections to the manner of 'by-passing', it would probably have been well on the way to completion by now. Admittedly, Wales is a special case: it has its own administration and its own budgets. But the provision of by-passes in England is patchy. Counties who have broadly taken pains and spent money to keep their roads of high standard sometimes suspect they are being penalised for that in cases where the environmental plight of residents, if not weight of traffic, make a by-pass urgent. And the accident of trunk road rating (the A5 through Welshpool is a trunk road, though generally not an excessively busy one) also distorts priorities.

The well-planned by-pass, then, can leave the village or smaller town like Odiham (or, for that matter, Welshpool) a better place to live in. At best it may restore it to something like its former tranquillity, and with a level of genuinely local traffic, it can often cope, for some years at least, without the irksome restrictions of double yellow lines to prevent local people from using it as the shopping and social centre it naturally is.

*Warwick: inadequately by-passed*

But the same is not necessarily or usually true of the rather larger town. Warwick, for instance, got a £3 million M O T-style by-pass in 1967, taking a great volume of traffic, which had rumbled dangerously and unpleasantly through its historic centre, away round to the west. But the respite was brief, and by mid-1970 the level of traffic through the town had built up very nearly to its immediately pre-by-pass level. There were several reasons for this. One was the growth in the total volume of traffic generally and in the West Midlands particularly. A second was that the by-pass was only a partial one. It carried north-south traffic, but not east-west traffic which had little alternative but to push through Warwick and neighbouring Leamington.

A growing proportion of it was, moreover, in some sense local, and this fact was at the centre of a running dispute between the local civic society and the county planners which was erupting when I went there to report Warwick's environmental plight for *The Times* in August of that year. The state of civic society/county planning office politics was a remarkable illustration of how such parties can have identical aims and respect each other's intentions, but disagree strongly on tactics. Both the Warwick Society and the county planning committee through their chief officer, Ronald Norris, wanted to free Warwick from the tyranny of through and heavy traffic while allowing reasonable movement for those who came there to shop or as tourists, and for the residents. But the county's plans for this were unacceptable to the society. This was because they involved demolition of valued old buildings in order to reconcile a pedestrian precinct with accessibility to a central bus station which the town council and a large body of the traders wanted; and because it involved a relief road which the society criticised as divisive and destructive of the town's social fabric and unnecessary from the point of view of strictly local traffic.

The quarrel is a familiar one. It occurs frequently in towns above a certain size, where the nature of the built-up area means either that a relief road must go wide and risk not attracting the traffic it was meant to take out of the town, or must cut into the urban fabric. If our planning and politics had already achieved for 'secondary road' building integration of roads and redevelopment through high spending on purpose-built 'environmental corridors' where insulation against noise and disturbance are built into the scheme from the start, and if the compensation code were known to be adequate, public opposition to such relief roads might often be minimal. But this is something we are only now on the point of achieving with motorways, let alone with the secondary road system. And so the difference of outlook between even the most enlightened official planners and the conservationists is magnified. The local authority planner sees more clearly the need to cater for the growing car population; the amenity society conservationists tend to say: 'Let the motorist who comes here stew in his own juice. The more you do to satisfy him, the more he demands.' And as between the car and the individual old building, they have no doubt where their loyalty lies.

There is one other aspect of the traffic situation in Warwick which is worth examining. It too concerns the effectiveness of by-passes. The long-distance lorry-driver's preference for his favourite pull-up on the narrow trunk road rather than the motorway café is legendary, though probably exaggerated. With Warwick, the planning machine failed to provide even the choice. The by-pass was built, but a surprising number of heavy lorries continued to plough brutally along the high street, shaking some of its finest old buildings including the sixteenth-century Lord Leycester's Hospital as they passed out of the town centre past the ancient West Gate. Why? Because their favourite transport café was on the old road out of town, just outside that gateway, and it scarcely made sense to their drivers to by-pass the town and then divert back to within a few hundred yards of its centre. The café owner, it appears, had wanted to resite his pull-up on the by-pass, but in planning terms he hadn't a chance. It is firm ministry policy to limit access points on by-passes for safety and traffic flow reasons, and transport cafés do not normally fit into this picture.

Leaving aside for a moment the commercial loss to the café owner, you may ask—as the Warwick Society asked —why lorries could not be kept out of the towns simply by banning them from the historic core within the old gates. The answer they got was that Warwickshire county police would find it extremely difficult to enforce such a ban. They hadn't the manpower, and on the whole the county planning committee preferred not to propose traffic regulations if there was little chance of enforcement. This seems to me to go to the heart of our attitude to motor vehicles, and as will be argued later, seems to require a new attitude of mind towards the 'freedom of the road'.

## Chapter Four

# LORRIES IN TOWNS

On this matter of environmental damage to small towns and villages with the misfortune to straddle main roads, the local amenity societies had little doubt of the culprit. It was the heavy lorry—its engine reverberating deafeningly in narrow streets, its exhaust pouring out unpleasant and sometimes harmful fumes, its wheels lumbering over pavements, and its load battering the corners of buildings on awkward turns. Two important developments on this matter followed the establishment of the D O E. First the hostile reaction of a wide range of interests consulted, from highway authorities to amenity societies, to the proposal to permit larger and heavier lorries on Britain's roads, and notably the massive indictment contained in a Civic Trust memorandum to ministers of damage done by lorries in towns and villages up and down the country. Second the D O E's decision, announced by John Peyton in November 1970, not to allow those larger and heavier lorries in spite of the road haulage industry's pressing arguments that they must have them to fit in with continental European practice.

The Civic Trust memorandum, published earlier that month, was submitted to the Department of the Environment in October 1970 in response to consultation by the then Ministry of Transport of it and other interested bodies on the proposals by lorry manufacturers for increases in maximum weight. This consultation was itself an innovation—very likely a product of the Crosland overlordship, and certainly of the growing public concern for environment which prompted it. The proposed increases were:

(a) articulated lorries: loaded weight to rise from 32 to 44 tons, length from 15 to 15½ metres;

(b) rigid lorries: loaded weight to rise from 28 to 30 tons;

(c) rigid lorry plus trailer: loaded weight to rise from 32 to 56 tons; and

(d) various, mostly smaller, increases in the loaded weight limits for smaller vehicles.

The Trust was not, of course, the only body to put in a memorandum arguing against increases, but its response is especially worth examining because it took the ministry's invitation to express a reaction as the cue for a broad survey among its 700 registered amenity societies not just on the specific proposals but on the impact of lorries on town and village environment generally.

As it pointed out to the minister, 'neither the Trust nor local amenity societies were specifically consulted about any of the other increases in the maximum permitted vehicle weights and dimensions which have been allowed since 1957, when the Trust was formed.' So they felt it legitimate to look into the actual impact of earlier changes as well as the feared and expected result of those proposed.

The ministry's original request for views, though as we have seen a welcome innovation, did not leave much time for consultation. In a letter to local societies dated 23 January 1970, they were asking for replies by February 10. A return from 300 of the 700 societies circulated was, therefore, a pretty good response rate in the circumstances, and on it the Trust was able to argue in a preliminary memorandum against the proposed changes—at least until more study had been carried out on their impact, until the stringent regulations were introduced limiting their routes and condition, and until such regulations were made capable of effective enforcement.

## Civic Trust indictment

The Civic Trust's final report was made public at a press conference early in December by its president and founder, Duncan Sandys, M P. It was largely the product of unremitting but scrupulously objective labour by one of the trust's staff, Arthur Percival, who knew from first hand of some of the problems from his home town of Faversham. The report's analysis of lorry nuisance and damage, together with a massive 325-page dossier of actual examples, opened many people's eyes to the seriousness and widespread nature of the problem.

Merely to list the forty-odd categories of nuisance used in the report to analyse incidence of damage among respondent societies is to give a glimpse of its magnitude. Societies had reported actual instances of noise nuisance, fumes nuisance, and vibration effects; of damage by direct impact to historic and other buildings, bridges, walls and fences, trees and hedges, street furniture, underground services (pipes, cables etc.), road and pavement surfaces and grass verges and banks. Under the heading 'road safety infringements' they provided instances of excessive speed, insecure loads, brake failure, power failure, steering failure or error, skidding, overturning, overloading, mounting pavements, causing danger to pedestrians and accidents generally.

The list then went on to congestion and resultant pressure for road widening, itself destructive to the environment; and ended with a list of fifteen other effects: blight; use of residential roads as short cuts; parking nuisance; need to strengthen bridges; mud-spray, dust and dirt; danger to overhead wires; damage to private roads; overtaking difficulties for other drivers; damage to watercourse banks; danger to other vehicles; pollution of watercourses, verges, etc., resulting from accidents to tankers; visual intrusion on account of size; height, resulting in expensive and/or out-of-scale bridges; vulnerability to theft of lorries left unattended; and overspill of slippery mud on roads.

Much of this, of course, could apply to motor vehicles generally. The lorry poses the conflict in a more acute form because it is out-of-scale. However carefully handled, a bull in a china shop is still likely to do more serious damage than a terrier—though both will probably be regarded as undesirable intruders by the china shop proprietor.

*Lorry damage: examples*

Many of the actual examples given in the report were horrifying both in their results and their senselessness. At Foulsham in 1968 a 15-metre lorry collided with a wall and brought it down. It fell on top of two women and a three-year-old girl and killed them. In the following year at

55

Chepstow an old lady was crushed to death against a wall by a lorry. At Leighton Buzzard also in 1969 an articulated lorry had difficulty in turning a corner. In attempting to do so, it brought down scaffolding which killed two pedestrians. These instances are cited not to make emotional impact—though that may be needed in order to focus public attention on the problems—but because they are all cases of large vehicles going where, in all good sense, they had no business to go: the bull-in-china-shop syndrome. As the local society commented of that last incident: 'This was not an "accident"—it was merely trying to take too large a vehicle through a country market town.'

But if accidents causing death and injury are too numerous from these causes, the toll of damage to buildings and physical environment is, in quantitative terms, more formidable by far.

Bewdley, Worcestershire, one of the historic towns listed by the Council for British Archæology as of special importance and also designated by the county as a conservation area, is just one example of repeated damage by direct impact. Traffic management schemes designed to ease traffic flow through its medieval streets has only, say the local civic society, worsened the problem by tempting lorries to go faster. In the three years preceding the Civic Trust report lorries crashed into ground-floor rooms of houses in the town three times, and several porticos of listed buildings were smashed repeatedly. The parish church was damaged by lorries twice in five years, once in September 1965 (stones knocked out of north wall) and once in December 1967 (articulated lorry extensively damaged northeast buttress, already smashed into by a bulldozer nine days earlier). Bewdley bridge, built by Thomas Telford in 1795-8 and notable for its three beautiful segmental arches, was damaged by traffic six times in the five years preceding the report. Finally, reported the Bewdley By-pass Committee, 'two other ancient and notable buildings have been so frequently damaged by passing trade vehicles that the owners have ceased to attempt to repair the damage.' The shell-shaped canopy over the front door of the high street house in which Stanley Baldwin lived has been continually demolished; and there was repeated damage to the canopy and drip course above Gillam's bakery. All this in just one small but precious town.

But Bewdley was by no means untypical. Stamford, Lin-colnshire, (again C B A listed and a conservation area) has had at least four listed buildings damaged by vehicle impact in recent years. Corners are especially vulnerable. As the Stamford Society pointed out in a restrainedly factual turn of phrase, 'The town is rather hilly and the damage is caused, in the main, by lorries getting out of control. This sort of incident happens about once a year. Repairs are in-variably in stone when (as is usually the case) a stone building is involved. This is expensive.' (Nor did such dam-age altogether cease when the town was by-passed.)

Two further random selections from the Civic Trust re-port's bulky appendices. In Tewkesbury two fifteenth-century cottages were in process of restoration when a lorry collided with them, apparently having skidded on a greasy road. The damage cost £1,000 to repair, but that sum scarcely takes account of the premium put on skilled and painstaking restoration work nor the discouragement to such efforts in similarly vulnerable situations. Blandford, Dorset, is a fine Georgian town, the creation mainly of two local architects, the brothers Bastard. It has many fine houses above unspoiled period shopfronts. Asleep over one of these shops one night in August 1969 were the manager of the shop, his wife and three daughters, when at 3.30 a.m. they were 'awakened by a terrific crash. The bed tipped and the windows and floor moved. I was frightened and screamed,' the eldest daughter recalled. 'After the crash there was dead silence for a few moments and then bricks started to fall, the windows shook and I could see daylight above the top of the window.'

What had happened? An articulated lorry carrying a load of bagged gravel and with a gross weight of twenty-two tons apparently skidded on the wet road. It finished up em-bedded in the ground-floor shop window, and the building had to be shored up. More than a year later the shoring still blocked half the carriageway and it had become clear that there would have to be extensive rebuilding.

And Yarm, Yorkshire: a Georgian town lying within the loop of the River Tees, on the trunk road carrying most of northbound Tees-side industrial traffic. This lorry traffic, in cluding some from engineering and chemical works, was extremely heavy; and it had all to go through the high street and over a medieval bridge, albeit widened in the early 1800s. There is no scope for diversion short of a full-scale by-pass. In 1968 and 1969 alone lorries hit and damaged that bridge seven times.

All these are cases where lorries both damaged valued old buildings and threatened life and limb. They are cases—and they can be duplicated hundreds of times all over Britain —where heavy vehicles were going where they should never be permitted. Sometimes they take a given route because as at Yarm, there is no other without a long diversion. Sometimes they go where they go to save only a minute or two, or out of lack of forethought or sheer perversity.

But sometimes it is through avoidable ignorance. Take the case quoted by the Civic Trust from that admirable but untypical London suburban weekly, the 'Ham and High' (*Hampstead and Highgate Express*). For the second time within months, it reported, a refuse contractor's lorry lay overturned in a narrow Hampstead street. It had overturned on a bend. The driver, according to the 'Ham and High', said it was the first time he had driven through Hampstead instead of via the main roads. 'I'll never do it again.' He added 'It's mad for lorries to go through there— but nobody warned me.' Quite often, then, lorries take unsuitable routes from sheer lack of any direction to the contrary.

The kinds of damage and danger cited are, one suspects, the tip of a sizable environmental iceberg. What it is harder to prove or even assess is the things people feel unable to do in their towns because of traffic danger and nuisance, the extent to which their lives are stunted by surroundings dominated by heavy traffic. Too many people never think of just going for a walk along their high street —because noise, fumes, overhanging wing mirrors from lorries, giant wheels mounting the pavements, make it unthinkable. Nor is the nervous strain of going shopping along a narrow pavement with a pram and a four-year-old in tow—because you have to go shopping and have to take the children with you—easily quantifiable. But it seems to me almost as barbaric, almost as heavy a burden on mother and children as our society allowed to be imposed since it forbade their employment underground in coal mines.

Other aspects of lorry damage are vibration and noise. There has been some tendency in the past for official experts to assert that vibration does not harm buildings. It is, indeed, difficult to establish a causal connection, but at least in the case of older buildings—certainly where the structure is a half-timbered one—the co-existence of perceived lorry vibration and structural deterioration is not just coincidence.

One theory has it that a sound building is unaffected by vibration, but that any weakness will be worsened by it. In the case of historic houses this is too nice a distinction to have any real meaning. Almost any building more than, say, 150 years old, however lovingly and carefully maintained, is likely to have weaknesses if that definition of weakness is used. And, if it is on a narrow high street used as a lorry route, it will suffer. The plain choice is: either you keep your lorries on such streets or your ancient buildings. You cannot have both at close quarters. To argue that a sound new building would not have suffered from a similar shaking is either fatuous or a piece of casuistry.

In any case, respondent societies to the Civic Trust survey believed vibration caused damage. It was both the effect feared by more societies than any other and the one of which they quoted most actual instances. But because of the difficulty of establishing cause and effect, still less legal liability, the financial hardship can be considerable. Liability for damage 'lies where it falls', and sometimes it falls on the shoulders of those least able to bear it—as a ninety-year-old Bath householder and his wife discovered. They lived in Newbridge Road, a notorious lorry route out of Bath towards Bristol. A 30-yard section of their 8-feet-high garden wall cracked badly in 1970, and the local authority called on them to repair it. The cost was estimated at something approaching £1,000. Normally in such cases the owner would be given fourteen days to carry out the work, failing which the local authority would do the work and present him with the bill. Common sense tells one that the use of a once quiet road for heavy traffic at least contributes to such damage, but even if this can be clearly established, there appears to be no easy or established means for the community to shoulder some of the cost.

## Effects of traffic noise

The effects of traffic noise on people's lives are easier to establish—though there is little more prospect of redress for those affected—and the Civic Trust appendices contained some harrowing instances. Reports of people made ill by noise, kept awake night after night, or sleeping only with the aid of drugs, came from all corners of the country. Nor are all the worst effects those of engine noise. Changing gear on hilly stretches of narrow high streets where the confined space redoubles the noise is one particularly deafening variant of this. But the rattling of the empty metal bodies of lorries was also a severe cause of complaint.

The 'iceberg' effect is probably present here too. As the secretary of the Oswestry Civic Society put it in answer to the Civic Trust survey, 'Having lived in the London urban area for many years, I can testify to the deleterious effect the present tonnage has both upon people and property. The noise can be quite intolerable, much of the "urban neuroses" being directly attributable to lack of sleep and rest because of noise.' The human animal is no doubt very adaptable, and can usually 'adjust' to shut out noise—but there is often a cost, physical or psychological, to such adjustment.

Nor should one ignore the serious secondary effect on use and value of places suffering the sustained onslaught of the heavy lorry, particularly at night. Old high streets and town centres are both very vulnerable to noise, as to other forms of lorry nuisance, and some of them are among potentially the most attractive residential and tourist areas. Traffic noise kills this. Private houses go over to commercial use or fail to command rents which will ensure their adequate maintenance; fine old market town hotels cannot let their 'best' rooms because of the rumble of the 3 a.m. lorry. Such hotels are, it is true, less economical to run than modern purpose-built affairs or out-of-town motels. But many of them could command premium rates from native travellers as well as history-conscious tourists from overseas, if they fronted on to a traffic-free or traffic-restricted town centre where restoration and repainting of attractive frontages no longer seemed a futile exercise.

## Civic Trust recommendations

The Civic Trust memorandum to the then Minister of Transport in February 1970 urged that weight of vehicles was inextricably tied up with the nature of the roads on which they operated. Compulsory routes for heavy lorries taking them clear of residential streets, town centres, conservation areas and minor rural roads, were essential for existing heavy lorries, let alone the proposed heavier ones, it said. It wanted much more careful study of such a solution before the 44-ton lorry and its brethren were considered any further. Later that year, having analysed local societies memoranda and looked at other evidence, the Trust submitted a further thirty specific recommendations. Many of these were concerned with the more effective enforcement of, or the plugging of gaps in, existing legislation. Engine noise (existing regulations largely unenforceable and very rarely enforced), body work noise, dangerous loads, vehicle maintenance, exhaust, speed limits, and drivers' hours were among them. Others called for more research—for instance, into vibration effects and the results of traffic management schemes on lorry damage and nuisance.

It is worth noting here that the Metropolitan Water Board experiences a great increase in burst mains in roads affected by traffic management schemes. They attribute this damage to faster traffic speeds and one-way flow. What damages water mains is likely also to damage other things: buildings, road surfaces, street furniture. Another recommendation called for a comprehensive totting up of lorry damage to roads, pavements and street furniture.

As for damage to individual properties, the Trust called for the establishment of a statutory duty on drivers of vehicles to report to the police accidents involving property. At present, while a driver is under an obligation to report an accident in which someone sustains cuts and bruises, he can demolish half a fifteenth-century cottage and, if he can back out and drive away quickly enough, may in practice escape liability. He is under no legal duty to report the incident. The owner's only redress is a civil action—if he can catch or trace the culprit. Of course, a duty to report does not ensure that the unscrupulous driver causing damage will report. But the establishment of a duty with penalties for non-compliance at least makes most people think twice about it. The setting up by the road haulage industry of a restitution fund for compensation to the owners of buildings damaged by hit-and-run lorries was also suggested. The industry was noticeably, if not surprisingly, slow to react to that suggestion. There were further recommendations for regulations limiting height of lorries and banning projecting wing mirrors which, in a number of cases reported by local societies, had struck pedestrians walking on pavements. And there was also one calling for noise insulation grants, similar to those given to owners and occupiers of property in the vicinity of major airports.

Next is a clutch of what one can call politico-planning recommendations. Some of them make admirable sense, and the thinking behind them may very well have begun to affect ministry decisions before the memorandum and before the creation of the D O E. In several points they were very similar to proposals being forwarded at about the same time by other amenity bodies, notably the Council for the Protection of Rural England. They amount to a case for segregation of heavy lorry traffic, prohibiting it from using the streets of historic towns, villages, shopping centres and residential areas wherever possible. In some cases the argument is that it may be possible and desirable to ban lorries even for access purposes by encouraging the establishment of interchange points where goods destined for or originating from a town centre could be transhipped to or from smaller vehicles such as vans. In the case of new warehousing and industrial developments, local planning authorities should be advised to look more carefully at the presence or absence of access routes suitable for heavy lorries when considering the planning applications.

Along with these came a couple of practical recommendations which could, if adopted, produce small but significant gains for residential areas troubled with lorries parked overnight. Establishment of official lorry parks should have high priority, it was urged, and meanwhile the ministry should ask operators to make reciprocal arrangements for parking in each other's depots. If this is ever put into practice, however, it is more likely to be because haulage interests are worried about thefts and hijacking than because of their concern for a good environment. The haulage industry lives, by and large, by quoting cut-throat competitive rates rather than by promoting for itself an image of responsible public concern.

Then the Civic Trust came out with three recommendations about electric vehicles. Briefly it wanted more spent on research, more tax discrimination to encourage the use of existing battery-powered vehicles for short-haul work; and more attention—possibly with similar fiscal encouragement—to hybrid petrol- or diesel-electric road vehicles.

Finally came a number of resolutions which together amount to a statement of the fashionable conservationist 'rail and water are better than road' philosophy. They called for the planners, again when looking at proposed industrial or warehousing development, to look carefully and give due weight to rail or canal access possibilities; wanted the government to think again about guiding more goods by rail before spending vast amounts on new roads; and pointed to the spare capacity on many inland waterways as a possible means of diverting some freight away from the roads.

These recommendations were put in restrained and tentative form as compared with those of some other bodies, whose apparent belief in rail and water as a panacea for all the ills of the internal combustion engine earns them an aura of cloud cuckoo land. (On the contrary platform, it may be noted, the Railway Conversion League's apparent belief that if you only turned nine-tenths of our railway lines into roads, most of the problems could be solved, is just a bit too high-pitched to convince realistic observers.)

## Heavier lorries: the DOE's decision

But now let us look at the D O E's reaction to the heavier lorry proposals submitted originally to the Ministry of Transport—a very different animal. On December 16, exactly a week after the publication of the Civic Trust report, Mr John Peyton, Minister for Transport Industries within Peter Walker's unified department, announced, to the consternation of vehicle manufacturers and haulage interests, that no increase was to be permitted in the existing 32-ton maximum weight for lorries. This brought home forcibly the fact that the Walker principle of 'making the polluter pay' did not apply just to things like chemical plants and factory chimneys. It was a broader proposition, and applied to them. Though, as Mr Walker said in his Cambridge open lecture in January 1971, without the D O E, this decision would probably have gone the other way.

Mr Peyton went on to say that he 'shared the concern about the effects of heavy lorries on the environment which had been expressed to him from many quarters, including not only local authorities and amenity societies but also many private individuals.' He was also tackling three kinds of quantifiable and controllable pollution by circulating new draft regulations on exhaust fumes, noise and power/weight ratios. Exhaust, he said, would be dealt with by making the appropriate British Standard on smoke control mandatory and by making it illegal to alter fuel injection equipment and engine speed governors so as to increase the amount of smoke, which is the main pollutant from diesel engines.

The proposed changes with regard to power/weight ratios of lorries were, it seems, aimed more at the nuisance of congestion than anything else—though anyone who has as a motorist got caught behind an under-powered lorry climbing a narrow hill on what passes for a trunk road is likely to take the view that low power/weight ratio also causes danger and pollution. The changes on this score do actually involve sanctioning some increase in weights in certain categories within the overall 32-ton maximum. But, as Mr Peyton pointed out, these are marginal and are designed to allow some lorries carrying a given weight to be shorter than at present. Both these changes were to come into force in April 1972. Noise control was to take a year longer—'in order to give the industries a fair chance to achieve what the minister regards as a demanding, though not unreasonable, standard.' This was a reduction in permitted engine noise by from 3 decibels—in most cases to a level of 86 dBA.

All this was admirable in intention, but sceptics observed that the main trouble about the old regulations, at any rate on exhaust fumes and noise, was not the levels prescribed (though these were certainly not exacting enough) but difficulty of enforcement and a failure to enforce them. Difficulty of enforcement seems to have been almost insuperable with the old noise standards—a negligible number of prosecutions since 1968—because controlled 'open space' conditions for applying the required test were seldom or never present in the noisiest urban situations.

Certainly there was sympathy for the inhabitants of lorry-polluted towns and villages among D O E ministers. Graham Page's twenty-two years as chairman and later treasurer of the Pedestrians' Association for Road Safety have already been mentioned. Mr Peyton, if not already sympathetic about noise, may well have become so since he moved into the M O T headquarters, St Christopher House, in Southwark. For as long ago as 1963 in his report *Traffic in Towns*, Professor Colin Buchanan gave an example of a newly completed office block where traffic-produced noise levels were well above those at which conversation can be conveniently carried out. Though the report did not say so, that office block was St Christopher House!

At the House of Commons press conference on December 6, 1970, at which the Civic Trust's president, Tory ex-minister Duncan Sandys, unveiled the damning report on lorry nuisance, he seemed to some journalists almost complacently confident that 'good sense would prevail', and that no public campaign to persuade ministers was necessary. With hindsight, it is apparent that he already knew the report's main point was to be conceded. But in welcoming the D O E's 'no' to heavier lorries when it was publicly pronounced a week later, Mr Sandys warned that this decision did nothing to relieve the tremendous environmental strains imposed by lorries of the present permitted size and weight. The Walker strategy of spending more to by-pass key towns earlier is good so far as it goes, but does not, for Mr Sandys' money, go far enough.

## Chapter Five

# PEOPLE AND CARS

*The voracious motor vehicle*

Most of the Civic Trust's recommendations designed to tame the lorry and put it firmly in its place made very good sense, and, as we have seen, the D O E grasped several of the prickliest nettles and showed an inclination to pluck out others later. Perhaps at this point, however, there is a danger of isolating the problems of the lorry from those posed by road traffic in general. Lorries are, it is true, polluters out of proportion to their numbers—by which I mean that in terms of exhaust smoke, certainly noise, certainly congestion, and damage to the environment which they penetrate, they are far greater nuisances than the private car. Moreover they are almost universally disliked—by householders, pedestrians, and other motorists. The danger is, then, that public opinion will pick on the lorry as a scapegoat for the results of its own motor-car indulgence. So we need to remember that, even if all the Civic Trust's admirable recommendations could be translated into practice by a wave of the wand, most of the problem of pollution by motor vehicle would still be with us. Imagine lorries banned from town centres and residential areas, and restricted to designated lorry routes; much of their cargo diverted to rail and canal; transhipped in any case at out-of-town entrepôts on to silent electric milk-float type or hovercushion vehicles servicing town centres. Imagine them, moreover, where they were permitted, all impeccably maintained to emit no smoke darker than the permitted shade, make no engine noise greater than 86 dBA, and not block other traffic by their sluggishness on those few stretches of narrow hill which, even in such a perfect world, we must presume still to exist.

Such a transformation, could it be achieved—and one hopes it gradually will—would bring great benefits especially to the kind of constricted town centre we have been looking at which was never meant to take such traffic and where the conflict is at its most brutal. But it would not remove all conflict between people—at home, at work, at leisure—and the motor-car. Peak hours would still amount to a messy battle between people on foot and people behind the wheel—with public transport, which ought to be the saviour of the situation, instead being martyred by it. Leisure and holiday motoring would increasingly create stagnation on out-of-town routes, to the detriment of both the pleasure seekers and business and commercial traffic— with the bus operator again having the worst of it. While in the large cities, and especially London, it is doubtful how far lorry bans and designated routes could be made to work (they could and should to a greater extent than at present), and quite unrealistic to suppose that they would make more than a comparatively small dent in the total traffic problem.

For though the lorry may be cursed and punished and put in its place, it is no more than the most virulent symptom of a disease from which we all suffer who have ever sat behind a steering wheel, or behind the man behind the wheel. We assume that the car, like the person on foot, has a presumptive right to go anywhere on public roads except where expressly and for obvious good reason banned.

## A fallacious fifth freedom

Moreover, fed by the energetic special pleading of motoring organisations, road haulage interests and the motor manu- facturers, this assumption—which was reasonable enough until the motor-car explosion began in the fifties—has tended to become elevated into a 'fifth freedom'. It bodes fair to become almost as sacred a part of the Englishman's heritage as freedom of speech. The Englishman's right to dwell unmolested in his own castle (itself in practice these days eroded by all sorts of nasty but sensible statutory powers given to gas board officials and the like) has tended to be replaced by a presumed right to drive the family 1100 or Cortina Estate broadly wherever he likes, whenever he likes.

Now it can be argued on a philosophical level that rights or freedoms of this kind must always be subject to the overriding consideration that, in their exercise, one is not permitted seriously to damage the rights of other citizens.

Or at least not to any unreasonable extent. The lack of specific remedies on the part of the householder whose environment is impaired by growth of motor traffic does not destroy this principle, any more than a no-entry sign at the head of a one-way street destroys the supposed principle of freedom to drive where you please.

The growth of personal mobility for the man in the street is, I think, even over and above its commercial benefits, the greatest social benefit the motor-car has brought. The metaphor of the car as the Englishman's travelling castle is not a chance one. For many families the car is an extension of the home, an extra room with the magic carpet quality of being able to release them from the drabness of the back-to-back terrace house or the desert of 'prairie planning' which edge-of-town municipal housing estates so often become. It is usually a very much more convenient way, in the present state of public transport, for Dad, Mum and their notional $2\frac{1}{2}$ children to get to most holiday destinations. They go from door to door, without having to bother about timetables, getting push-chairs and baby luggage on and off buses which may be late or over-crowded, the strain and tedium of Saturday holiday queues at mainline stations, or doubts about getting a bus or taxi at the other end. And, in terms of *cash paid out at the time of travel*, an appreciably cheaper way. Though, as we shall see, that is very different from overall cheapness.

As to commercial road traffic, the use of the lorry has grown because of a similar ability to do the whole removal job, from door to door, without the transhipment involved in rail or water transit. But, as we have seen, the similarity breaks down when one looks at more than the crude mechanical feasibility of door-to-door operations, and begins to pose a slightly different proposition. Not the engineer's question: Can this object physically be moved from A to B by this means? but the social and political question: Can it be moved *acceptably* from A to B by this means? And just as mechanical engineers generally, as a profession, have been slow to build in ergonomics (the science of building machines to suit human beings) into the creative stages of their technology, so broadly have civil engineers, in town halls as in ministries and elsewhere, been slow to take into account a broader, bigger kind of ergonomics:

the science and art of recasting our towns and cities to fit
the human beings who live and work in them, rather than
to suit individual and pressing functional needs—like
remedying a road bottleneck between Knightsbridge and
Hyde Park Corner. Still, all this said, the motor vehicle—
private and commercial—constitutes one of our twentieth-
century society's biggest boons. What we need (*pace* my
friend Terence Bendixson, who has been writing a book
called *Can We Kill the Motor Car?*) is not to kill the beast,
but tame it. Tame it, I would say, by creating a new fiscal,
social and psychological framework for its use.

## Changing motoring economics

I put fiscal first because this seems to me the *sine qua non*
of changed attitudes to motor-car use. The private motorist
has been continually barraged in recent years by propaganda from the A A and the R A C to convince him that he is
over-taxed. He is invited to reduce his rear window visibility
with a little sticker saying 'Cut motor taxes'. In fact a little
more thought ought to convince him that, at least in his
own selfish interests, he should want them kept at their
present level. A lower vehicle tax, for instance, would tend
to bring more cars on to his overcrowded roads more
quickly, while in political reality leaving less money for
their improvement.

But this argument really misses the central point about
present motor taxation—that it is its nature rather than its
level which needs changing. Take our notional private
motorist with his wife and statistical 2½ children. He
probably does not find it all that easy to produce an annual
lump sum of £25 for his five-year-old Morris 1100. If he is a
prodigal fellow, this may constitute an annual financial
crisis ending in a pencilled note on his windscreen hopefully
informing the authorities 'Tax in post'. If he is a prudent,
careful chap, he may have made some minor, planned sacri-
fices to pay, not just for the car, but its regular upkeep,
depreciation, insurance and—imposed on top of all these
necessaries—tax.

The case of the citizen who finds car ownership a strain
is posed here because he is, broadly, the new motorist who
is adding to the car population. But my main psychological

proposition is almost certainly true of other and better-heeled motorists. It is that, once the car owner has paid the overheads on his car, his instinct will be to use it in order to spread those overheads. And in marginal cases where the vehicle tax has had to be scraped together it may sometimes actually preclude any course other than intensive use. The tax may have taken the money he might have spent on a rail season ticket.

How do you counteract this present fiscal invitation to car owners to use their cars as much as they can? One simple way would be to transfer the weight of motor taxation from the lump sum vehicle excise licence to fuel tax. Then for every mile he drove—and especially for every mile in congested conditions—the car owner would be paying, and be aware that he was paying, a premium rate. This device has the virtue of simplicity, but there are at least two serious objections apart from the political resistance which would come probably from motoring interests and certainly from oil interests.

The first objection is that to make motor taxation take the form of a tax on mileage rather than on vehicle ownership would be inequitable. It would hit the ordinary family motorist harder than it would the owner of the Rolls or the driver of a company car, even assuming that the 'ordinary' motorist is driving a car which gives him a high mileage per gallon. More important, it would fall as heavily on the man in a country district, who has no real alternative to running his own motor vehicle, as on the suburban commuter who might travel by train or bus, and should be encouraged to do so. This would still be true even after allowing for relative lack of congestion in country districts.

The second objection is that such a tax would probably not work as intended. Suppose vehicle tax were reduced to a nominal level, and petrol duty doubled, what would be the likely effect? The reduced vehicle tax would probably boost car sales a little, but the higher fuel duty would simply provoke resentment without very much restraining the use of these newly-bought cars. It would certainly cause resentment from the vast majority of car owners who had to suffer the higher fuel duty without immediately benefiting from the cut in vehicle tax. Two points stand out here as especially significant: once you have a car, you tend to use it; and the vehicle tax, while most motorists appear to believe it is too heavy, is still a relatively small factor in the total cost of running the normal car.

## The 'black box' solution

A more radical and possibly more effective way of recasting the motor taxation set-up would be to cut both vehicle tax and purchase tax substantially, while raising fuel tax to discourage mileage. But even if it were politically feasible, either from an electoral point of view or with the intended adoption of value-added tax, the same two objections would to a large degree still hold good.

How, then, can we impose a premium on use of motor vehicles at congested times and in congested areas? Two main types of solution have been proposed: the blunt instrument of restraint imposed by making it difficult and expensive to stop or park on arrival; and the 'metered use' or 'black-box' answer examined, in some detail, with other solutions, in the Smeed Report of 1964.

There is little doubt that the 'blunt instrument' approach, which—in so far as they attempt to restrain car volumes in their cities—is the mainstay of most local authority planners today, does broadly work. Traffic flows, like water, or even quicksilver, run where there is room for them, and when there is no more room, draw back. There are at least two disadvantages to this approach, however.

The first is that the motoring community—and more important, the communities through which their vehicles pass —have to tolerate a continuous and continuing state of congestion or near congestion in peak hours. As far as the communities through which the roads run are concerned, this makes for 'bad environment', while in the motorist it induces bad temper, frustration, accident proneness (especially on release from a jam) and political pressure for more road space. So, politically, it is counterproductive. The motorist has chosen to drive that way, feels he has a right to go that way, and resents being impeded.

The 'black box' solution avoids this crucial friction element. The motorist, at least if he wishes to use his car regularly in a congested conurbation, has a sealed meter fitted into his car which is activated by impulse from cables buried in the road. These would vary from very frequent in the city centre to non-existent on quiet rural roads, and could be variable in the sense that extra impulses could be set off by a time clock in busy periods or even automatically as traffic built up, there or some distance away. The meter would, by this means, tot up a 'congestion tax' of whose individual, almost minute-by-minute constituents the motorist would, or could, be aware. The choice of whether to use his car or not, and which route to take, would then be his; it would in principle be a rational one; and the price he paid would—like other items in his car budget—be, in a sense, self-imposed.

## The persecuted motorist fallacy

This question of true choice is, I think, crucial. And it goes to the heart of the sham world in which the motorist, as a motorist, has come to live. First of all, in Britain, he inherits in greater or lesser measure something of the ethos of those early twentieth-century days of the pioneering motorist. From the days of green flags carried on foot in front of cars to restrict their speed, and of A A patrols not saluting when a police speed trap was operating, came a sense of injustice at the hands of government. It all became a battle for the rights of the oppressed motorist, and this is still reflected in the public attitude and statements of both the A A and the R A C. (The other—and much less often expressed— side of the argument is, of course, that in many ways the motorist is an extraordinarily privileged creature and it is the people whose living conditions and journeys to work by public transport he ruins who are the true oppressed and victimised classes. That view is no more extreme than the customary motoring lobby one.)

But more to the point in the present context are the economic shams. The buyer of a car is given the impression that, in buying vehicle, insurance and tax disc, he is buying the right to drive it anywhere he chooses, by any route and at any time he chooses. He also usually tends to assume that he may drive at any speed that seems to him safe, even if illegal, if there are no policemen too obviously looking for speed limit infringements. None of these assumptions really stands up in our modern urban society, because the mass pursuit of such supposed rights is (*a*) increasingly not possible in certain circumstances (like peak hours on radial routes into a large city) and (*b*) an act of collective selfishness which hurts other sections of the community. The false assumption, albeit a tacit one, which many motorists make is that, in paying their vehicle and fuel taxes, they 'commute' (in the true sense of the word) the damage they do to the community. There is no real justification for this assumption. What we need to do is to relate the cost of vehicle use to damage caused by individual journeys at particular times of day and week—and this the Smeed 'black box' would do admirably. In contrast to the 'blunt instrument' of parking restraint, which lets the motorist in, but makes life very difficult for him on the way and when he gets there, the black box metering system is a 'fine instrument' with an almost infinitely variable disincentive which can be linked not only to congestion but to an index of relative environmental damage. Like most fine instruments, however, it is not cheap.

## Problems of traffic control

Before looking at the black box's cost and disadvantages, however, let us examine another aspect of motorist/authority friction: speed and other traffic restrictions. It is worthwhile to do so because they are a potent and growing source of environmental damage. Motorists who drive—as most of us do at least occasionally—at 40 m.p.h. through a 30 m.p.h. residential area, are damaging the residents' environment. So is the driver who turns right at a banned right-turn sign designed to exclude or minimise traffic. It seems to me there are two common factors in such situations: poor communication; and artificiality in the message authority intends to communicate.

Take artificiality first. Consider the dual two-lane road running out through the suburbs of almost any large British city. It often has a 30 m.p.h. limit on it, justified by ribbon residential development on either side. Perhaps it bisects a cohesive community, and children and shoppers need to cross it continually. But 30 m.p.h. for a two-lane, one-way carriageway is artificial and absurd to the man behind the wheel, so he drives at 40 m.p.h. or more. Perhaps there is little you can do immediately about that situation. The homes and the road should not be together. But its lesson is clear. It is futile for the government to provide a road whose design standards encourage traffic to travel at one speed, and then seek to mitigate the damage by imposing a lower speed limit.

The motorist's subconscious reaction, is, it seems : 'This is a blanket, overall rule. It cannot sensibly apply to my particular circumstances at this particular time' (as clearly it doesn't at half-past midnight on a clear dry night with no pedestrians about). The motorist's completely understandable failure to reconcile the general rule with his own case has brought speed limits into disrepute, so that now we have reached the state, at least in the Greater London area, where there is a recognised 'tolerance' of about 8-10 m.p.h. in which the police rarely prosecute for breach of speed limits. Indeed traffic flows have become so geared to this, that if a serious attempt at enforcement were made, London's road traffic would probably grind to a halt.

One device which has been little resorted to in Britain but which could, at least on congested main roads, help to restore credibility to speed limits and raise the motorists respect for them, is the continental practice of variable light signals. Placed at intervals along a road, these can be designed to let him drive fast when the road is clear, changing to progressively lower speeds at the approach to congestion or to a traffic light which has changed or is changing to red. The motorist quickly comes to appreciate that these signals are meaningful in the particular, current road situation. With the growing computerisation of traffic lights in our larger cities, there would seem to be an opportunity here to build variable speed limits into the system.

A prime example of motorists' failure to comply with a different kind of traffic sign—both because of poor communication and artificiality—was brought to my attention early in 1971 by a colleague, George Jones of *The Times* parliamentary staff, who lived in Gloucester Terrace, Paddington. Indirectly the G L C's Westway elevated motorway was again the villain of the piece. When Westway was about to be opened, it became apparent that, at least for an interim period, Gloucester Terrace, still a pleasant and quite stylish residential street, would become in effect a slip road for northbound traffic seeking to get on to the motorway. Residents and others protested, and the G L C, while arguing that this was only a temporary route, agreed to cut Gloucester Terrace half way along with a 'partial no entry sign' which would apply for twenty hours a day though traffic would be permitted to pass it during the peak hours 8 a.m. to 10 a.m. and 4.30 p.m. to 6.30 p.m. The theory was that as long as the interim traffic scheme continued, through traffic would be kept out of Gloucester Terrace except in rush hours. But in a thirty-minute period on a weekday morning when the ban in law applied, I counted fifty-two vehicles illegally passing the no-entry sign and only five turning off (though they were not necessarily doing so because of the sign).

The faults of the Gloucester Terrace situation were threefold: the partial no-entry ban probably seemed a highly artificial nonsense to many of the motorists who understood it; the no-entry signs put up there were inadequate and impossible to read and take in at the speed at which most motorists were likely to approach them; and they were not effectively enforced. (The Metropolitan Police gave this an understandably low priority among competing claims for its time and attention. Individual police officers probably also considered it a nonsense, though since it remained their duty to enforce, they would obviously not say so publicly.)

This particular case also highlights the importance of clear communication. It is doubtful whether the Gloucester Terrace no-entry signs would have been disregarded anything like as flagrantly as they were had they not been a plain, unilluminated disc with exception plates in fairly small letters below. The G L C in reply to criticism said they were waiting for illuminated no-entry signs which were on order but had long delivery times. It is at least arguable that, when the credibility of a traffic regulation is involved, means should be found to delay the coming into force of the regulation until all the hardware is installed and ready to switch on or be uncovered.

A more effective way of signposting that partial no-entry ban would have been to instal, at the junction and on its approaches, signs which lit up—either by time-clock or manual operation—when actually in force. Other variants or additions could have been red traffic-light type stop-lights switched on during the periods when entry was banned, and/or green diversion arrows. This kind of signposting is clear, meaningful and credible in the sense that the motorist, knowing it is geared to specific circumstances of time and place, is likely to react instinctively to it—rather than hesitate and then drive on. Had some well thought out combination of advance illuminated warning signs and time-varied diversion signs operated at Gloucester Terrace from the outset, it seems very unlikely that more than a small fraction of drivers would have ignored the ban.

This kind of case is really part of the broader argument that physical road conditions should assist traffic regulation rather than running counter to it. Some planners and engineers indeed argue that physical constraints are very much more effective than signs commanding or exhorting. The city planning officer of Norwich, Alfred Wood, a pioneer of pedestrian streets and the art of keeping the car in its place, argues that one 'sleeping policeman'—a ramp or corrugation in the road surface—will do more to keep vehicles down to a reasonable speed than a whole battery of legal regulations backed by penalties but not credible because unlikely to be enforced.

This is a problem which should be tackled urgently, because devices to exclude through traffic from residential neighbourhoods are now being increasingly tried out by local authorities. It would have an extremely unfortunate effect on progress in this direction, as well as on the credibility of traffic regulations and on road safety, if the only result of a proliferation of no-entry signs over the urban or suburban townscape were to be mass disregard for them by puzzled or irate motorists. There are other and better methods of keeping the car in its place.

The basic 'philosophy' underlying this chapter, then, is that we have to find ways of persuading the individual motorist to do what is right by the community, rather than exhort, command and indict in a vacuum of generalised propositions which appear to apply less and less to the individual man or woman at the wheel reacting swiftly to individual situations. In order to restore a meaningful connection between law and policy and the individual motorist, we need better communication—whether in road direction signs, traffic signals or advance warning of traffic chaos and congestion; and an effective stick-and-carrot device (whether black box or something else) which puts a premium for the individual vehicle owner on what, collectively, amounts to anti-social behaviour.

The black box solution might have to apply just to the half-dozen largest conurbations where both traffic pressures and the cost of road works needed to remedy them are out of proportion higher than the environmental cost. If this were the case, then occasional visitors could be charged a flat fee per day (a combination of colour coding and the technology of built-in decay should be able to produce a limited-life sticker to aid policing).

There is an argument (as often advanced by those from the provinces as by Londoners) that the problems of the capital are, at least as far as traffic congestion is concerned, different in kind, not just in degree, from those of other British conurbations. There is an element of truth in this. and, partly for that reason, I leave further discusion of the London problem to the next chapter.

# PART III

# Battle for London

---

*Chapter Six*

## CHANGING LONDON

*The growth of London*

If William Dunbar, who thought fifteenth-century London 'the flower of cities all', were brought back to life and to the capital and commissioned to do a reassessment of his poetic judgement, he would have to take account not only of a transformed capital city, but of the whole nature of cities. And the most radical rethinking would be occasioned by the changes of only the last seventy years.

The London that Dunbar knew was a city of a few thousand people, stretching from Ludgate in the west to the Tower in the east, with a quite separate settlement gathered round the centre of royal administration at Westminster and a tendency for noble lords to build grand houses (any other nation would call them palaces) in the stretch of country between. Covent Garden really was a garden, Clerkenwell and Shoreditch still villages on the fringe of the built-up area.

By the beginning of the nineteenth century London's built-up area had spread from these twin centres a distance of not much more than a mile and a half, including a broad semi-circle round its southern bridgehead at Southwark. Marylebone, Clerkenwell, the Sloane Street area were in, and Newington to the south. But Islington, Kennington, Bethnal Green and Paddington were still villages—London-orientated, but distinct, with their own agricultural and commercial life and a population whose existence was geared to London's, though they were not of it.

It was for the Victorians to give the boundaries of London their great push outwards, building early on, incidentally, its first planned major by-pass, which they called simply 'the New Road'. Planners today think of it as the northern boundary of what they call 'Central London'. It is, as Marylebone Road/Euston Road/City Road, one of the major in-town traffic routes. By midway in the century, the first census showed London's population, within what was later to become the County of London, as over 2.3 million. Fifty years later it was 4.5 million. Then it fell again as the spread of public transport—electric tram, bus, and especially underground and suburban railway—gave the urban millions their chance of the better environment: the suburban semi with its own garden, apparently with unspoiled English countryside on their doorstep. That dream proved a mirage for most of them, but at least they were no longer packed in in squalid conditions at densities of 150-200 people an acre.

The purpose of this oversimplified sketch of London's history is to show how two big changes occurred, and to distinguish between them. First, as we have seen, came the spread of the metropolis, caused by exploding population, greater mobility (supplied by mass public transport) and a certain spread of prosperity which allowed the lower middle and artisan classes to live at some distance from their work.

But the point to be borne in mind about this is that people still did live in the middle of London, either because they chose to or because they had no choice in the matter. Even the City in the early 1900s had some 27,000 people living within it. By the 1960s its resident population was not much more than 4,000—largely caretakers of great office blocks or of livery halls, plus a few dedicated eccentrics like Sir John Betjeman. No one lived over the shop any more. City merchants—and they scarcely called themselves that any more—were driven in their Rolls from Virginia Water and the Surrey Hills. And this seems to me to point to a second, and one suspects more significant change: dissociation.

## Commuter city

When the first city merchant to do so took his family without the walls to a mansion among the green fields of Holborn or Whitechapel, his involvement in the then London of the Square Mile was in some degree lessened, even if he walked through its streets each morning to reach his business. But in a socially mobile society, it is arguable that for any outward-looking mercantile community with aspirations for its progeny, something of the sort was bound to happen. Indeed, if you wanted to have progeny at all, it was sensible to get the family away from the plague-ridden centre.

What matters is not that everyone lives in the centre, but that a reasonable number of people do so in reasonably attractive conditions and with a sense of resident community. The City of London arguably lost that in the 1930s, and is now undergoing the trauma of a very expensive blood transfusion at the Barbican, with quite a few sceptics among the business community who say the operation isn't worth it anyway, and that the Square Mile should stick to the business of making money. 'If it goes dead at night,' they add, 'well, we're not here to notice.' And a totally commuting population has in their eyes, one suspects, at least the merit of making things tidy.

As far as the Square Mile is concerned, that is an argument that deserves a hearing—though I should add I find it a soulless one. But to the school of thought which regards the growth of cities on the European model as at once something organic and productive of excellence, the 'dead centre' argument is anathema. This school cites American cities, and in particular Los Angeles, as an awful warning to European town planners, of the sort of results commuter dominance may produce.

Some of the features associated with the rise and fall of the great American city can, indeed, be detected in London. The familiar pattern of the middle-classes moving outwards through suburbia leaving an unfashionable and tawdry belt of tenement houses—or, as we prefer to put it with dry statistical euphemism, 'multi-occupation'—was already occurring in Victorian inner London in the twenties and thirties, although it was not complicated then by racial or colour stigma.

*Inner London's new popularity*

It is sometimes argued these days, in favour of violent resuscitation of the heart of London by eight-lane motorway, that the gravest peril the capital faces is the flight of 'all save the very poor and very rich' from the inner areas. Personal experience makes me doubt that this is either a very novel or a very imminent danger. I clearly remember, as a child living in Highgate in the forties, regarding virtually everything south of the Archway bridge (the then boundary between Middlesex and the L C C's domain, between Tory Hornsey and Labour Islington) as beyond the pale. My parents and grandparents had all lived in Islington; my grandfather ran a small and scarcely viable woodworking business there. The area was cheery if drab, but certainly beyond the pale in residential terms. If not wholly slum and council, it seemed so—apart, perhaps, from a small pocket round Canonbury Square.

Yet look at Islington now. My relations who moved out to Highgate and Muswell Hill thirty-odd years ago regard the house-prices with incredulity. What happened there—and has happened or is happening to other areas like Kennington, Camden Town and (even more to the point) certain streets around Waterloo Station—is that middle-class awareness homed almost simultaneously on to the advantages of cutting travel time to work and the attractions of eighteenth- and nineteenth-century domestic architecture—even in terraces! 'Semi-detached' became in such circles not so much an irrelevance as a term of abuse.

A fashion, you may say, which may pass in a decade or less. One doubts it. For the fashion is not frivolous, but backed by bourgeois economics and utilitarian considerations of *lebensraum*. In the mid-fifties an up-and-coming young professional sought to buy a semi-detached with three bedrooms and a space for another over the garage (if the local planning officer would wear it) and caught the 8.15 in from Grove Park. Today's bright young professional buys a vertical strip of Victorian townscape behind which are a dozen rather scruffy rooms and a walled garden rather more than twice the size he would get if he chose a comparably-priced 'town house' in Dulwich or Sydenham. He has room to expand, can get out of earshot of the children (if any), and jumps on a bus or tube at about five to nine which, even allowing for a half-hour later start, is his journey time just about halved.

Those are the practical advantages of life in the inner city, which has also been made more tolerable by smokeless zones and small-bore central heating pipes. There is in places a shortage of parks and open spaces, though this is to some extent being slowly rectified. But it does not seem to have halted the middle-class invasion of Islington (notoriously underprovided in this respect). Presumably this is because middle-class families are more aware of recreational opportunities further afield, middle-class husbands here go to work by public transport, and middle-class wives can drive the family car.

There is also the distinct possibility that building societies, proverbially slow to catch up with house-buyers' even quite modest forays away from the ordinary, will set their seal of approval on Victorian inner London with something like the same warmth that they now welcome the sound 1930s semi. Admittedly, there is much more that can go expensively wrong with a 100-year-old house, but are the skill and standard of workmanship of present-day building trades operatives so superior, and modern houses so universally free of serious faults? I doubt it.

Another important, though rather intangible, factor is, I suspect, a new generation's attitude towards class barriers. There is a reaction against the class apartheid of the one-class commuter suburb. Young professionals these days believe in integration. In theory, at least, they would like— or believe they ought to like—the idea of having working-class neighbours. Sometimes this admirable principle is carried sturdily into effect with a degree of real neighbourliness.

More often it means in practice a negative lack of any snobbishness but with a minimum of real contact. In other cases, having coarse-tongued Cockney neighbours is welcome provided they are round the corner, or three houses along, rather than next door. Victorian party walls are not always sound-proof, and if the neighbours are squabbling, it may seem somehow more acceptable if they do so with middle-class fluency (even in the use of four-letter words) than a distressing Plebeian unsubtlety.

So, all in all, a fair guess may be that large tracts of inner London with durable, adaptable Victorian houses will become desirable to the middle classes, who will learn to

rub shoulders with the increasingly indistinguishable plebs
—their neighbours, if not in house-to-house terms, then at
least in pockets. And this is healthy. How balanced the
mixture depends in part on whether we find a way to
finance more rehabilitation of Victorian houses for rent to
the less well-off.

Inner London, which faded for social and transport
reasons in the first four decades of the twentieth century,
could bloom in the second half—not with the rank growth
of the ugly, budget hotel and office block, but as an inner
city both economically and socially healthy, its comfortable,
often elegant urban fabric cared for and carefully patched
rather than torn apart and replaced. Of that, more in later
chapters. We are, however, in danger of spoiling it all because we mistake the features of urban life that those who
live in a great city really value.

## Two kinds of city

There are, it has been argued, two approaches to the city:
the characteristically European approach: evolutionary,
adaptive, but for reasons of space and tradition valuing and
guarding what is there; and what may be called the 'disposable American' approach which has been broadly true of
many US cities. This second approach, one suspects, is less
born of a car-owning and -using society than of the attitudes
of the frontier. Buried deep in the American ethos is the
notion that you can always move on, further west, into
the empty, unexploited lands, if your present resting-place
becomes uncomfortable or irksome. Possibly this—as much
as the lack in the middle west of very much in the way of
history or the tangible manifestations of it—has governed
the traditional assumption that you could tear a city apart
and put up something not only bigger but better.

Then came the realisation that space, in the sense of
limitless prairie and forest there for the adventurer to take,
was actually running out—along, possibly, with such other
natural resources as clean water and clean air. To this one
can, not too fancifully, attribute two recent features of
American life. Had not the fervour of the conquest of space
something more in it than simply the competitive urge to
outdo the Russians? Was it perhaps tinged by a streak of

fear at the loss of that traditional American escape, 'the Frontier'? And the ecological backlash of the late 1960s and early 1970s, which culminated in the quite amazing decision of New York State's hard-headed legislators to ban supersonic flight above certain very stringent noise levels—surely that had some root in a desperate fear that, as a nation, the Americans had been prodigal of their patrimony, and had unthinkingly applied 'frontier' values just once too often.

Putting aside such whimsy, the fact remains that Los Angeles—often held out as the classic case of the American big city—is not a city at all in the European sense. The centre no longer dominates the suburbs—the suburbs dominate the centre. In practical terms this means a very high proportion of Los Angeles' down-town area devoted to road space. The 'centre' has ceased to be a place in which people care to live, and increasingly they prefer to work elsewhere too. Los Angeles is *par excellence* the polycentric city. The centre has to some extent become one monumental, fantastically expensive and complicated motorway interchange. It is a place to go through rather than to.

## San Francisco's good example

That not all Americans want their cities to go that way is shown by San Francisco, 350 miles up the Californian coast. There the voters of three maritime counties in a referendum authorised the funds for a public transport system designed expressly to save the central city from engulfment by the motor-car. The Bay Area Rapid Transit system often actually runs along the central reservations of the motorways, where it can be seen to go faster than motorists' legal speed limit.

Not only is there tempting park-and-ride provision at out-of-town stations, but the stations themselves and the trains offer the commuter a degree of comfort and elegance, which Londoners would think quite lavish, to tempt them to leave the cars out of town. It can be done; it costs a lot of money; but arguably the true costs are less—much less—than the mass construction of urban motorways right into the centre.

Ah, the sceptic will say, but none of this really fits London. What is proposed here is a modest and overdue amount of urban motorway building—and not radial, suburb-to-centre motorways, but orbital, suburb-to-suburb ones. The danger here, urge apologists for the G L C's Ringway system in toto, is not that London will die through the surgery of the ringways, but that it will die of the economic effects of congestion through lack of them; that living conditions in the centre will become intolerable not as a result of weight of fast-moving traffic on purpose-built motorways, but as a result of that traffic congested on unsuitable existing routes.

## A polycentric London

The Greater London Development Plan does indeed propose a modest degree of polycentrism, with major shopping and employment centres at such places as Kingston, Croydon, and Lewisham in the south, and Ilford, Wood Green and Ealing in the north. But the strategy is to take a useful amount of strain off the centre and peak-hour commuting; not to compete with it. As the Greater London Development Plan puts it, this would leave rather more room for national and international, as distinct from local and regional, functions. Central London in this strategy remains in principle a place to live in, and certainly to go to for leisure-time purposes. And it remains, too, the big commuting magnet, but with, hopefully, a little of the power turned off.

Even so, argues the G L C, if even that degree of decentralisation is to be achieved, and the Londoner's increasing expectation of making non-commuting journeys by car satisfied, Ringways there must be. It is no use having countermagnets, if their pull is seriously impeded by lack of road space.

## Ringway strategy and arguments

The Ringway strategy postulates four irregular but broadly concentric rings (see Figure 3). Taking them from the centre outwards, they are Ringway 1: what used to be called the 'Motorway Box', with its corners at Hackney Wick, North Kensington, Battersea and Kidbrooke; Ringway 2: improved North Circular Road north of the Thames, new eight-lane motorway running through places like Eltham, Beckenham, Streatham and with links across the river by bridge at

Wansworth and by tunnel at Thamesmead; Ringway 3: running about twenty miles out from the centre, with its down-river cross-Thames link provided by a duplicated Dartford-Purfleet tunnel; and Ringway 4 some five to ten miles further out than that.

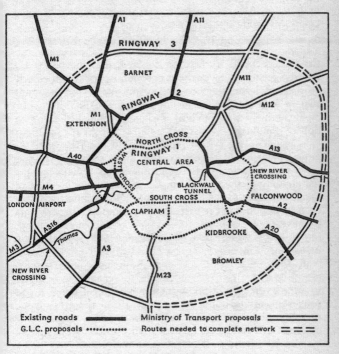

FIGURE 3. Proposed London ringways.

Of these four Ringways, only the innermost is wholly a G L C affair. Ringway 2 (north) is Ministry of Transport; Ringway 3 a G L C responsibility only for roughly one-third of its length. For this reason, as well as for the strength of opposition they generate, the Ringways have in the public mind been imbued with more importance the further in they are. Yet in terms of their functioning as by-passes, the outer rings ought to be regarded as more important than the inner ones. One reason is that traffic, say, from the Channel ports to the Midlands can beneficially on both environmental and cost grounds be diverted round London as far out as possible. The economic facts are that a mile of motorway on Ringway 1 costs on average upwards of £12 million; on Ringway 4, calculated on a comparable eight-lane basis, more like £1.5 million.

The by-pass argument should not be overstated. There is a road-planners' statistical law, too often validated in practice for its broad truth to be doubted, that the bigger the built-up area, the lower the proportion of traffic which will be seeking destinations beyond or outside it. But assuming that in a year or so's time the French and British governments actually start building a Channel Tunnel, the proportion of genuinely by-passable traffic could greatly increase.

In principle the G L C is committed to the view that the outer rings should be constructed first. Their critics have often been sceptical of this, and the doubts remain because the building of these outer rings is in other hands—those of the Department of the Environment—and because they have been busy building the east and west sides of Ringway 1 in advance of everything else—by special Ministerial dispensation—even while the Greater London Development Plan inquiry was in progress. The critics argue fairly convincingly that, once traffic gets used to an inner orbital route, it will be difficult, if not impossible, to persuade it *en masse* to alter its habit and take a newer but longer (even if less congested) orbital route further out. If, on the other hand, the outer rings are established before 1 and 2 are anything more than fragmentary, there is a fair chance that genuinely by-passable traffic will learn its orbital lesson and never bother to penetrate into the suburbs.

These and other arguments about the Ringways were the dominant theme of the marathon Greater London Development Plan inquiry which opened at County Hall in the autumn of 1970 and threatened to run right through into 1972. The Ringways were criticised for a variety of reasons. It was said by some opponents that such massive sums (the G L C's Ringway budget, with inadequate allowance for associated secondary road building, had by 1971 risen to £1,400 million compared with £1,100 million in 1967) could be better devoted to housing and social services; that more passengers could be carried more economically by new tube lines which would cost less; that the destruction of homes to clear the line for the motorways was something London, with its chronic housing shortage, could ill afford; that such examples of motorway building as the GLC had to date provided gave one no confidence that they were other than ruinous environmentally; and even that London was essentially a radial city, and the planners' attempts to create orbital movement to new counter-magnet centres was an expensive and undesirable irrelevance.

Another criticism frequently expressed of the Plan was that the GLC's motorway plans were the one firm element, with programmed dates for large stretches and money lined up. Most other features of the Greater London Development Plan were to a greater or lesser extent pious expressions of the desirable. But on closer inspection it appears that weakness was to some extent inevitable, because of the nature and limitations first of London local government; second, of the new-style structure plans of which this was, unfortunately, the first to be subject to public inquiry.

For the 1964 reform of London government produced in the town planning field what has ever since been the bane of local government officials there—a blurred overlap of functions. The GLC is broadly the strategic authority, concerned with primary roads, overall balance and matters of 'metropolitan importance'—and in that last definition there is endless room for argument and rivalry. Much of the meat of planning, therefore, would fall to the individual plans of the thirty-two London boroughs. The new notion of a structure plan, moreover, is of a written statement of aims, without the detailed, down-to-earth (but inflexible) zonings of the old-style development plans. For these two reasons the Greater London Development Plan inquiry was bound to appear to many people exasperatingly abstract. The primary road proposals were the one important element that was tangible and firm, because the GLC's responsibility there was not shared.

*The GLDP inquiry*

Put at its lowest, the Greater London Development Plan

inquiry has had great value as a safety valve. It has provided an arena where anyone with a serious point to make about the moulding of London's future could come and make it, get a fair and sympathetic hearing and feel that what he was saying would at least be borne in mind in the panel's deliberations. How Mr Frank Layfield, QC, and his panel coped with the magnitude and complexity of the material they were fed is past my comprehending. Yet their questions showed they did, and by no means necessarily on the G L C's terms. Objectors ranged from the eloquent and perceptive to a few that were fatuous windbags, but in general the arguments were remarkably well-marshalled. What were the main motives for opposition to the plan and the cross-currents which affected them?

## Reasons for opposition to GLDP

First—and perhaps so obvious that one might lose sight of it—is fear. There can be little doubt that the main generator of opposition to the Ringways was the individual householder's fear that he would be uprooted with inadequate compensation from an area he was content in and where he felt at home. Alternatively, and bulking larger of late, came fear of what may be called the 'Acklam Road syndrome'—the family home not demolished, but left raw and exposed to a hostile motorway environment. The owner-occupier particularly fears this, because his mobility depends on an asset which may be rendered unsaleable.

Underlying such fears is a general feeling of insecurity—of not knowing. In theory, for instance, a prospective purchaser should be able to discover whether the house he is considering is affected by motorway plans. But searches sometimes go wrong. There have been too many cases in which plans for roads are well known in the locality, but because they are not formally 'proposals', solicitors conducting searches for prospective vendors have been told that nothing is 'proposed'. And then again the actual consultation process, to be meaningful, leaves open the possibility of route modifications, which again breeds a sense of insecurity. If the authorities are open to argument about exact alignments—as clearly they ought to be—then their route cannot be 100 per cent firm, and the information given to prospective vendors, though honest and sensible, is imbued with an element of doubt.

Much of this sense of insecurity would, it is plain, be dispelled if we had a fair and complete compensation system. This ought to err on the generous side—a notion to shock district valuers, perhaps, but, I shall argue, justified on longer-term economic grounds as well as those of social justice. It should take in a broad enough swathe of land to allow, in appropriate cases, comprehensive redevelopment calculated to minimise the intrusion and disturbance of the motorway expressly built with that as one of its purposes.

The new compensation code would also, even where no compulsory purchase of marginal motorway lands was sought, require the road-building authority to purchase from any owner-occupier who wished to sell because he feared either permanent or temporary impairment of his surroundings : and as far as occupiers not owning property were concerned, a duty to rehouse would operate in similar conditions. There are, of course, objections of cost. But it is likely that such a new system of compensation would quickly begin to pay for itself. In the first place, the realisation that compensation would be sure and adequate for house-owners, whether their homes were demolished or only depreciated by the nearness of the road, would remove much of the objection to some motorway routes, and could perhaps even be accompanied by a speeding up of the present rather lengthy procedure for contested road lines.

There is, certainly, a limit to the extent to which the procedure can be concertinaed without loss of fairness or thoroughness. But West Germany, for example, seems to have a fair and acceptable system of objection and appeal which takes appreciably less time than the present D O E procedure in Britain. One suspects that a great many of those affected would rather have a slightly quicker and less elaborate procedure, than have the right to wring the last ounce of opportunity out of the present procedure and be kept waiting longer to know their fate.

The notion of a road-building authority purchasing a broad corridor of land to be redeveloped at the same time as the road is constructed is also expensive. It has been finding some favour of late, but more among town planners

than among road engineers or politicians. Yet in certain circumstances this too might actually show a profit.

Take, for example, a stretch of motorway which runs
through a shopping centre 'ripe', as the property men say,
for redevelopment—that is, drab and run-down but well-
located. It runs on through an area of substandard terrace
housing of no great visual quality and no very great sense
of community or identity either. There is a new tube line
planned for the area. In such circumstances, 'corridor' redevelopment is likely to be quite a profitable undertaking as
well as environmentally more acceptable.

Perhaps the motorway is put through a succession of cuttings and cut-and-cover tunnels, with buildings either
straddling the road with good side and top noise insulation,
or turning blank backs (again with sound insulation built
in), and thus holding most of the noise in a deepish, man-
made canyon. The two kinds of cases which then still fall
to be argued are (a) those where the strictly economic deal,
even in the long term, is a bad one, and corridor treatment
can be justified only on environmental grounds; and (b)
cases where the chosen, or perhaps the only, route presents
problems which money cannot resolve.

## Quality of London threatened

Intertwined with fear of the personal economic consequences of the Ringways, however, were a number of cross-
currents of reasoning and sentiment about London as a
place to live and work in, which often came out at the
Greater London Development Plan inquiry because almost
every hobby-horse and pet aversion could be fitted some-
where into the framework of the inquiry, by being turned
into an objection against one or more paragraphs of the
statement. Some on the face of it unlikely points for a
strategic plan inquiry were well and convincingly argued—
for example, the deplorable tendency of certain borough
engineers and surveyors to chop down mature forest trees
and replace them with ornamental species such as the
flowering cherry. This was the complaint of a remarkable
body called Women on the Move, whose 'coordinator'
Mrs Irene Coates (author and playwright as well as feminist
propagandist) had lent a rare energy and address to the

Bedford Park Society's fight to save the planes, horse-chestnuts and sycamores which were as much a part of the townscape of that splendid Victorian suburb as Norman Shaw's spacious three-storey houses.

I mention the Bedford Park trees case here because it seems to me to illustrate a complaint which emerged again and again in the Greater London Development Plan inquiry, as it does again and again in the arena of public participation in planning, especially in London, that though such and such a group of planners have looked honestly and not unintelligently at the situation in a particular area, with obviously more knowledge and expertise at their disposal than any local resident is likely to have, they have somehow 'missed the feel' of the place. It is almost as if they had planned it entirely from maps and documents, and could say they knew what it looked like only because they had seen it from the wheel of a car in a traffic hold-up.

## A warning to planners

And this may well be so. Top planners are busy administrators, tending a political machine into which they feed a synthesis of the information they have themselves been fed. But if I were writing a rule-book for planners, almost, I think, Rule 1 would be that the top planner should regularly make time to spend an hour or two actually walking round a neighbourhood to be affected by future planning decisions—quietly observing, getting the feel of the place, then perhaps chatting up one or two casual passers-by or waiters at bus stops. He might then even try knocking on one or two random, unprepared front doors. Just occasionally, that is.

Out of whole sections of the Greater London Development Plan hearings, then, emerged a composite picture of what Londoners liked about their city. Different groups, of course, treasured different qualities, but there was a surprising degree of overlap. They liked its parks, its riverside —the tidal, industrial reaches as well as the central historic and pastoral suburban stretches; its fine townscapes and obvious set pieces—but they also liked squares and gardens; its street markets, 'village' shopping centres (even with traffic), and untidy tangles of narrow lanes, They liked places they could identify, with a strong visual or other character (like the smell of cabbages in Covent Garden)—well-worn places they had perhaps grown up with or come to terms with over the years. In fact, if one can gather together the sense of a whole string of objections to the planners' efforts to prepare a better environment for the London of the year 2000, it was: 'Take care how you meddle with our familiar surroundings. You may be confident you can do better. We aren't. And we are the people who will have to suffer the disruption of change, and live with your mistakes.'

When one remembers how confidently architects and planners adopted the now discredited housing solution of mainly high-rise blocks for a population mainly of families with young children, or looks at the brave new Elephant and Castle shopping precinct, by this time six years old and still half empty, one has to concede that even the most talented planners are not infallible.

## The Whitehall inquiry

This response may be seen as part of a wider reaction to the 'clear and redevelop' school of thought, and found a sharper, more concentrated and eloquent expression at the Whitehall inquiry of July 1970. The old Ministry of Public Building and Works, and its predecessor the Ministry of Works, had had plans for at least ten years for replacing Whitehall's Victorian government office blocks (inadequate both in space and working conditions for a modern civil service) with a fine, new purpose-built administrative complex.

The notion of a comprehensively planned series of linked blocks on either side of the southern end of a pedestrian Whitehall finally took shape in the Martin/Buchanan Plan of 1965. (Sir Leslie Martin was the overall architect/planner, Professor Colin Buchanan the traffic consultant.) At the time, though many preservationists reacted sharply to the proposed demolition of Sir George Gilbert Scott's and J. M. Brydon's splendidly imperial but utterly inefficient Home Office/Treasury/Foreign Office blocks, the public mood then was 'Break no eggs, get no omelettes', and the civil service seemed hungry for its omelette.

The Martin plan, moreover, did envisage retention of

that familiar London landmark, Norman Shaw's fortress-like New Scotland Yard—another grossly inefficient building to work in, which the Metropolitan police were then preparing to quit without, at least operationally speaking, any great regret.

By the time the politicians had got round to trying to implement the first stage of the plan, however, things had changed in several respects. The Ministry of Public Building and Works had decided they could not get their required office space without demolition of both New Scotland Yard and the Georgian Richmond Terrace, which runs from the Embankment to Whitehall at the northern end of their clearance site. Conservation had become an 'in' thing, and the Labour Minister of Public Building, Mr John Silkin, who emerged determined to push through what he saw as a long overdue scheme for the decent housing of civil servants, found himself confronted with an environmental overlord in the shape of Anthony Crosland able to force on him a public inquiry which he might otherwise have been grateful to dispense with, on the basis that this was a matter primarily for Parliament and the Crown.

Finally, the general election of June 1970 produced a Conservative government whose regional policies, in so far as it had any, most emphatically did not include being seen to build Whitehall palaces for bureaucrats if there was a chance that they could instead be reduced in numbers, or at least eased discreetly into the provinces or the suburbs. So the Whitehall inquiry began with a disclaimer from the Ministry of Public Building and Works counsel that the new administration was in any way committed to its civil servants' plans. Consequently there was a greater feeling that this was a genuinely open question the inquiry was examining than is the case with most public inquiries involving proposals by government departments.

The main opposition to the Whitehall project had been expected to come from a body known as 'the Joint Committee'—a body principally representing the Georgian Group, the Victorian Society, the Society for the Protection of Ancient Buildings and the Civic Trust, whose function is to coordinate action against such threats to historic buildings and townscape. The strength of all these bodies at a public inquiry is in the star witnesses they can produce.

In this case they included Professor Sir Nikolaus Pevsner (Victorians), Lord Euston (S P A B), Duncan Sandys (Civic Trust), and Sir John Betjeman there independently but very much on their side. Mr Sandys was able, with the authority of a man who had held six different ministries, with offices on both sides of the river, most splendidly to rebuke the official contention that civil servants must always be clustered round their political masters, and their political masters be within 'division bell distance' of the House.

The weakness of all these four bodies at such an inquiry is, however, that in varying degrees they lack the technical or financial resources to mount the kind of case they would wish, arguing in well-researched detail positive alternatives to demolition as well as, negatively, the virtues of the buildings they wish to preserve.

To the rescue sprang two worthy champions from unexpected quarters. The G L C, in the shape of its Historic Buildings Board then energetically and glamorously presided over by Lady Dartmouth, held firm where Westminster City Council had capitulated. Its Surveyor of Historic Buildings, Ashley Barker, presented a detailed and meticulously argued case for keeping not only Shaw's Scotland Yard and the Regency Richmond Terrace, but also No 47 Parliament Street, the old Whitehall Club by the Victorian architect Parnell, now used as the London *pied-à-terre* of the Welsh Office.

Then—which is more important—he was followed by a senior G L C development architect, Robert Shaw, who showed in detail how a great deal more usable office space could be put inside the Scotland Yard façade at much less cost than the Ministry of Public Building and Works had dreamed possible. He was the more able to do so, incidentally, because the G L C had been preparing plans for building extra office space into the central courtyards of their own in some ways rather grandly impractical County Hall building just across the river.

The second unexpected champion was Peter Shepheard, then just half way through his two-year term as President of the Royal Institute of British Architects. His intervention was unexpected because R I B A presidents have not usually involved themselves in public controversy about building plans. But Shepheard thought this was a special case—because the planning machinery was being wrongly used, and because of the importance of this chunk of London scene —and allowed himself to be persuaded to join battle. He argued three main points.

First, he argued that the piecemeal approach represented by so narrowly-briefed an inquiry was architecturally and in planning terms disastrous.

Second, he maintained that a cleared site with all buildings demolished did not necessarily produce better architecture, and was not essential to the effective use of this particular site.

Shepheard's third argument was linked with this, but turned on æsthetics. Counsel for the ministry had striven to show that individually the three buildings in dispute did not amount to much and that the learned witnesses who now defended them had often made only passing or slighting reference to them in the past. Professor Pevsner was particularly open to this tactic. Counsel pointed out, for instance, that in the *Cities of London and Westminster* volume of his monumental *Buildings of England* series he had devoted only eight lines to Thomas Chawner's Richmond Terrace, calling it solidly built and 'solidly designed' but 'uneventful'.

This is, as we shall see, a frequent lament of developers, both public and private, who find themselves overtaken by the rising tide of conservation. There is a complete and devastating answer (which Pevsner gave at the inquiry with a wry, sad smile). It is, in essence: 'Our judgement was fair enough when it was written in the early fifties or before. There was then so much to choose from, and a relatively low level of public appreciation for much of it (particularly the Victorian). It seemed pointless to do much more than make a selection. Now the public is much more appreciative—but, thanks to you developers, there is much less left. Which makes this building's retention all the more desirable.'

But to return to Peter Shepheard. He was confronted with the argument that, though some people might consider the individual buildings in dispute pleasing, they would not fit in well with the new buildings the Ministry of Public Building and Works proposed, and were anyway part of a present rather untidy jumble. To which the R I B A president retorted that it was the untidy jumble which gave that end of Whitehall the character people liked. A variety of street scene, if the ministry architects were good enough to meet the challenge, could keep for Whitehall the processional feeling it gave at present—not one monolithic block, but a progression of buildings and styles. This argument, which Ministry of Public Building and Works counsel not unkindly called the 'sweet disorder in the dress' argument (after the poem of Robert Herrick) is in fact central to almost all conservationist arguments. So indeed was Peter Shepheard's linked point: that it is not simply the individual buildings that matter, but the townscape, the urban scene, call it what you will, and everything in it and about it, that goes to give a sense of place and visual identity.

There is a connection here with the case presented for the retention of the two New Scotland Yard blocks by Ashley Barker, the G L C's Surveyor of Historic Buildings. His argument was two-pronged. He of course presented the architectural and historical case for keeping these two buildings: the north block by Norman Shaw himself, the south block, nearer Parliament, put up twenty-two years later, but to Shaw's designs, and the two linked by Sir Reginald Blomfield's splendid iron gateway. But he also argued, as a shrewd, professional conservationist would, that the Yard's façade to the river was part of London's visual heritage, a view embedded in popular history (and fiction), and internationally known.

'If ever there existed a building on which architectural and historical interest combined, we have one in Scotland Yard,' he told the inquiry. 'If we recognise the civilisation of Florence through the treasured palaces of the Medici and the Pitti, we should see the civil order of London reflected in Scotland Yard and value it as highly.' Shaw, he argued, had 'celebrated the genius of London's police in a monument which the architectural connoisseur and the man on the Clapham omnibus could both understand.' But whereas the architectural historian might, in a sense be able to make do with photographs and detailed drawings, the layman could not. If you took that view away, you robbed the common man of a part of his patrimony.

98

*Chapter Seven*

# BATTLE OF THE RINGWAYS

## 'Destroyers of London'

To people who loved London as it was—the London environment that visiting New Yorkers raved about as they once had about our policemen, and visiting town planners asserted now made it the most human and civilised of any big city in the world—the villains of the piece, its destroyers, appeared as three in number. First came the planner with untried theories about how people would want to live in future, and too little awareness of how they in fact lived now. Second was the developer, public not less than private, who tore down the shabby but familiar, and after a year or so of noise, dirt, vibration and dislocation, gave back something which was unfamiliar, prohibitively expensive and, perhaps most important, failed to fit in with the pre-existing patterns of people's lives, to be, visually and socially good neighbours with the place in which it was planted.

And third—the biggest villain for most London conservationists—was the road builder, who not only threatened immense destruction and seemed no respecter of much-loved places, but who brought severance and alienation of communities not just on a well-chosen few acres, but in continuous linear swathes. As the Chiswick Motorways Liaison Committee, a local umbrella organisation for ten local amenity groups, put it, an eight-lane motorway was like plonking down the equivalent in area of a small municipal park full of fast-moving noisy traffic across a neighbourhood—and another, and then another, in line until the end of the route.

The Chiswick Committee's evidence to the Greater London Development Plan inquiry was an example of what an impressive case local amenity groups, when they pool their resources, can produce. It touched deftly on several sensitive spots in the G L C's case for the Ringways—small rate of financial return; in-built assumptions in the London Traffic Survey; imbalance between hard cash commitment to roads and lack of it to public transport investment; and escalating cost. Then it went on to challenge the theory of increasing demand or suppressed demand for orbital movement. It struck out hard and with some shrewdness at the 'doubtful and . . . arrogant assumption that the old community patterns of London have now served their purpose and should be replaced by a system which will leave Chiswick within twenty minutes' drive of Greenwich and destroy both in the process.'

## Impact of roads on people

But they were almost certainly at their most effective when they got down to explaining to the inquiry what the local impact was of six- and eight-lane motorways, not on maps of no matter what scale, not on the drawing board, but on the ground. They tore to shreds the G L C's bland assumption that a railway line can be assumed to sever the neighbourhoods it runs through if it is not in a tunnel, and that the insertion of a motorway alongside would make relatively little difference.

This might be true of multi-track railways like that between Waterloo and Clapham Junction but, the Chiswick Motorways Liaison Committee pointed out, many railways in London were two-track affairs in cuttings or on the level, with frequent pedestrian routes crossing them. often at 'natural' level. The visual and physical connections across them were such that they were scarcely experienced as barriers at all, it argued. A six- or eight-lane motorway was quite a different matter. And to prove its point, it produced photographs of such a railway (fairly typical for south London) in its suburban setting, then of the railway with a six-lane motorway, superimposed, at ground level.

'Instead of the existing situation of a community well linked across a 30 foot railway we now have an impenetrable swathe of railway and motorway up to 200 feet wide splitting the community completely. A subway 250 feet long is a very different prospect for a pedestrian to the existing crossing facilities on the level or by means of small road- or footbridges. For some indeed such a subway becomes unusable. We submit,' went on the committee. 'that this is the reality of the severance caused by a motorway: a massive and total disruption of the community through which it passes, and something for which Londoners are ill-prepared by the soothing words of the G L C when it refers to routing its motorways along existing "cracks" in the urban fabric.'

## Subtopian subways

The point about subways being 'unusable' to some people is certainly one that needs making again and again. In one sense, of course, vandalism and hooliganism can render them unusable, and within months of the opening of West-way there were complaints of both from the tenants of nearby council flats. What the Chiswick Committee were, of course, saying was that, for a small but nonetheless important minority, a subway of any length induces a phobia in them so that they physically fear to use it.

There are, it must be admitted, subways and subways. If well designed they can, in certain places, be attractive, focal points of community contact. They can have shops and gay, vandal-beating mosaics and good lighting. They can be an asset. And G L C road men tend to talk sometimes as if, within the permissible environmental tolerances of their huge budgets, this and so much more can easily be included. All one can say is: It hasn't happened yet. Though great care may be taken to work out and cater for the expected pedestrian flows in various directions, with ramps (quite rightly) as well as steps, the end result of most G L C and L C C subway-building to date has been to produce a confusing, deterring maze of squalid, ill-lit concrete rat-runs.

Of course people use them—for journeys they have to make, at least—and in terms of road (rather than certain other kinds of) safety they are no doubt an improvement. But in environmental terms? First, there is, I suspect, the iceberg effect again here: the walks people no longer take, the social contacts they no longer have at doorstep and street corner. What of the half-blind old-age pensioner in Walworth who used to toddle down to the Elephant of an evening, with friendly lights, warm smells and Cockney voices all the way, and always someone to see him across Walworth Road?

His new route would be through the subways, where there have been one or two unpleasant incidents lately—one poor old chap beaten up, they say. And anyway he doesn't care for those subways. They look a mess. And such a stench sometimes. So he doesn't go. A sentimental, untypical picture perhaps. But there is enough truth in it to be disturbing. Subways of this kind *are* off-putting, even to the self-confident in daylight going about their business. When the trips are 'optional', leisure-time ones, the deterrent effect is bound to increase.

## 'Cracks' in the urban fabric?

Before leaving the Chiswick Committee's evidence, let us look a little more closely at the 'railways divide communities anyway' argument which it so firmly nailed. Other amenity and anti-motorway groups had made this point, including the Blackheath Motorway Action Group, which was fighting a programmed section of the South Cross Route through the environmentally very vulnerable Blackheath conservation area. The GLC's 'safeguarded route' (that is one on which, though no final ministerial approval had been given for construction, all planning applications were normally refused) ran along railway for the whole stretch from Kidbrooke to Lewisham.

The railway is all plain two-track, much of it in cutting or tunnel. It does not obtrude, either visually or in noise terms. I can state this flatly because it runs behind and almost under my house. Traffic noise from the A2 half a mile away is, when the wind blows from the east, much more disturbing than the sound of an electric train 200 yards away in a cutting. In the shopping centre at Blackheath Village trains going under the bridge are not noticeable.

Indeed, far from severing communities, the railway in commuter districts often provides a focus. The shops are near the station, people converge on the area. Destroy that and you destroy, in a sense, the heart of the community. Nor is there much doubt that eighteen months to two years of demolition, excavation and building work does destroy such a centre, commercially and socially—probably beyond the power of man or money to resuscitate.

## Buchanan's Greenwich/Blackheath study

This fight for environmental standards—and for such intangibles as the ingredients of a sense of community—to be given due and early weight by planners and road builders even though not so amenable to quantification as motorists' travelling time and compulsory purchase costs, received immense assistance in the spring of 1971 from a report to the G L C from Colin Buchanan and Partners. It was on the environmental impact of G L C road proposals in the Greenwich/Blackheath area, and the G L C commissioned it because of the weight of articulate protest and influence, official and private, that this middle-class suburb characteristically brought to bear.

There was some suggestion at the time that the G L C leapt in to commission Buchanan because the then minister responsible for environment, Anthony Crosland, would otherwise have commissioned a government study. Indeed there was quite a flood of complaints in local amenity circles that Buchanan, already a G L C roads consultant, would not be sufficiently independent in his approach. But as soon as the Buchanan team began actually talking to local interests, this criticism sank without trace and the erstwhile critics of the G L c's choice of consultant began to talk much more optimistically about the probable outcome of the study.

To be fair to the G L C road planners, Greenwich/Blackheath—a green wedge driven south from the Thames across an otherwise rather drab area of Thames-side London—presented an almost intractable problem, at least on the basis of the design and cost standards to which the road plans were originally prepared in the 1950s. The Royal Naval College on the river frontage—described by Kenneth Clark in his Civilisation series on B B C T V as 'the greatest architectural unit built in England since the Middle Ages'—presented a façade which even they were bound to regard as inviolable. Behind the Naval College came the narrow Romney Road, carrying an increasing weight of Thames-side industrial and commuter traffic into Greenwich town centre, which badly needed by-passing; and then the grounds of the National Maritime Museum, again part of the same Greenwich set-piece and guarded by powerful official watchdogs.

Behind it was Greenwich Park, a Royal Park, not a G L C one, of which Robert Mellish, when briefly Minister of Public Building and Works in the late sixties, said: 'They will put a road through it over my dead body.' Up the hill a mile from the river, the park wall gives on to the open plateau of Blackheath, fringed by a necklace of Georgian and Victorian houses, but crossed by heavy A2 traffic, whose disruption of an otherwise largely unspoiled scene was already much resented.

Beyond the Heath lay Blackheath Village, its narrow and now inappropriately named Tranquil Vale choked with north-south traffic, but still a genuine village centre. Beyond the village, a large private estate of high visual character and high property values. All this stretching two miles south from the river. And through it the G L C reckoned it needed to run three major roads: (1) a by-pass for Greenwich; (2) a widened A2, because peak traffic flows were such that even the pedestrian crossing locals had for years demanded was calculated to cause acute traffic jams (and therefore refused); and (3) the south cross route, or southern side of Ringway 1 (the so-called 'Motorway Box'), from Kidbrooke to Nunhead and New Cross.

Of these the A2 widening was probably the least controversial. There was a general assumption (perhaps at that time optimistic) that the G L C could be persuaded or forced to put it in a cutting, so that its visual and severance damage to the Heath might well be less than the existing busy road. In Greenwich the G L C produced a two-stage plan. Ultimately they wanted a tunnel by-pass under the park, but an interim scheme for pedestrianising the area round the market, though accepted by the borough, was bitterly opposed by the Greenwich Society.

Their argument, broadly, was that Greenwich had waited too long for relief from through traffic to swallow a scheme which substituted severance of the community along one line for severance along another, and which passed 'on stilts' so close to Hawksmoor's St Alfege's church (in order to pass over a road and a railway in a cutting) as to offer a classic case of wanton damage to historic environment. But the gravest threat was almost certainly the motorway, which the G L C road planners had decided, for want of a

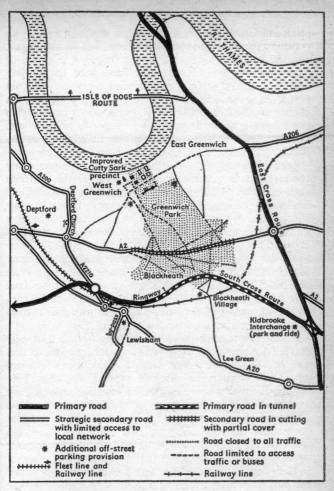

Primary road

Strategic secondary road with limited access to local network

Additional off-street parking provision

Fleet line and Railway line

Primary road in tunnel

Secondary road in cutting with partial cover

Road closed to all traffic

Road limited to access traffic or buses

Railway line

FIGURE 4. Greenwich-Blackheath proposals: 1991 strategy. (*Based on a map in the* Greenwich and Blackheath Study, *Colin Buchanan and Partners.*)

more acceptable solution, to take along the Kidbrooke to Lewisham railway line, on the strength of the later discredited railways-are-cracks-i the-urban-fabric theory. And this meant six (later revised to eight) lanes of motorway whose construction would clearly tear the heart out of Blackheath Village.

However the G L C roads chief, Peter Stott (now joint director of planning) had lived nearby as a boy. He regarded the village as disposable and replaceable. There was not, he told me on one occasion in 1968 or '69, very much special worth keeping in that bit of Blackheath. The remark was revealing, because it was clear he was thinking (*a*) of individual buildings of architectural or historic importance (*b*) of the actual line of the motorway and its immediate margins. Though the village and a whole stretch of Blackheath to its west had just been designated a conservation area by the other local authority concerned, Lewisham, the concept of townscape, and of a living place as a whole, did not, at least at that time, appear to weigh very heavily with him.

This was an attitude which the Buchanan study of Greenwich/Blackheath rejected entirely. Though the safeguarded route was for the most part aligned to minimise housing loss, it said, the houses threatened in Blackheath Village formed 'an integral part' of the village. 'To lose them would be a serious matter not only for the individuals who lived there, but also for the life of the village.'

Moreover, the study went on (paragraphs 232-3): 'Blackheath Village would suffer serious disruption while the South Cross Route was being built through the heart of its shopping centre. About one-fifth of the shops would be directly affected and the group of properties to the south of the railway would be separated by the width of the proposed route from the main part of the Village. Tranquil Vale'—one of the two main shopping streets—'would have to be closed to traffic for a time, although this inconvenience could be avoided were it possible to build a by-pass to the east of the Village (spanning the railway and motorway alignments), before construction of the South Cross Route was begun. . . .

'In the long term there is the risk that the upheaval to trade and shopping habits during the construction period could do permanent harm to the Village as a shopping centre. Some people would transfer their custom to other centres . . . and the remaining Village shopkeepers would suffer a loss of trade. Even if it were possible to rebuild the shops on a deck over the sunken road, it is difficult to see how retailers whose premises were destroyed to make way for the road could be temporarily rehoused and to be sure that they could be offered premises in any redevelopment at rents comparable to those charged for their former properties.'

That, incidentally, will ring ominously true to many all over the country who have seen well-established shopping streets destroyed, often for the building of new shopping centres rather than of roads, only to find two or three years later that, if they were traders, they could not afford the new rents; or, if they were shoppers, that the new shops were the wrong shops, were the right shops but much more expensive, or—quite often—remained empty for a further period of months or years.

These considerations were by no means unique to Blackheath, even though it had been able to make out a case for special consideration. They, or similar factors, could apply—as the Buchanan team made clear—to other less articulate and influential London communities affected by the Ringways.

The study then went on to the appraisal of various alternatives to the official route, and it is interesting to note some of the environmental criteria they used. There were two sets of these. The first was: Category (A) *Impact on people's lives*, and this included: (1) number of households displaced and condition of dwellings; (2) how long people had lived in them; (3) loss of schools and disturbance to children's lives; (4) loss of shops and effects of this; (5) *severance*—which they defined as 'the effect that the road will have on the movement pattern of the local community' and which would be seen in terms of 'the loss or disruption of existing pedestrian and vehicular routes, and the extent to which the new route would cut through a "cohesive area".'

Point (5) was a notion local amenity groups had been trying to implant in the minds of road planners for years—though it was no fault of Professor Colin Buchanan that it had failed for the most part to take root there. The idea was implicit in his *Traffic in Towns* report of 1963—though broadly all ideas bar one in it have taken seven years to begin to be put into effect. The exception was the argument that new purpose-built primary roads were needed in towns if a severe degree of restraint was not to be imposed on the motorist there. On the whole, the road planners and builders took that notion (sometimes without the 'if') and forgot for the time being about environmental areas, distributor systems and other inconvenient or expensive accompaniments to it.

But back to the 1971 Buchanan team's list of tests of environmental damage. Impact (6) on people was loss of open space, measured in relation to the possibilities of alternative provision (an interesting one, that, because it attempts to give a weight to relative irreplaceability); and (7) loss of job opportunities through removal of factories or offices.

Category (B) was *Impact on environment*, which, if anything, is harder to quantify than impact on people. Some of this category's five heads are, in fact, ascertainable fairly objectively; others are not. The five were: (1) the extent of the area affected by traffic noise from the new route (objective tests) and the vulnerability of the activities in this area (less so); (2) the total area from which the new route would be visible (wholly objective): (3) the visual disruption that it would entail to areas of high quality, e.g. the Heath (considerable degree of subjectivity); (4) the number of listed buildings and other buildings of merit lost or affected (subjective—but officially endorsed subjectivity) and (5) the acreage of land to be acquired, and its present use (elements of both?).

## Cost-benefit and other values

I go into some detail on the objective/quasi-objective/subjective nature of the Buchanan team's twelve tests not because I am critical of them—I regard them as an admirable attempt to redress imbalance in pre-existing methods of 'costing' motorway proposals—but because Buchanan and Partners have, I believe, sometimes been criticised by some fellow professionals for allegedly being 'unscientific' in their approach. I think this criticism is unfair, and is rooted in a fallacy which is itself 'unscientific': that if you cannot quantify effectively a factor by conventional statistical tools, you either leave it out or give it a low value which is the 'best result' achievable by techniques not meant to cope with it at all.

If Professor Colin Buchanan was ever in danger of falling into that trap, he ceased to be so after his experience as a member of the Roskill Commission, when he sensed quite early on that the Roskill research team's use of cost-benefit techniques was going to lead to results seriously biased against environmental factors. The twelve tests applied in the Greenwich/Blackheath study may therefore, I hope not too fancifully, be seen as representing a determination not to fall into a similar trap when giant roads rather than a giant airport were under scrutiny.

The Buchanan study was not, of course, in any sense anti-motorway. Even had the terms of reference permitted this, such a posture would have been quite out of character. The Buchanan stance ever since *Traffic in Towns* has been, broadly, that motor traffic would grow in the cities, though a measure of restraint would have to be imposed if the cost —economic and environmental—were to be kept in reasonable bounds. In so far as traffic was allowed to grow, however, it would need new roads to replace and augment the old, unsuitable ones; and to do otherwise than plan to supply them was to invite worse environmental conditions, not better.

## Greenwich/Blackheath conclusions

This view was again spelt out in the Greenwich/Blackheath study. 'Critics of the Greater London Development Plan have claimed that the new routes will have so disastrous an effect that the present situation is to be preferred as the lesser of two evils, particularly if it can be relieved to some degree by management methods, by minor road works and by improvement to public transport. We have tried hard to find a long term solution on these lines, but we have failed' (paragraph 256). Unless there was more road space, no elbow room existed for improving traffic conditions and the likely result was further erosion of the residential environment.

Again in their conclusions the team specifically met the point of those who saw transportation strategy for Greater

London 'in terms of cut and dried alternatives—*either* to build motorways *or* to prevent car use and improve public transport; *either* to squeeze the last ounce of capacity from the existing road system *or* to keep traffic out altogether in the interests of environment.' Their work, they said, showed 'that if movement and environmental objectives are to be realised, all these policies are likely to be required— but the mix will differ with the needs and problems of the different parts of London.'

If the report provided a broad endorsement for the GLC's view on *whether* new roads were needed through this part of London, it answered the equally important questions of how and where in terms distinctly unflattering to the official choice of routes. The application of the twelve environmental tests described earlier to the safeguarded route for the motorway and a number of alternative alignments on an A/B/C/D: least impact/some impact/more impact/ most impact scale gave it a preponderance of D readings matched only by the two outsiders among the choices— elevated motorways several miles to the south, which were bad also on cost and movement effectiveness grounds.

In the end the Buchanan team came to the conclusion that a long bored tunnel under the Heath, by-passing Black-heath Village and costing £11.5 million more was the only solution that could be considered satisfactory in terms of environmental impact. And this caused them to ask : is it right to spend so much money on this area? They found part of the answer in the Greater London Development Plan's own statement of policy on 'areas of special character' which talked of 'protection of character, scale and quality of main open spaces and fine buildings,' 'the preservation of distant views,' 'the promotion of traffic-free pedestrian enclaves,' and 'the assimilation of major road proposals without damage to character and environment.'

To introduce a motorway anywhere into an existing city is difficult, they added. 'To do so across such a sensitive area demands, in our view, that no risks should be taken on the outcome of the exercise.' The question was also partly answered by the cost of the total 'package' of which the re-aligned South Cross Route formed part. They proposed cutting or trimming to a more modest level several of the GLC's secondary and local road schemes, notably the motorway spur to New Cross. More modest improvements would work just as well, they argued. The total cost would not be substantially greater than the original G L C proposals.

What were the main ingredients of this 'package' for the study area? In summary they set them out as follows:

1. Existing A2 to be widened to four lanes and put in cutting across the Heath, with 'sensitively' sited pedestrian bridges. This proposal they suggested G L C should examine urgently for (a) feasibility and (b) its effects on roads outside the study area.

2. Investigation, somewhat less urgently, into four major proposals:

(a) the tunnel route for the motorway.

(b) the feasibility of by-passing Greenwich by bridges to and from the Isle of Dogs—expensive for the modest by-pass Greenwich town centre needed, but quite economical if the benefit to dockland redevelopment, and of extra river crossings relieving the Blackwall and Rotherhithe tunnels, were considered.

(c) improvements to rail services, possible extension of the Fleet Line (planned for Lewisham) to Kidbrooke, and

(d) park-and-ride facilities to tempt the motorist to leave his car and go on by public transport.

3. Development of a district road system within the strategic routes (A2, South Cross and Isle of Dogs), including a modest single carriageway two-lane by-pass to take the north-south through traffic out of the Blackheath Village shopping centre.

4. Various small road improvements, including widening a bottleneck on the hill by which the A2 approaches the Heath and closing some side roads on the Heath.

5. Traffic management schemes, particularly exclusion of heavy vehicles from the A206 through Greenwich (a road that runs like a circular one-way race track round Greenwich town centre, and on between the Naval College and the Maritime Museum).

The report ended with a note of reservation and caution. The study had been of Greenwich/Blackheath. That did not mean it would necessarily form a valid part of an inner London road system. Further studies were needed to make sure (a) that the proposed package did not worsen conditions in adjoining areas not studied; and (b) that the study area was not getting too much priority over other areas. The implication was clear: the G L C should be doing many more studies at this depth and should have started on them much earlier.

The report's appraisal of the G L C by-pass proposals for Greenwich town centre was also fairly damning, and bore out the view that the highway engineers and planners were not nearly so good at getting the environmental implications of a road right as the engineering ones—even when, as in this case, they claimed that it was designed as much for environmental relief as for traffic flow improvement. The G L C's scheme, said the Buchanan team, would be disastrous for St Alfege's church, would divide one part of the town centre from another, and would cut the main pedestrian routes from riverside to park.

All these points had been made by local critics of the scheme, but had been brushed aside by the G L C, and accepted by the borough council as a price to be paid for curing greater evils. The G L C scheme (which, I must say, when I first saw it I regarded in the same light as the borough council) was now shown up for what it was: a steam-hammer-to-crack-a-walnut solution. It also seems to have reflected a fallacy commonly held, not only by planners but by conservationists too: that you either have all or nothing—total pedestrianisation, or total traffic.

The report's interim answer to Greenwich's anguish was simple, neat, and very much less expensive than the G L C's or most of the alternatives put up locally. Traffic management—including a weight limit here, a road closed to all vehicles save buses there—would take the vast majority of through traffic via the newly completed East Cross motorway on to the A2 (which would need widening anyway). Truly local traffic would not be seriously inconvenienced and would still be able to use most of the local roads, though its weight, the team estimated, would not be such as to cause serious nuisance and would certainly be only a fraction of the present levels.

The report's proposal (3) needs elaborating. 'Secondary' roads have been a constant refrain to Buchanan and Partners' pronouncements at least since his North-east London report to the G L C in spring 1970. Professor Buchanan believes most of the proposed London motorways will be needed, but he also believes that they will be ineffective and environmentally disastrous if the G L C and boroughs skimp on the supporting network of high-grade feeder roads.

## Some lessons for road planners

The total road system can be seen as a series of sieves or filters, one over the other. The sieve with the coarsest mesh is urban motorways, the primaries. Below that Buchanan sees two distinct categories of secondaries. Below them come the finest mesh, district and local distributors, beneath which finally are residential and other enclaves (somewhat misleadingly called 'environmental areas') which are intended to be free of through traffic. The theory is that long-distance trips are caught by the motorways, medium-distance ones (for whom motorway interchanges are too widely spaced, or no convenient primary route exists) by the secondaries. Trips to local primary schools and shops are probably on the finest mesh.

But leave out the secondary meshes and medium journeys are perforce made on lesser roads where the environmental impact is not sufficiently cushioned—roads with houses and shops fronting them. Buchanan's fear has been that a concentration of attention and resources on the primary routes would cause those concerned to duck or postpone their responsibility to construct high-grade, purpose-built secondaries, and that the routes which in fact serve this purpose will be the traditional main shopping streets of London's suburbs.

I have devoted this much space to Greenwich/Blackheath not just because of its intrinsic importance (which the Buchanan team and the G L C both accept), nor because I live there and know what is involved—but because this study was a crucial landmark and has lessons for all of London and for planning generally. Let us attempt to extract the main lessons.

First, the exercise showed that an honest intention on the part of road builders and the politicians who control them to do the environmentally fair and right thing does not ensure that it will be done. They need to devote as much detailed care and effort early on to getting that aspect right as they have traditionally done to getting the cost and engineering aspects right.

Second, it showed that, in planning roads, we need to see them from the start in terms of the total cost-benefit for all the people they affect. To take account just of vehicle-users' needs, with 'environment' as a negative factor operating at a late stage when ideas have crystallised, is no longer good enough.

Third, and following on from this, it shows that there is more to these environmental factors than a fine view or two, keeping noise levels down, and avoiding demolition of one or two listed buildings. The social impact, the effect on the complex pattern of people's lives, is at least as important, and may apply as much to Deptford or Willesden as to Blackheath or Hampstead.

Fourth, it shows that the introduction into debate about road proposals of an independent, uncommitted party gets the other two parties—proposers and opposers—out of their entrenched battle stations and into a useful dialogue, and allows genuine alternatives to be tested professionally (more of this in Chapter 14, Participation).

Fifth, it shows that, under pressure of increasing public hostility to the effects of urban road building, the public, politicians and professionals are now for the first time ready to look carefully at the expensive implications of *Traffic in Towns*.

A significant indication of this was provided, a few days before the official publication of the Greenwich/Blackheath study, by the Greater London branch of the Institution of Highway Engineers. They invited Mrs Ann MacEwen, the Buchanan partner in charge of that study, to speak at a seminar on Traffic Restraint and Conservation.

In a fairly forthright paper on the subject, she told the assembled road engineers (male almost to the man): 'It is not good enough simply to push the traffic through, and let the locals reap the environmental consequences. Remedial measures may be costly—for example, putting a road in cutting, bridging to avoid severance, double-glazing, planting to conceal car-parks—but this is part of the real cost of the proposals.'

She taxed them (and though she diplomatically included planners and architects in her stricture, the cap fits some of the company better than others) with doing 'an immense amount of unnecessary and irretrievable damage . . . by thoughtless application to historic areas of standards and rules of thumb which may be satisfactory elsewhere—but spell total ruin to the subtle form and pattern of an old town.' 'In essence,' she said, 'the mistake is to give too high a priority to the needs of the motor vehicle.'

Instead of building high-grade and expensive dual carriage-ways and underpasses to link two bottlenecks, as the Hyde Park underpass had done, they should think rather in terms of narrowing some roads (what a splendid and daring suggestion to make to road engineers!).

She was also preaching the wider purpose of road building. The D O E's so-called 'cost-benefit criteria' measured only the benefits to road users. Yet when you build a new road and perhaps—as Buchanan and Partners had proposed for Bath—put it in a tunnel under the town, the purpose was 'not simply to avoid the frustration and waste caused to motorists and vehicle users. It is to save the towns, to improve the quality of life in them, and to conserve historic areas which are as much a part of the national heritage as the paintings in the National Gallery or the scenery of the national parks.'

She also cautioned them—and here she might well have been thinking of Greenwich—to beware of dismissing local amenity societies as 'busybodies or cranks, with subjective opinions.' They, together with local architects and archæologists, had much to add to 'official sources and wisdom' because of the real concern and affection for places they knew intimately. There is nothing like going and looking at a place on the ground and talking to the folk who live and work there. But on to other thoughts on other aspects of London.

*Chapter Eight*

# PARKS AND THE RIVER

*The pattern of London parks*

In this chapter let us examine two of those features of London which both objectors to the Greater London Development Plan and the G L C say they cherish. Parks and open spaces is one of these; the Thames the other. A third feature is the character of some of the older residential districts, where not only Georgian or Victorian houses survive, but the townscape, the town plan and something of the atmosphere of the period. But that third aspect we leave to discuss in Chapter 9 under the heading 'urban conservation'.

London has historically, and is lucky to have, four main sets of parks. First there are the Royal Parks, originally the Crown's private places of pleasure opened to the public as an act of sovereign graciousness. They are now as much public parks as any others, though administered for historical reasons by the Department of the Environment (before November 1970 by the Ministry of Public Building and Works). Second there are the 172 parks which were administered by the old London County Council and since 1965 by the G L C, some of which have now been transferred to London borough councils; and third, the original borough-administered parks—in inner London, the old L C C area, usually quite small ones, but in the outer boroughs including some really quite large areas.

A fourth rather special category are the City of London Corporation's parks and woodlands, all of them save the smallest outside the actual Square Mile of the City. Epping Forest is the largest and probably the best known, and it also administers Burnham Beeches in Buckinghamshire. But closer in—with little justification save that of history and available finance—the City also has a number of other open spaces in such scattered and improbable places as Highgate, Kilburn, and West Ham, Kenley, Coulsdon. Riddlesdown and Farthingdown in Surrey, and West Wickham and Hayes in Kent.

Some London open spaces come under none of these management structures. Among these should be mentioned Wimbledon and the adjoining Roehampton Commons, run by independent boards of 'conservators'.

If the City of London's curious but valued collection of open spaces has any dominant characteristic common to most of them, it is of more or less natural-seeming woodland or common which, with one or two exceptions, all its open spaces possess. The Royal Parks, by contrast, with a total area in and around London of 5,500 acres, are notable for their finely landscaped quality. They are parkland in the Capability Brown sense of the term, and this character has been carefully maintained, sometimes it seems to the exclusion of recreational facilities needed in some of the areas these parks serve.

The G L C parks system, at least until the transfer in 1971 of some 125 of their number, was, with a total of 7,615 acres, the largest under a single administration. It included, and still includes, such large, nationally-known open spaces as Hampstead Heath, Battersea Park and Blackheath, and ranged through strategic, medium-sized open spaces like Victoria Park in the East End to quite small areas, sometimes amidst the tightest packed urban areas, such as Hammersmith and Southwark Parks and Lincoln's Inn Fields.

## The G L C parks philosophy

Historically the role of the old L C C parks department, following that of the Metropolitan Board of Works before it, had been to extend the amount of open space available to Londoners by buying, as the opportunity presented, parkland and open estates which became available—for the most part, in the nature of things, on the edges of or outside the largely built-up area of the then County of London.

In post-war years the role of the County Hall parks department has perhaps changed its emphasis. An enlightened administration has concentrated less on adding to the acres —though this exercise has by no means ceased—than on extension of the opportunities they offered for public enjoyment. In terms of entertainment, the provision has been excellent, ranging from the brass and military band concerts (which one associates with the Victorian bandstands

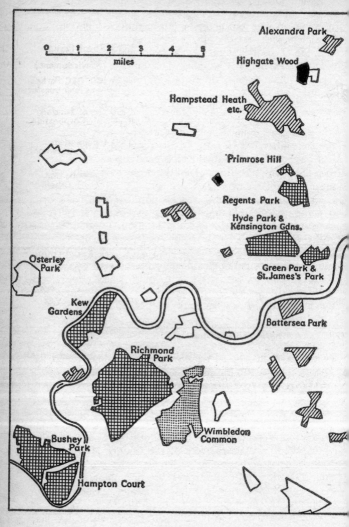

FIGURE 5. The London parks

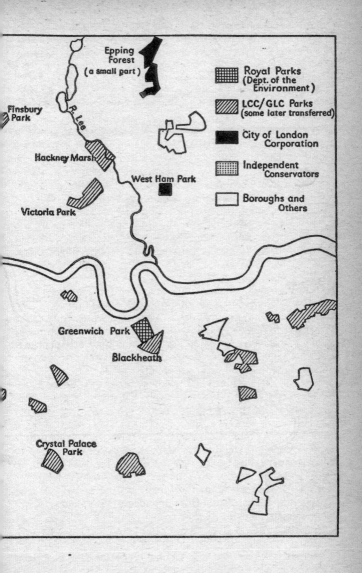

Epping Forest (a small part)

Royal Parks (Dept. of the Environment)

LCC/GLC Parks (some later transferred)

City of London Corporation

Independent Conservators

Boroughs and Others

Finsbury Park

R. Lee

Hackney Marsh

West Ham Park

Victoria Park

Greenwich Park

Blackheath

Crystal Palace Park

of conventional municipal parks throughout England) to open-air symphony concerts, chamber music recitals, jazz, ballet, children's entertainments and poetry and prose recitals. The scale and scope are properly and admirably metropolitan, and even when they relied on public transport to a greater extent than is now the case, people came from quite distant suburbs to Kenwood, Crystal Palace, Holland Park and the Ranger's House at Blackheath for these activities.

Sports were also rather better catered for in LCC/GLC parks than in many others—certainly than in the Royal Parks—though provision nonetheless lagged well behind demand and need. But the other outstanding feature of the County Hall parks administration has been to my mind its admirable play provision for children. Its adventure playgrounds, its one-o'clock clubs for small children, mobile zoos, pony rides—these have brightened the days for countless thousands of London children who might othervise have been at a loose end, bored and potentially 'at risk' in one way or another.

Behind such facilities and activities there seems to me to lie a whole difference of 'philosophy' and approach. The attitude of most municipal authorities towards their parks has, traditionally at least, been that trees, lawns and flower beds, well cared for in horticultural and arboricultural terms, are a delight and tonic to the citizenry and, incidentally, a useful place for children to play safely and perhaps let off a little steam—though preferably under fairly tight supervision. This is basically the negative parks philosophy. The LCC/GLC attitude is what one can call the positive one. It says: 'Here is an open space. What can we do with it to maximise public use and benefit?' Some people who regard themselves as staunch defenders of good environment rather deplore some of the results. Many of them, for example, do not care for garishly paint-sloshed timbers roughly secured to mature trees, or pieces of old rope dangling rubber tyres from branches. And a good many Londoners deplore the fact that about fifteen acres of Battersea Park is given over to the noise and vulgarity of a funfair (though the more valid criticism of the Battersea funfair is surely that it is too tame and tawdry; noisy and vulgar is what a funfair arguably should be).

But increasingly the light has broken through. People have come to accept that the alternative to turning over a corner of your park to rough and ready, minimally 'controlled' opportunity for children to get some 'adventure', is to find, too late, that they are getting it in other ways and places—dangerously on demolition sites, vandalistically and dangerously on the streets, or destructively and to the disruption of their elders' peace among formal flower beds and forbidden shrubberies which offer them little that is permitted but the frustration of their energies and adventurous instincts.

The attitude of the County Hall parks administration towards landscape has also been more positive and enlightened than that of most parks departments in Greater London. The G L C, like the L C C before it, has a distinct 'house style' reflected not only in parks' notice boards—neat, clear, but unobtrusive—but in its use of the materials and tools of the landscape architect. The term is significant. While all too many council parks departments, in and out of London, still think in terms only of herbaceous borders and neat beds of salvia, the L C C long ago understood that landscape was something that could be moulded and given character and functional usefulness—if seen and treated as a whole, not in little bits.

Its attitude to trees is in tune with this. It knows how to keep them healthy by careful surgery, not butchery. And while local councils in some areas still wring their hands in despair that vandals have destroyed their ill-protected saplings, held to puny stakes and surrounded with an ineffectual skirt of chicken wire, the G L C runs a tree bank. It plants out not saplings, but 20 ft semi-mature forest trees, and puts a sturdy 6 ft by 6 ft by 6 ft wooden cage round them if there is still any danger. If Peter Walker wants, as he has said, landscape architects' influence to be on a par with that of accountants, he might do worse than seek means to encourage their use as consultants by the more backward municipal parks departments.

Of course, the broad comparison of County Hall excellence with borough backwardness admits of exceptions. There are enlightened parks administrations in some boroughs, among them Harrow. But in general terms the contrast is clear. Why is this? There are, I think, a number of reasons. The very size of the G L C operation produces advantages. It provides a careers structure with top posts that attract officers of talent and imagination. It demands, in this as in other spheres, that elected members give their officials a greater degree of practical autonomy, a greater freedom of manœuvre, than local borough parks committees have in practice generally been ready to allow. And the size of the budget means that the imaginative proposal is less likely to be objected to as an expensive extravagance than in the smaller set-up.

## The parks transfer battle

It was these and other factors that led a strong body of opinion in London to oppose the handing over of part of the County Hall parks system to the boroughs. This the G L C, under the 1963 London Government Act, had a statutory duty to carry out. In principle, of course, as the former leader of the London Boroughs Association, Mr Godfrey Taylor, strenuously argued, local authorities with populations of upwards of a quarter of a million were more than capable of looking after parks and open spaces; and it was a little unfair of opponents of the handover to argue (largely on the basis of inner London) that they were incapable when, in many cases, they had scarcely ever had the chance to prove otherwise. Small parks and public gardens apart, in many places in the old county it had always been the L C C that made all the running.

On the other hand, when men with the narrow horizons of the herbaceous border mentality are entrenched, as officials and councillors, an increase in the scale of responsibility does not necessarily produce the desired change in outlook. As evidence of this I quote the words used by the leader of Kensington and Chelsea Council, Sir Malby Crofton, to *The Times Diary* in 1968, in seeking to justify the proposed takeover of the G L C's Holland Park by his borough. What his council sought to administer, he said, was 'the cutting of grass and the tending of flowerbeds.' Sir Malby, I believe, intended no irony; but it was a remark that utterly damned his council's aspirations in the eyes of both landscape architects and amenity society members, because it was deeply indicative of the 'negative', 'herbaceous border' approach to parks management.

As Mr Leslie Ginsburg, architect and the Civic Trust's planning adviser, put it in November 1971 (at a joint meeting of the Institute of Landscape Architects and the Design and Industries Association), 'There isn't really a proper organisation in most boroughs to do the job. Borough landscape work isn't really landscape work at all. With a few honourable exceptions, it is gardening and tree hacking.'

Nor is this distrust of borough parks departments and borough engineers in London restricted to professionals with a vested interest or sympathy for a vested interest. It is shared by many ordinary citizens who like the old avenues of planes and other forest trees, and react sharply to plans to replace them with supposedly tidier, ornamental varieties —as the case of the Bedford Park trees, discussed later, shows.

Perhaps the most powerful argument which swayed those who argued for keeping the G L C parks administration intact was that of 'established excellence'. To throw away decades of effort spent in building it up to a standard rare in parks management, and to dismantle an existing efficient and progressive organisation in the hypothetical belief that the separate organisations of thirty-two London boroughs would all, or mostly, be able to match its standards—that, they argued, was altogether too much of a gamble.

The argument, indeed, was in some ways akin to that successfully advanced for the retention intact of the L C C education service. The difference was that education at that time carried altogether more political weight, and a device for preservation of the County Hall education service—as that constitutionally nonsensical but practically admirable body, the I L E A—had been written into the London Government Act before it reached the statute book.

All that the defenders of the G L C parks administration were able to achieve was (a) a sensibly delayed action for the transfer, and, more important, (b) a provision for the G L C to retain parks and open spaces which were 'for the benefit of an area of Greater London substantially larger' than the borough concerned—an elastic definition which looks as though it has turned out to be very nearly all-important. For it rapidly became clear as protest about the handover grew vocal in 1968, that the protesters and the G L C were often talking about different things.

The opposition to the transfer argued how monstrous it was that the capital's great open spaces, the heritage of all Londoners, like Hampstead Heath and Battersea Park, should be balkanised among councils ill-equipped to care for them. The G L C, however, was applying itself to settling cash terms for handing over, not such familiar parks of metropolitan importance, but the small and medium-sized ones— used largely by local people and, it could be argued, little known to the wider London public.

However, the G L C, locked in some tough bargaining with the London Boroughs Association (some of whose member boroughs in the inner areas were very reluctant to accept parks in their areas unless the G L C agreed to cushion fairly handsomely the rate burden they would acquire), was somewhat inhibited from refuting this misconception. While negotiations were still going on it could not say exactly which parks it would be keeping and which handing over.

In the event, the final transfer deal was much less catastrophic than had been widely feared. The G L C kept 47 out of its original 172 open spaces, and the acreage is even more significant: 5,530 out of a former total of 7,615 acres. It includes all the major open spaces and chains of open spaces, including Hampstead Heath and all the adjacent parks (Kenwood, Golders Hill, Parliament Hill, etc.) Black-heath, the too little known Bostall Woods/Abbey Woods chain between Shooters Hill and Thamesmead, Hainault Forest and Hackney Marshes, Wormwood Scrubs, Crystal Palace and Peckham Rye, and Holland, Battersea, Finsbury, Southwark, Victoria and Brockwell Parks.

Some of these—Hampstead and Blackheath—were never in fact even theoretically negotiable, because of the terms on which they are held and managed by the council. But the really significant part of the list contained parks like the last eight named—medium-sized parks of between 50 and 200 acres, which were a marginal category under the Act and could have gone either way. Apart from haggling over financial terms by boroughs reluctant to take up new responsibilities without a handsome dowry (and some of the Labour boroughs like Southwark were anyway politically opposed to the transfer), another factor became very clear. It is shown clearly by the attitude of Haringey (at that time a Conservative borough) towards receiving Finsbury Park, whose 115 acres were almost entirely within its boundaries.

The transfer of this park broke down basically because, though in Haringey, Finsbury Park is probably used very much more by the citizens of neighbouring Islington, and Haringey were not inclined to accept this rates burden predominantly for another borough's benefit. (Islington—also at that time Tory—was incidentally another of the inner boroughs which was distinctly unenthusiastic about the handover.) In reality, in the inner areas at least, the borough boundaries do not make sense for parks provision of more than a purely local kind; and the realisation by councillors of all parties of the practical and financial implications of this were, I suspect, the main reason why the cookie crumbled as it did.

## Parks: some criticisms and problems

Two other responsibilities which the G L C, probably sensibly, retained in the final package were its role as developer of riverside parks and gardens—clearly a strategic role in many places; and its responsibility for creation of new open spaces in the inner areas, such as the emerging North Camberwell and Barnsbury ones—chains of parkland being carved out of the built-up area of tightly-knit nineteenth-century inner London which so lacks them. It is a long, difficult and expensive business, tied in with slum clearance and urban renewal, and as such better tackled by the G L C.

On the manner of creating the North Camberwell open space, rather than the concept of it, the G L C has come in for some quite severe criticism recently. One of its own landscape architects, Mr Michael Ellison—speaking in a private rather than a G L C capacity—told that same joint meeting of the I L A and the D I A at which Leslie Ginsburg was so critical of parks policy, that he thought the actual implementation of the North Camberwell scheme was sadly lacking in imagination and flair. What could have been a splendid opportunity, he said, had been reduced to 'triangles of grass, acres of black top, and carefully chosen, beautifully maintained forest trees in quite a range of species'. It did little to enliven or enhance a rather drear part of London, he complained, and added that the 'cheapness, nervousness and botanical purity of the scheme are a loss of the fabric opportunities. The only life tempted into it is sniffing dogs.' The opportunity had been grasped, but the grasp was, so to speak, shaky and ill-judged.

His basic argument, was that 'parks provision' as such was an out-of-date concept. We should be talking more in terms of usable pedestrian space, with trees and gardens and squares valued as the asset they are to adjoining property. As roads were widened and pavements stayed the same—though more vulnerable to traffic noise and disturbance—we needed to plan consciously to provide strolling and sitting space for resident Londoners, commuters and the growing migrations of tourists. Neither engineers nor parks administrators were geared up to cater for this need.

Mr Ellison also advanced, on the same occasion, an interesting theory about open space use and need, which appeared to suggest that small, local open spaces were in practice more important and useful than large ones. He based this on a survey carried out by the G L C parks department at the end of the sixties which, he said, showed that Londoners needed a hierarchy of parks from the large 'regional' open space to which people were prepared to travel some miles, down to neighbourhood open spaces of about two acres of which there should at least be one within a quarter-mile radius of every home.

The question of priorities for limited available resources can all too easily be ignored by those proposing ambitious extensions of existing open spaces. The furore over Witanhurst, a magnificently sited mansion at the top of Highgate West Hill, was a case in point. The threat of development led many people who loved Hampstead Heath to urge that it and its grounds should be added to the Hampstead chain of open spaces as an extension, just as land between Jack Straw's Castle and Hampstead Garden Suburb had been added in the 1930s.

But the likely cost was formidable—a probable £1.5 million in compensation to the developers who had already received outline planning permission from Camden Council. Others thought it shocking, if public funds were being suggested, that the spending of such a huge sum should be proposed for the marginal extension of open space in an area already abundantly provided with open space. It should be spent on more urgent social purposes—schools, hospitals, housing—they said; or if on open spaces then in areas like nearby Islington where whole districts lacked anything more than small gardens or public squares.

The argument was in fact a confused one, and one needs to separate several distinct questions; the intrinsic value of the house, Witanhurst; its value as part of the view; the effect of the proposed development on the view; and whether the estate ought to be added at considerable expense to the Heath. Anyone who knew and loved Hampstead Heath and the view from it of the Highgate heights would be likely to want to preserve that view, but that is not the same thing as saying they would want to spend scarce resources making it into a park and preventing all development.

One possibility which suggested itself was the compromise of allowing low-rise, private development in well-landscaped surroundings so as to preserve the view (some compensation would be payable to the developer, but homes in such a revised scheme would command top prices), with the house bought and retained for public or community purposes and a right of way established through the site connecting Highgate Village with the Heath. In the event Mr Walker called the case in at the end of April 1971, and at the time of writing a decision was still awaited.

But to return to Michael Ellison. He argued that Inner London, large parts of which were chronically under-provided with parks, needed open spaces to serve not only its 3.1 million residents, but also its daily influx of 3.5 million commuters and its annual influx of tourists, whose numbers were currently increasing at a rate of 1 million a year. If adequate provision were to be made for those who lived in the inner areas, then these commuting and package tour populations must also be allowed for, and planned for not in vague general terms, but with precise overall policies.

He and Mr Ginsburg both complained that the Greater London Development Plan ducked this question. It contained little more than vague statements of need, and pious but equally vague statements of intention. There was no blueprint, let alone machinery, for London open space provision. 'The G L C is opting out of its responsibilities for landscape,' said Mr Ginsburg.

The reason for this is, I think, pretty plain. The London Government Act saw the G L C as the strategic authority, but blurred the demarcation line between what is and is not strategic. This demarcation problem has created constant bad blood with the boroughs, and parks was an area in which the G L C thought it could avoid unnecessary bad blood. So it passed the policy buck to the individual boroughs—which in the case of inner London is no answer at all.

Mr Ellison's solution was an interesting and constructive one. He accepted that the transfer of responsibility was taking place, and implicitly that the G L C was unlikely to fill the policy vacuum. But he also demonstrated convincingly that it was nonsensical for the inner London boroughs to try to plan open space provision on an individual council basis. The inner boroughs, he said, should form a consortium to carry out the job. This idea has many attractions. It could provide a career structure and enable the recruitment of specialist skills in a way that the boroughs could not. Indeed, the lack of a career structure had been early recognised, in May 1968, by Mr Godfrey Taylor who as leader of the London Boroughs Association was then already negotiating the terms of the handover with the G L C.

The L B A in general avoided questioning the quality of the service provided by the G L C parks department, and indeed did it the compliment of asking that certain services —one o'clock clubs for small children, entertainments and mobile zoos among them—should continue to be provided on an agency basis. In the public eye, this may seem to meet the worst practical objections to the handing over of a given park—and the G L C provided such amenities not just in its largest open spaces but in the small and medium-size ones. (For example, the fifty-eight acres of Maryon and Maryon Wilson parks at Charlton, in which much of the Antonioni film *Blow-up* was shot, is considerably more attractive to children because of visits from G L C mobile zoos and of pony and pony trap rides.)

But one cannot but be doubtful about this agency arrangement as anything more than a short-term expedient. The individual boroughs are buying the service, and though they may be unlikely even in times of financial stringency to cut such popular items as I have mentioned, they will almost certainly tend to fight any extension or improvement which costs money. This factor may damage the G L C department in two ways: it may find itself providing, frustratingly, a second-class service for cost reasons in parks handed over to some boroughs; and it may find that borough resistance to paying more for a better service rubs off on what it can do in its own parks. An agency could prove the worst of both worlds. This would certainly be so if it gives some boroughs an excuse for not setting up the necessary parks administration, either individually or, better, on a consortium basis.

Mr Ellison's theory of open space provision is admirable in its flexible view of what constitutes 'open space', and where and how it can be used. It breaks free of the traditional view that a park is a park unless it's a garden. But his thesis that the local open space has in many ways greater usefulness because it is more accessible to people's homes calls for one reservation. This reservation is based on increasing car ownership and mobility. As we shall see in discussing the country park phenomenon (Chapter 10), people —including families—are prepared to drive quite long distances to rural 'open spaces' if the attractions are great enough.

In a large conurbation, this is already partly true of the 'urban countryside' provided, for instance, at Hampstead Heath or Kew Gardens. This does not, however, upset the Ellison argument. These are planned excursions made typically at week-ends or other times when the family car is available. The small local open space serves a different purpose: it is within pram-pushing, four-year-old or old-age pensioner walking distance from home, in circumstances where there is no family car or it is not available. These are sunny-half-hour rather than Sunday afternoon places. And here—as in talking about public transport provision—the distinction between cars per household and availability of cars to the household cannot be too much emphasised.

If a consortium provides the best available answer to

lack of adequate policy and management structure for parks in inner London, what can fill the immediate vacuum in skilled talent and counter the entrenched herbaceous border mentality? Probably the most hopeful answer is as has been suggested earlier, the use of consultants. In this field, as elsewhere, even the best and most far-sighted professionals can find themselves so tied to day-to-day administration and short-term problems that they are unable to stand back and take the long, broad look.

## Adventure at Markfield

A good, recent example of the sort of thing which a borough parks administration and a consultant working together can produce was unveiled in April 1971 in a densely populated area of Tottenham with all too little open space provision. I went to look at it with an interest made all the keener because, eleven years earlier, I had spent a week helping out as a (totally untrained) supply teacher in a junior school there, and had therefore glimpsed the problems. The borough concerned, Haringey, splits broadly along the line of the main railway out of Kings Cross—socially, politically, and more to the point here, in terms of open space provision, it is well heeled to the west (Highgate, Muswell Hill, Crouch End), while to the east (with the exception of some areas round Wood Green) it is underprovided. Here are the flatter lands bordering the Lee Valley, which were densely built over in the nineteenth century with rather mean terrace houses for artisans. South Tottenham is very much the wrong side of the tracks.

Here there existed a small, dull, functional recreation ground called Markfield, and alongside a disused sewage works and associated pig farm. The social scientist would not be surprised in this situation that bored youngsters broke bounds and enjoyed themselves gloriously, adventurously, but dangerously and destructively among the derelict filter beds and in the pumphouse which held a fine old steam beam engine. Some people in Haringey council apparently were surprised. It certainly and understandably had them worried.

So for several years they spent £2,000 a year on a 24-hour-a-day security guard, with Alsatian dogs, to 'stop people from damaging it and themselves.' Then, much to their credit, they decided—in the light of the Lee Valley regional park plan of which the area would form a part—to let the kids in for adventure instead. They brought in a leading landscape architect, Mary Mitchell, and spent £30,000 (some of which was recoverable in a government derelict land grant) in turning these 6½ acres into Markfield Action Playground.

Some 75,000 tons of subsoil acquired by dint of making part of the area a free tip, were imported, and Miss Mitchell used these to create grassed hills and mounds and ridges. These have two purposes: to screen the playground from the park and adjoining railway lines, and to provide interest both visually and as play features. Children enjoy running up and down hills and hiding behind them. But much of the old sewage works structure was retained and turned to good account. The filter beds, cleared of rubble and dirt, provide separate spaces for roller skating, archery and other such activities, and for play equipment like climbing frames.

In the pumphouse, the beam engine was to be preserved as a working museum piece, but other empty parts of the building were already on the first day serving for table-tennis and netball or volleyball.

One magnificent grassed hill, on which Haringey planned to have an artificial ski-slope, was clearly going to be a great favourite among the children for running up and down, sitting and standing on and looking out from. It gave a vantage point rare in these flat Lee Valley lands, with views across the neighbourhood and of the occasional container-train edging its way round the curve of the railway embankment on to the main line.

Below, in yet another concrete length of old filter bed, Haringey's jeans-and-sweater-clad play leaders were already, on this first day of opening and to the landscape architect's relief and delight, with half a dozen local children rapidly knocking together a typical adventure playground structure of old timbers, six inch nails and gaudy paint. No one looked too much askance. The climate is changing. The borough's director of recreational services admitted frankly that a few years back he had been apt to recoil with horror from such structures, but had come to realise their value to the youngsters and the community as an alternative to vandalism, danger and needless conflict with the law.

Possibly in Haringey's case the catalyst was a Conservative council majority elected in the sudden floodtide of 1968 and discovering at first hand what the problems of this proletarian, mixed-race district really were. They needed to prove that they cared. Haringey was learning the lesson—which many politicians and quite a few architects have still failed to absorb—that environmental upgrading is not just, or even mainly, a matter of visual æsthetics.

For as others have learnt (including Tower Hamlets council, quite recently, in the Isle of Dogs), you do not cure decades of environmental neglect by simply planting trees, using bright new materials, colour schemes and lettering styles, and putting in the odd play-space for toddlers. That is to invite the old vandalism to try its aim on new targets. You also need what the industrial group dynamics men call 'motivation'. Local people—and especially young people— need to feel the improvements are theirs, to get involved.

Otherwise it is all an alien exercise by uncomprehending and uncomprehended outsiders—something to be smashed up first, and laughed at afterwards, in that order. Markfield Action Playgroup and other exercises like it, provided there is adequate and sympathetic play leadership, can be part of that positive motivation. Even so, in some areas— like the Isle of Dogs—environmental upgrading will be an uphill business with constant setbacks. But without it, the area is almost certainly doomed.

## London's neglected river

Mention of the Isle of Dogs brings us conveniently to another of the key London features which the Greater London Development Plan inquiry showed that people were concerned about. London's attitude to its river has for well over a century now been a two-faced one. The Thames was the object of a good deal of sentiment and poetry, but, if you did not actually live on those green and pleasant upper reaches above Chiswick, the Thames was something to be recognised because it was there, a barrier and an impediment rather than an asset and an avenue.

What has changed this in the last decade or so is the movement of shipping downstream as vessels grew larger and required deeper berths. It is neither a new phenomenon (the St Katherine and London Docks were built in an earlier age for just such a reason) nor in any way unique to London. It was foreseen—dimly—both by public and the authorities. Yet what took both by surprise was its suddenness. And it changed everything.

## The South Bank blossoms

For years the G L C and Lambeth and Southwark boroughs had looked forward to redevelopment of the obsolescent warehouses which fronted the south bank of the river from Waterloo Bridge to Tower Bridge. Then, in 1970 and 1971, it was (to employ the pop man's graphic phrase) suddenly seen to be 'all happening'. Consortia were formed; Sam Wannamaker's and Christopher Plummer's dreams of reconstructions of Globe theatres and a neo-Shakespearian quarter were suddenly taken seriously by everyone (except perhaps cynical newspaper reporters); ingenious architects juggled with provision for the riverside walk, demanded by the G L C, so as to boost their permitted plot ratios for redevelopment; and men in County Hall and the Royal Fine Arts Commission worried about preserving vistas of St Paul's across the river.

The suddenness of it all was to large extent more apparent than real. Plans had been going ahead steadily on several projects for quite a time. But a number of factors, other than the dominant one of the decline of shipping to the wharves and older docks, did come together to contribute to the effect. The West End had been becoming increasingly difficult for developers for years. There was less land there, it was more expensive, and both Westminster and Kensington and Chelsea had become increasingly sticky both on demolition of listed buildings and on planning applications for redevelopment.

At the same time, the tourist boom—with the annual influx of visitors rising by a million each year—created great demand for new hotels. Partly because suitable sites were running out, partly because of increasing opposition to loss of homes and residential character, the traditional post-

war area for this—the West End and near the air terminals
—was clearly not going to provide for this much more. And
tourists, in many ways more appreciative of London's neglected treasures than the natives, were well known to be
drawn by the river.

Then, in January 1970, the G L C succeeded in persuading
the minister, after a public inquiry, to rezone the warehousing area as 'West End'. Offices and hotels could come
and were welcome. Other factors probably included the fact
that the National Theatre, after years of false starts and
disappointed hopes, was now seen to be rising on its new
site (the third to be marked out for it) immediately below
Waterloo Bridge; the decision in favour of a Thames Barrier; the steadily increasing cleanness of the river, with
fifty-seven varieties of fish to be found by 1971, including
bass caught at Greenwich; and the feeling of developers
that under the newly elected Tory government the climate
was right for redevelopment.

Not everyone liked what was happening. There was
great nostalgia for the old wharves and warehouses, and
for the little lanes and alleys which ran down to and along
the river, not only on the South Bank but on the north side
below Blackfriars Bridge where the City Corporation's relief
road and North Bank redevelopment had resulted in acres
of old Victorian buildings being bulldozed into the gap behind a new river wall. A great deal of this was *post hoc*
sentiment for buildings which had never been much regarded during their working lives; part of it was the result
of the new enthusiasm for all things Victorian; and part a
reaction to the destruction of the familiar and informal and
its apprehended replacement by buildings and roads on an
alien, less human scale.

These were, of course, generalised fears, just as the defensive reactions were not always applied to the best of
the old buildings. The new architects have tried in varying
degrees and with varying levels of success to make the new
developments pleasant for people to work and live in, and
wander through. And in one or two instances the problem of a viable new use for an old commercial building on
a valuable site has been solved—the Samuel Pepys pub and
restaurant at Brooks Wharf, Garlickhythe, though playing
in rather extreme form to the gallery in the person of

American tourists (and probably derided by the purist for its beams and its wimples) is a case in point. Smith's Wharf next door at Queenhithe could have been, I think, with advantage incorporated as handsome public rooms into the new hotel building there, but for economic or other reasons a cleared site solution was preferred.

## Redundant dockland

A bigger worry, however, concerned the wider dockland area. Because of the container trade revolution, aided to some extent by the steady transformation of the nature of dock labour under the Devlin new deal, not just the wharves but the greater part of the nineteenth-century dock system below Tower Bridge was being displaced, more rapidly than had been thought possible, by deep water berths at Tilbury and elsewhere downstream. Economy of scale dictated larger vessels and larger vessels meant unloading or trans-shipment downriver. This had happened with oil and other bulk cargoes years before. Shellhaven and other oil port installations in the Canvey area had pointed the way. The Port of London Authority's own £3 million grain terminal upstream of Tilbury followed in 1968. The arrival of containerisation meant that the application of this law of economy of scale could not long be delayed for other cargoes.

So here, potentially, was a vast area for re-development —six miles of riverside and more—stretching to the fringes of the City. The G L C grasped the nettle with the first section of P L A land to come on the market, St Katherine's Dock, set guide-lines for balanced development, invited comprehensive plans from developers, and chose an imaginative scheme put up by Taylor Woodrow—a hotel, conference centre, public and private housing and a marina for small boats. Work on the £22 million project started in 1970 and, despite some criticism from idealists who complained that the private homes had the best river views (Taylor Woodrow, after all, needed to sell them to make the project pay), it looked like being, both economically and environmentally, a success.

But St Katherine's was not by this time the real worry. It was after all only 27 acres out of 5,000 or more. And,

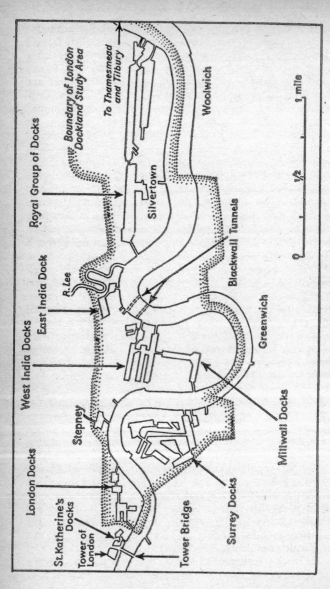

FIGURE 6. The London docks

nearest central London and hard by the tourist attraction of the Tower, it was probably the choicest site from a development point of view. The real fear was that the great opportunity presented by the London and Surrey Docks (already closed by early 1970), and the West and East India, Millwall and ultimately the much larger Royal groups of docks behind Woolwich reach, would be muffed —that instead of seizing the opportunity to transform the environment of East London, by planning its redevelopment as a whole, the government, the G L C and the boroughs would talk piously of the need to do so, but in practice sanction relatively piecemeal development of a disappointing standard and with little relation of one site to another.

The G L C, it is true, did set up an internal study of the Surrey Docks area and intended to produce a discussion paper on future action. But they seemed inhibited from taking a longer look, at least publicly, at P L A lands which were not yet available. Whether the G L C would, left to its own devices, have acted strongly enough to push through an integrated solution one cannot tell. Many planners and others doubted it. And certainly a Tory G L C would have found itself on uncertain ground had it ever needed to tell the entrenched and in some ways very insular Labour masters of Tower Hamlets that their developments were planned with too narrow horizons, too low an environmental standard and would perpetuate the ruinously one-class character of dockland society.

## Mr Walker's Dockland Study

In the event they were saved from any such embarrassing possibility by ministerial intervention. On April 28 1971, Peter Walker announced in a House of Commons answer to Bob Mellish, Labour M P for dockland Bermondsey, that he was in effect freezing 5,000 acres of dockland (2,000 of them ready for redevelopment), stretching from the old London Docks in the west to Beckton in the east, for eighteen months pending a full study by planning and economic consultants. The fact that Mr Mellish, then chief whip, broke with parliamentary convention to put down the question, shows how important this Cockney Labour leader, born and bred in London's dockland, considered the matter.

He had been desperately afraid that the opportunity for improving this traditionally down-at-heel segment of London was not going to be taken. Even if the threat of a vertical-take-off airport on the Surrey Docks site had by that time receded a little, the prospect for a really imaginative deal for East London from the Tory G L C had not looked good. Mr Walker had a month or two earlier promised the House of Commons that he was determined not to have a piecemeal redevelopment.

Mr Walker was in no doubt about the importance of the decision. It was, he said, the most exciting one in its potential he had taken since the D O E came into being. Rarely in any large city could such a huge area only two miles from the centre have become suddenly available in this way. It provided an opportunity unique in this century, and it would have been 'tragic' had it been missed. 'I am determined,' he told Mr Mellish, 'that this opportunity shall not be lost by allowing haphazard development.'

All in all the decision's reception publicly was one of welcome. But Mr Walker had prepared the ground well. Consultations with Desmond Plummer and other G L C leaders, as well as the leaders of the borough councils involved and the P L A as the big landowners, had been extensive.

One interpretation of the decision—perhaps uncharitable, but with more than a grain of truth in it—was that the minister was saying to the G L C, as well as to the boroughs, 'You're incapable of doing the job, so I'm taking over.' And this would be a serious indictment of the 'largest local authority in the world' which prided itself on its strategic, 'regional' outlook. In so far as it was true, however, Mr Walker had spared no pains to save any hurt feelings. There were worries about the effect of the study on developments that the boroughs—particularly Tower Hamlets—were already on the point of starting, and, for the P L A's part, its effect on their ability to sell their redundant land without delay. But no one publicly had anything but good to say of it.

Let us look more closely at what the minister was doing. He had given a team of consultants a £250,000 brief (half paid for by the G L C) and an eighteen month deadline. Led by Mr Alfred Goldstein of civil engineers R. Travers Morgan and Partners (one of the Roskill technical team), the team consisted of engineers, planners and valuers, and was backed by a retainer to the London office of Robert Matthew, Johnson-Marshall as advisers on planning and environmental matters. They were to look at this whole area of disused or obsolescent docks, decaying and derelict commercial properties, outworn housing, poor public transport and generally thoroughly drab surroundings, and come up with ways in which it could be redeveloped. They would probably, said Mr Walker, suggest a number of alternative options. On the basis of these the D O E and the other authorities concerned could agree a plan.

In the meantime, all applications for development, however minor and detailed, would be referred to the G L C—and the G L C presumably would then pass them to the consultants and/or the Department. Means would be found to deal with 'urgent development applications'—a potentially elastic proviso, but it looked as though he meant to construe it restrictively—and if before the end of the study there was general agreement that such and such an area was ideal for, say housing, then development would go ahead without waiting for the full answers.

This sensible second proviso brought special praise from the leader of the G L C's Labour opposition, Sir Reginald Goodwin, whose Southwark constituency included the Surrey Docks. 'Exactly the approach I would have hoped for,' he commented. His only reservation was that he would have liked the upstream Southwark area between London and Tower bridges included (the reason why it was excluded was probably because the go-ahead had already been given for a good deal of development on that stretch). But of the study decision as a whole he said, 'It is an extremely good proposal and entirely welcome.'

So fulsome, indeed, was the chorus of eulogy from even unlikely quarters politically that one began to wonder where the snag was. The truth is, of course, that the announcement of a consultant's study is the pill sugared. It is towards the end of the exercise that people begin to taste the real flavour of the thing.

## Problems of dockland

The point about poor transport is one worth elaborating on. The plight of the East End, originating in nineteenth-century poverty and overcrowding, was compounded by poor transport in many areas, and by a working-class ghetto attitude in local politics and therefore in planning. In the immediately post-war area, the aim was to build homes for East Enders rendered homeless in the blitz, and a mixture of medium-rise blocks of flats and rows of terrace houses were the generally adopted answer. Even the L C C's Lansbury development in Poplar, for its day an enlightened piece of planning, did little—indeed could do little—to dent the one-class character of the area. Who, bar the odd devoted doctor or social worker willing to move there as well as work there, wanted to live in the East End if he had not grown up there?

But then of course, London was still turning its back on the river. It was only a decade or two later that Len Deighton and other well-heeled explorers saw the attraction of converting warehouses with views and terraces on to a tideway now largely freed from both water and air pollution—and sewage and pre-war dockland fogs—and from the weight of commercial shipping. And this links with the point about public transport. The river not so much winds as loops through this section of dockland (see Figure 6), and there are no bridges—only (until the Blackwall duplication of 1967) congested, fume-filled road tunnels and well-used but time- and energy-consuming foot tunnels.

The Isle of Dogs, traditionally a tight, inward-looking community, was accessible by road and public transport only from the north. Its buses ran along a long, drab cul-de-sac to serve a dwindling residential and working population who sought independent means of transport if they could. Silvertown, between the Thames and the Royal group of docks, is similarly an island cut off from the main radial line of road and tube communications into London. If anything it looked more to Woolwich across the river by ferry or foot tunnel than to its hinterland. What was needed was some line of communication running more or less straight, east-west, cutting across the loops and bends of the Thames to link these pockets and islands so that the river ceases to be a barrier.

The first suggestion that the G L C were considering this in the summer of 1970, when it became known that they were reconsidering the notion of a Greenwich by-pass by double river crossing through the Isle of Dogs in the light of the road links needed for any effective redevelopment of the island. This was the solution that Colin Buchanan and Partners soon afterwards suggested, and its history illuminates the difference between looking at projects locally and in the broad view.

When first proposed by a member of the Greenwich Society as a solution to their traffic problems, it looked ridiculously expensive. Seen from an environmental point of view alongside the G L C alternatives, it looked the right answer but still expensive. But, as the Buchanan Greenwich study pointed out, the real answer was in terms of its benefit to both sides of the river. And looked at from this point of view it becomes primarily a means of revitalising the Isle of Dogs, and only secondarily the salvation of Greenwich.

The earlier distortion of relative values derives from two causes: (a) Greenwich, though by no means an entirely middle-class area, had an articulate, determined and often quite expert and influential pressure group; the Isle of Dogs, until its much publicised but rather suspect 1970 'U D I', had none. (b) Everyone was guilty of thinking in the old ruts, which saw the two sides of the river as separate. Even the G L C was in its own rut—the established project for a major route along the south side of the Thames, of which a Greenwich by-pass in Greenwich formed an apparently essential part. Mercifully Peter Walker, whatever other criticisms may be made of him, is not often guilty of rutted thinking.

What made the Dockland Study most hopeful and meaningful, however—even though the study decision antedated it—was the government's choice of Foulness for the third London airport. One of the main arguments in Professor Buchanan's dissenting Roskill opinion had been the positive effect a Foulness site could have in redressing the west-east imbalance in London. and it was certainly one of the factors that made Mr Walker argue in Cabinet for Foulness.

If a healthy mixture of development is to be the prime instrument of transforming East London, then there could be no more powerful generator of this than a major airport to the east. Tourist hotels on the tideway, technologically advanced industry making sophisticated high-value, light-weight products, more and a greater range of owner-occupied homes, from service workers directly or indirectly owing their jobs to the airport to the executive pads of sales managers with international territories—all these should be attracted.

And even though the airport was a good seven years off when the Docks Study was announced, the Foulness decision could well already have added to the attractions of some kind of development on East End Thames-side. From that point of view, too, the study and its associated freezing of development may not, following two days after the Foulness announcement, have come any too soon.

## Fast river transport

Nor, when we talk of improved communications for dock-land, should we miss the fact that the river itself—so much used in Pepys's time to avoid the traffic jams of Whitehall and the City—has until recently been largely neglected as a contribution towards better public transport. It has been consistently treated—despite gallant attempts in the fifties to run a 'water bus' service—as something for tourists and fine Sundays.

Now the matter is beginning to be seen in a different light, partly because of faster craft like hydrofoils and hovercraft, partly because the movement of commercial shipping to deep water berths downriver means that there are fewer objections to the more intensive operation of such craft. The GLC did in fact in 1969 commission a report from a subsidiary of the Bowring group, Hoverprojects Ltd., on the feasibility of such services.

The resulting report, which came down in favour at that time of the Russian-built hydrofoil as the more economical and dependable craft, showed that such services could, if the initial outlay were covered by a GLC capital grant, offer fares at services comparable with or a little lower than existing rail services. They would do so at attractive frequencies (about ten to fifteen minute intervals) and the journey times for short hauls like Charing Cross to Greenwich would be quicker, while for longer distances like Woolwich and Thamesmead they would be about the same.

The idea of such a fast commuter and tourist service was strongly supported by Mr Roderick Doble, Town Clerk and chief executive of Greenwich borough, whose riverside stretches from Deptford Creek to Thamesmead. He knew that hotel development on a council-owned site at Greenwich depended on good (preferably waterborne) tourist transport, and that commercial development down river at Woolwich would be helped by it. The British rail service on the Greenwich line, though quite fast, was of half-hour, off-peak frequency, and not comparable with the underground; but British Rail, apart from losing the confidence of marginal travellers who now drove or went by other routes when they could, seemed to have lost its own confidence. It argued that a rail route running near the riverside did not justify any greater frequency of service because its catchment area was only half that of a line not bounded by the river: the river as a barrier again. The argument has some force, but was basically a counsel of despair as far as local people were concerned and regarded by them as a recipe for running down the service.

Greenwich and the Hoverprojects managing director, Mr Ron Shaw, were anxious that a pilot service should be tried out in the summer of 1971, but difficulties over making craft available on a charter rather than sale basis postponed the start until the following year. The capital cost of the fast river service would certainly be tiny as compared with building a new tube line or main road for the same distance, but if such capital investment was coming anyway, as part of dockland redevelopment, some people wondered whether there would be room or money for the river service. The Thames barrage, which was approved after the fast river service study, did not affect its running.

But what of the airport? Was there room for a water service all or part of the way to Foulness for air passengers who wanted to reach central London by river. One cannot but feel that the project remains an attractive one, even with the changed situation created by the airport siting and the Docks Study. Its role might be that of a premium service for those prepared to pay more for the pleasure and comfort (in the sense of escape from sardine rush-hour conditions on trains), and the service could still probably be fast even with extra stops on the north bank.

This premium character might have been of doubtful viability when only Greenwich, Woolwich and Thamesmead were involved, but the addition of north bank locations with mixed development providing some premium commuting, and the airport (or a stop for the airport) gives some hope that it could pay. As a tourist gateway to London this stretch of the tideway, with its mixture of existing historic buildings and the new environment promised by Mr Walker, would be by no means inferior to any of the routes from Heathrow.

Noise is a problem, but not, the Hoverprojects researches suggested, nearly so great as might have been feared. The real difficulty is in the time-scale, in relation to the nine years of Foulness gestation. By the spring of 1971 Greenwich's and Thamesmead's need for that fast river service was already urgent. The premium commuter might be marginal to transport as a whole, but it looked like being a key factor both for tourists (the proposed new hotel at Greenwich appeared to hang on it) and the better-off buyers and tenants for its waterside private housing whom Thamesmead needed if it was to be the healthy social mixture the G L C was committed to. The attraction of a fast, regular, frequent all-weather service to Charing Cross which the project offered as an alternative to overcrowded, unreliable peak-hour trains through Southern Region's notorious bottleneck at Borough Market Junction looked like a factor that could possibly sway the balance for potential Thamesmeaders. One hopes the G L C—or the minister—sees its importance.

# PART IV

# Conservation

---

*Chapter Nine*

## BATTLE FOR THE TOWNS

*Preservation and conservation*

Conservation has become a vogue word in its application to the urban scene just as to the countryside, and in the urban context too stands in danger of being misunderstood, misused and adulterated. Often it is used more or less as a synonym for preservation. There are at least two respects in which it is basically different. First, preservation is broadly speaking negative or protectionist. Its attitudes are defensive and rarely contain any element of 'attack'. Second, it has been traditionally concerned with two objectives—to prevent destruction of valued old buildings, and, since decay and tampering with detailed appearance are as serious threats in the long run as demolition, to maintain the fabric of such individual old buildings structurally and visually.

The emphasis was, however, on individual buildings, and what public opinion largely desired to save was the substantial historic house which was threatened by decay or demolition, or the individual house in a group whose destruction or alteration would spoil the group.

So the state mechanism of listings for historic and architectural importance, statutory protection, building preservation orders and historic buildings grants were all directed towards the individual building and its individual owner, with more often than not only an implied reference to the townscape of which it was part. There may have been another historical factor here. In a climate which set individual rights of property on a pedestal to the point of resenting even benevolent encroachment, direct and separate dealings between the owner and the public authority, or the state, were the only acceptable method.

If this point seems a little exaggerated, let me give an example of how the ultra-possessive attitude which resents all interference is still sometimes found even in London. In 1970, the G L C's Surveyor of Historic Buildings, Ashley Barker, wrote on behalf of his committee—then headed by Lady Dartmouth—who is not, one would have thought, unduly associated in people's minds with an excess of collectivism or denial of the rights of private property—to the owners of some rather fine mews houses in Kensington on which the balustrading, they had noticed in making a tour of the area, needed repair. They were offering them grants for this work. In one case, the response was a lengthy and ingeniously abusive letter from the house-owner roundly asserting that whether or not he made repairs was solely his affair; it was monstrous that the G L C should be handing out ratepayers' money for such a purpose; and he trusted that the Tory majority at County Hall would live up to the principle of non-interference in private property and recommend the winding up of the Historic Buildings Board forthwith. Mr Barker, I believe, treasures that letter as a rare surviving example of robust Victorian rococo.

So preservation looked chiefly at individual buildings. Two factors occurring in the late 1950s and the 1960s worked for change. Wholesale demolitions for redevelopment made preservationists and the public realise that to safeguard the individual building was not enough if all around it changed. Half the character and value of an urbane Georgian town house is lost, they realised, if it is dwarfed by a tower block crowding in on it, or has to rub shoulders with one of the uglier variants of supermarket architecture. More pointedly still, they began to argue, what is the point of listing a row of six Tudor cottages if the road builders then come and cut away their urban context by widening and traffic management schemes which leave them stranded as an island growing daily tattier in the midst of a sea of diesel fumes and traffic vibration. The group, the townscape, was what needed to be protected and enhanced, they perceived, not just particular buildings, however much valued for their architecture or historic connections.

The logic of this took them one stage further. A townscape might have great charm and character without possessing any listed buildings at all. This was especially so, before systematic listings of Victorian buildings began, of nineteenth-century urban townscape. And this brings us to the second change: that in the climate of opinion towards things Victorian in general, and Victorian buildings in particular. The change has been rapid and remarkable, and the Victorian Society—founded in 1958—has been on occasion surprised by the rapidity with which the tide has turned. It and amenity groups throughout the country have striven valiantly to defend both individual Victorian buildings and the urban scene of which they form part. Nonetheless it is not unduly cynical to see the change in wider public attitudes as partly as much an expression of scarcity value as the boom in Victoriana which has opened and filled so many antique shops. Our first observed change, the depredation of the developer, has made people more aware and appreciative of what is left.

## Civic Trust facelifts

One of the pioneering exercises in treatment of townscape as a whole was applied to a very largely Victorian street scene: Magdalen Street, Norwich. In 1958 this shopping street was down-at-heel and tatty, a big ingredient in its tattiness being the individual do-it-yourself basis of house and shopfront painting and shop signs. The Civic Trust, founded by Duncan Sandys two years earlier, wanted to demonstrate that, given goodwill, and a sympathetic architect's skill, such a townscape could be dramatically upgraded for little more than the cost of repainting which shopkeepers would have undertaken sooner or later anyway.

The technique is in essence to remove clutter and then use carefully chosen harmonising colour schemes to emphasise the good architectural features both of individual buildings and of the group. At first sight it seemed that the greatest difficulty would be to get the agreement of dozens of different owners to participation in the scheme, including multiples in remote head offices, often with nationally-familiar shop-front styles which they would be reluctant to modify. In fact the Norwich scheme largely overcame this. Its principle of facelift by architectural harmonisation leaves room for flexibility, compromise and ingenuity by the coordinating architects. And in practice it was found that once two-thirds or more of shopkeepers and other frontagers agreed to participate, most of the others tended to come in. Of those who refused, almost all finally succumbed when the actual repainting showed up their own properties as drab and unmannerly odd men out.

Magdalen Street was both a great success on the ground and a tremendous propaganda success. Other places followed—market towns like Chesham and Haddington in Scotland; city shopping streets like Burslem's; villages like Holt in Norfolk, and even suburban centres like my own Blackheath Village. And the real snag turned out not to be getting people to join in schemes in the first place, but protecting them from erosion by outsiders. Thus visitors to Norwich today find that the considerable charm of Magdalen Street townscape was first shattered by a supermarket front which is totally at odds with its whole character—at odds with its essentially domestic scene, out of harmony with the overall colour scheme, and with lines that interrupt the rhythm of the streetscape. When that happens, the rot very often sets in. Such a breaching of the dam is a precedent which lets in other ill-mannered incursions; it is also a discouragement to those who have taken part in the scheme and learned to appreciate and care for their street.

What have been unkindly called the Civic Trust's 'tarting-up' operations have proved of tremendous value in making people aware of the good qualities of neglected urban townscape and in emphasising the visual importance of the group rather than the individual building. It can be argued that they have provided better value for money in improving the environment of our towns than almost anything else that has been done, including thorough but expensive work by expert consultants and detailed and lavishly produced conservation studies, the production costs alone of which would in some cases have gone a fair way to paying for such a paint-up.

But Civic Trust facelifts are not, and do not claim to be,

much more than skin deep. They are, in the current jargon, 'cosmetic treatment' rather than radical remedy. Psychologically they are good 'cheer-up' stuff, but—as we have seen—do not solve the basic conservation problems, such as the vulnerability to redevelopment of important unlisted buildings.

## Conservation areas

It was this which led the Trust's founder-president, Duncan Sandys, to build into his Civic Amenities Bill of 1967 the concept of the conservation area. This was to be designated by the planning authority—that is, by the county or county borough, or, in London, the London borough—on the basis, not of the galaxy of listed buildings it might and often did contain, but of the area's special character.

It did not, as listing does, carry a presumption of no change except for exceptional reasons. It rather sought to ensure that change when it did occur was sympathetic to what already existed. It did not ask planning committees to say no to new building; it sought rather to create a climate in which they could insist on new neighbours being, architecturally and in planning terms, good neighbours. I distinguish between 'architecturally and 'in planning terms' because there is rather more to this than the visual. An unmannerly new use for premises, such as noisy industrial activity in a residential area, or the generation of a large amount of new traffic on narrow streets, can erode an area's character quite as much as a façade which does not fit or a new building out of scale.

The second important point about this part of the Civic Amenities Act (another section of it attempted to tackle the problem of dumped cars and other large items of litter) was that for the first time it embodied in legislation on historic buildings not just the negative concept of protecting the urban scene, but the positive one of enhancement. Preservation had been a defensive stance. Conservation, following up the spirit of the Civic Trust facelifts and now given statutory support, went over to the attack.

Later disillusioned comment has sometimes complained that this part of the Act was 'a confidence trick'. It had no teeth, critics said. This is true. Practically speaking, it was an enabling Act. The only real duty it laid on planning authorities was, if they designated a conservation area, to advertise any planning proposals submitted to them for development within that area and allow time for comment and discussion. The duty to designate was very generally expressed, and if a planning authority chose to designate few, or even no, conservation areas, there was no effective legal compulsion. The statutory duty was no more than a powerful lever for local opinion in favour of conservation if it existed.

Nonetheless, as a propaganda device to focus attention on areas of fine quality or character, the Act was immensely successful. It gave local amenity groups a means to cajole, and sometimes shame, their local planners and councillors into recognising their urban heritage at a time when they were all too prone to sweep away whatever was down-at-heel or physically sub-standard regardless of its visual and social value. Perhaps even more important, in many cases it gave local authority architects and planners a means to overcome lethargy, disinterest, ignorance and sometimes plain philistinism among both their councillors and their fellow officials.

## The Burtons' St Leonards

A good example of the first category of persuasion is provided by the little town of St Leonards in Sussex—administratively part of Hastings county borough. St Leonards was the first planned English seaside resort, conceived and laid out between 1820 and 1860 by James Burton, builder of much of Georgian Bloomsbury, and his illustrious son Decimus. It consisted essentially of two linked sections: a colonnnaded sea-front, including the Crown House, where the Burtons, with a characteristic eye to fashion as a generator of business, invited the young Princess Victoria and her mama in 1834; and the delicately landscaped Tapshaw Valley behind it, which James Burton dotted with romantic Gothic and Regency style villas.

The elder Burton was also responsible for the carefully laid out commercial district behind his fine Assemby Rooms—streets reserved for traders ('Mercatoria'), washerwomen ('Lavatoria') and so on. Along the sides of the valley, it is often difficult to tell just which of the pretty villas were the work of James and which of Decimus, so well did father's and son's work harmonise. The essence of the landscape, however, is that everything was to scale. This scale was delicate: until the 1930s nothing occurred to disrupt it.

Then this sense of everything in proportion was sadly breached by a medal-winning chunk of concrete 'ultra-modern' called Marine Court—a massive block of flats on the sea-front demonstrating horribly clearly the principle that, other considerations apart, it is not too difficult to give a hundred people fine views if you are heedless to the fact that you are ruining landscape, seascape, skyscape and townscape for everyone else who lives in or comes to a place. The 1950s, however, scarcely showed any greater awareness of the need to keep to scale. While Marine Court breached the colonnaded seafront, Quarry Court—a sore thumb of a block of flats, strangely and sadly designed by the architect chairman of the Hastings Preservation Society—arrived to stick out square and bulky into the valley. Quarry Court is smaller than Marine Court, but proportionate to the scale of the landscape, it does almost as much damage as that massive piece of 1930s iconoclasm.

The biggest and most recent threat, however, came from the expansionist plans of Hastings Further Education College. This institution first built itself a large and really rather handsome—though unfortunately sited—three-storey building above Decimus Burton's charming 1850s crescent, Archery Gardens. The building was out of scale, but at least set back up the side of the valley, which minimised its impact. In 1966, however, the college unforgivably added another three storeys on top of this first building; and by 1970 the Hastings Further Education Committee were openly proposing to demolish Archery Gardens and construct another huge, alien block sticking out into the Tapshaw Valley, dwarfing both James Burton's Assembly Rooms and the remains of the seaside colonnades, and wrecking what was left of the original, gentle, small-scale landscape of the valley.

But some local people did care. In 1968 the newly-formed Burtons' St Leonards Society had persuaded, cajoled and partly shamed Hastings Council into designating St Leonards a conservation area, and in the trial of strength which developed in the council between the powerful and well-mobilised education committee and the planners and conservationists, the act of designation, plus public and private propaganda by the society, was crucial.

A 'visitation' arranged by the society from Georgian expert Sir John Summerson and others eloquent and skilled in the politics and psychology of conservation did much to cancel out the local political weight of the education lobby.

I should stress here that I am not for a moment implying that conservation and education are natural or inevitable rivals. Quite the contrary. It is rather that the college authorities had got themselves on the wrong site for a large, modern, educational institution—a mistake which more than one education authority made in the post-war decades when the scale of development required was not always at first appreciated. But, like others, they were loath to admit it. For an expanding institution, the St Leonards site, surrounded by narrow, hilly residential roads with several convalescent homes and similar establishments, was quite unsuitable. Those pleasant, narrow lanes became increasingly lined with student cars, while a new student car park—carved out of the town at considerable financial and environmental cost 300 yards across the valley bottom —lay almost unused.

Why is it, one asks oneself, that our further and higher educationists—traditionally the great defenders of civilised values against mere materialism—so often in the 1960s seemed to be caught in the posture of ruthlessly destroying the finest bits of townscape in the districts on which they are quartered? The question presents itself the more forcibly because of the parallel between what this county borough council's education committee sought to do to the Burtons' 'Little-Bloomsbury-by-the-Sea' and the very thorough-going philistinism in the cause of *Lebenstraum* practised by London University's development planners in Burton's London Bloomsbury.

In both cases the answer is to some extent a historical one. When Hastings placed its college where it did, it thought in terms of quite a small affair, and wanted it inside the county borough boundary. Then came the urge to extend and expand. But once an education committee—or a university senate or council—has spent money on a site, they are loath to move away or, alternatively, split campuses. (Like hospital administrators, they hold that scarce resources must be concentrated into ever larger single units, or units on adjacent sites.) But in St Leonards there seemed a very good chance that they would be made to, and the principle established that if education cannot live quietly and well-manneredly with its Georgian and Victorian neighbours, then it should go elsewhere.

Developers of educational campuses are developers in much the same way as developers of shopping centres: there may, indeed, in some areas be a higher social priority for improved shopping and entertainment than for improved education buildings. All that is different is the administrative process and the financial pay-off. But it remains development, to be governed by the same constraints of planning and conservation. The education developer has no divine right to tear down Georgian or Victorian townscape where a commercial developer would not be permitted to do so. In the case of St Leonards, split campuses or a move to a new 'green field' site would surely not have been such a tragedy. Better that successive but transitory generations of healthy young students should have to travel to their lectures and seminars (as a large proportion of British students do anyway) than that a rare and good environment should be destroyed for those who live in it and appreciate it year-in-year-out.

And that, of course, was the point of the St Leonards battle: not, as some people might have assumed, the history and sentiment attaching to the young Victoria's seaside visit and the historic buildings surviving from that period; but the need to conserve all that was left—and despite earlier incursions a very great deal was left—of an elegant, civilised and truly urbane environment.

While conservation areas, amenity societies, and the growth of feeling for the character of places which they express may have come just in time to save St Leonards, they were clearly a decade or more too late for Bloomsbury. Why is it that strength of feeling could save the one —relatively so little known—and fail to divert administrative determination in the case of the other. Burton's nationally known achievement in planned urban development?

## The rape of Bloomsbury

The answer, surely, is twofold: partly a matter of timing, partly a question of the scale of commitment and cash involved. By the time that London University's demolition men shocked the conservation-minded public into outraged protests at the destruction of Woburn Square in 1970, the climate had certainly come to favour quite strongly the conservation of London's Georgian townscape.

Had the plans that involved demolition of this and other fine Georgian terraces been drawn up in the late sixties and subjected then to university and public debate, Bloomsbury—or very much larger stretches of it—would probably have survived. The university would quickly have become adept at building behind preserved or reconstructed façades, at infilling sympathetically where the townscape was less crucial, and perhaps at putting underground much of the large and bulky bits of buildings, like engineering laboratories, which cannot easily be made to suit the scale of the Bloomsbury townscape. And, because university administrators are accustomed to making a virtue of necessity, they would have been proud and enthusiastic about conservation, instead of regarding it—as they sometimes seem to—as reactionary and obstructionist.

They might on the other hand have decentralised to a far greater extent that they have. (There are great merits in having students living as well as working in the centres of great cities, but not in numbers which dominate, nor on encapsulated university campuses which do not integrate with the social fabric of the town.) But when the Woburn Square demolitions provoked their agonised but vain protests, Sir Leslie Martin's plan for a cleared and rebuilt university precinct in Bloomsbury was already ten years old. And at the time when it was discussed and approved—both by the university and the planning authorities—Georgian architecture, Georgian squares, Georgian town planning were not held in the same esteem as they are now. Partly once more a matter of progressive demolitions enhancing scarcity value, no doubt—but not entirely. It is, I think, arguable that had the university campus plan come fifteen years later, or conservation areas and the public climate

which goes with them arrived fifteen years earlier, Bloomsbury would have been saved.

## Designation—and then?

So conservation areas were both an expression of the new
climate of opinion which saw that comprehensive enhancement was needed as an alternative to comprehensive redevelopment, and a tremendous stimulus to the growth of
that climate. How does the device work in practice? Very
often the local planning authority is nudged into designating an area, as was the case at St Leonards. In other cases
an enlightened planning authority with the resources to do
the job is ahead of public opinion. In either case, the first
move nominally is the authority's.

It advertises its intention to designate an area, usually
having done some preliminary survey work to discover just
what features of value exist in the locality, what scope
there is for improvement and just where the boundaries
can be usefully and sensibly drawn. It has probably also
put out feelers to local amenity groups and other bodies to
see how they react to the idea and to prepare them for it.
Then after the prescribed period the minister confirms the
designation.

At this or an earlier stage the planning authority will normally take some steps to explain to the wider public what
a conservation area is, why this particular area has been
selected, and what opportunities and plans there are for
enhancement. Sometimes this is done by means of public
meetings, sometimes by exhibitions, often by the publication at cost or less of an explanatory booklet. Any or all of
these can additionally attract news or feature coverage in
local newspapers.

Designation should wherever possible be accompanied, or
quite quickly followed, by some action on the ground by
the council concerned—for instance, tidying up, removal of
visual clutter, tree-planting, traffic management measures
to exclude or limit through traffic and so on. At this stage
it is vital to involve the local community in what is being
done, as well as such statutory bodies as post office and
electricity boards who (for example) may be persuaded to
'underground' some of their overhead wires. In some cases

a Civic Trust type facelift, or a renewal of a previous face-lift operation, can be made to coincide with, or serve as a follow-up to, designation. Some kind of village or local fete or carnival may be a way of attracting local people's attention and focusing it on what is being attempted. This the local planners need to play by ear according to circumstances. But maximum 'grass roots' involvement in the creation of a conservation area is not only democratically desirable but—as we shall see in Chapter 14 on Participation—essential to the meaningfulness and success of such an exercise.

Once a conservation area is designated, much depends on how determined, enlightened and skilful the planning authority is in its attitude towards development proposals. There is no magic in conservation areas. Apart from the requirement to advertise development proposals mentioned earlier, all a conservation area can do is to change the climate of assumptions that councillors, officials, residents, developers and—to some extent—the D O E have towards the place. But with that one exception, the Civic Amenities Act made no difference to the planning procedures. Refusal of unsympathetic development still has to be justified on planning grounds—of which, indeed, the existence of a conservation area may be one—and will be subject to appeal to the minister.

A skilful and enlightened planning officer will generally seek, not to exclude change and development totally, but to guide it into acceptable places and forms. He will know that without some change, transition, modification, the area is likely to decay and become ossified; but it is very much easier to state the principle of sympathetic development than to apply it in practice. The course is a tightrope one between economic, and sometimes social, stagnation on the one hand, and the visual and environmental damage brought about by too much change, too sudden change, or the wrong sort of change in the wrong places.

Suppose you save a Regency terrace in a conservation area, for instance, but allow a degree of infilling in back gardens. As a planning officer you will not be popular with those whose back garden privacy and green views are diminished, but you may nonetheless have taken the right course. But suppose that infilling generates extra traffic on narrow roads and at already congested junctions to the tune of forty or fifty extra cars. If that happens, then the damage to the conservation area's sum environment may be almost as bad as if you had in the first place recommended approval for new buildings which involved demolition of the terrace.

Enthusiasm among residents for the purposes of designation can be a tremendous bonus, especially if it expresses itself in efforts to improve the appearance of their individual houses. It is not necessarily or exclusively, however, concerned with the intangibles of good environment. When the London Borough of Lewisham designated its Blackheath conservation area, forty out of fifty households in one residential street just outside the boundary of the area petitioned to be included. Their road, leafy, tree-lined, and with pleasant, large but undistinguished Edwardian houses, was, they argued, more worthy of inclusion than many which had been included, and designation would be an encouragement to good maintenance and enhancement.

The borough planning officer, Stephen Byrne, took their point and recommended to his committee that the area should be extended. In that case the motive for petitioning was predominantly that of enthusiasm for upgrading their environment, but this was not, one suspects, unmixed with a shrewd eye to property values. Certainly designation of this and other roads not in the sought-after S.E.3 (Blackheath) postal area was quickly noted by local estate agents, who under the postal address S.E.13 (Lewisham) of properties for sale could now add 'in the Blackheath conservation area'. Designation almost at a stroke added hundreds of pounds to the values of properties in the area; though it should be added that Lewisham's development control policies as applied to the conservation area, and its encouragement to positive enhancement, will in the long run have a very much bigger effect.

One word of caution here: though designation and its follow-up should generally boost property values in a predominantly residential area, it can have the reverse effect where it restricts or removes the possibility of industrial, commercial or even larger-scale residential development. The owner of a large Victorian house of whom a developer has an option to purchase with a view to putting up forty flats in a five-storey block is not likely to be overjoyed when he learns that conservation area policy causes the planning authority to jib at anything over three storeys because it would spoil a fine skyline and generate too much traffic, and that the developer no longer considers his property worth buying on that basis.

## Conservation progress

As a propaganda exercise, conservation areas have broadly speaking been a remarkable success. By June 1970 the Civic Trust—which was keeping a careful watch and publishing the fruits of its observation in a periodic bulletin, *Conservation Progress*—was able to announce the 1,000th conservation area. A year later the number had increased to 1,500. The first 1,000 were a revealingly varied bunch. They included historic streets, squares, village greens and their surroundings, and town and city centres.

One hundred and thirty of them were in London (mostly in the suburbs), 475 in villages, and 395 in towns and cities outside Greater London. They varied in size from a couple of buildings *and their surrounding landscape* (significant inclusion) at Oak Street, Cossley, in Dudley county borough, to the entire 800-acre Hampstead Garden Suburb estate (London Borough of Brent). But the picture was patchy in the extreme. Local planning authorities varied not only in their willingness to make early designations, but in the way they drew the boundaries, in their positive follow-up, and in the extent to which they allowed the act of designation to affect their day-to-day planning decisions.

Among county councils, for instance, some—like Kent and Warwickshire—produced a steady stream of careful reports leading to designation and within two and a half years of the procedure being available had given conservation status to a very large number of their most attractive villages and parts of towns within their boundaries. Oxfordshire, by contrast—and it was not the only 'black sheep'—had infuriated amenity organisations (notably the county branch of the C P R E, chaired by Barbara Maude, energetic conservationist wife of Tory M P Angus Maude) by producing only a handful of designations. Heritage towns like Banbury and Bicester were afforded conservation areas status only belatedly and apparently only under pressure and by June 1970 the county had made only five designations (compare neighbouring Warwickshire's seventy) of which incredibly only one was a village.

The county council pleaded lack of money and resources; the conservationists complained that conservation—and indeed overall environmental policy—had too low a priority in the county. On the face of it, however, there were worse black sheep than Oxfordshire. At the time of the 1,000th designation, at least two counties—Norfolk and Northumberland—had not made a single designation (though Norfolk at least argued that it wanted to complete thorough preparatory work first).

In the county boroughs, the picture was also patchy, with some omissions difficult to understand. Brighton, with its superb Regency terraces and squares, had not by June 1970 made any designations. Nor had Edinburgh, whose old and new towns were candidates which could have needed very little deliberation. Other councils' designation policies showed a curious sense of priorities. Bristol, for instance, fairly early on designated Henbury village in its outer suburbs, then followed this up with Stapleton, another attractive village preserved in the interstices of its urban fabric. But as late as June 1971—three and a half years after the power to create conservation areas had become available— it had done nothing, formally at least, towards giving conservation area status to Regency Clifton, its original eighteenth-century suburb of Kingsdown or, indeed, what remained of its old walled merchant city, with gates built into the walls of its churches.

Some conservationists in Bristol thought that this was because their city council, with its strong Merchant Venturer tradition, was too sympathetic to prospective developers; others that its planning was too road-orientated, and that it was not prepared to designate any area where this might inhibit road building. Its officials and councillors, who had really done rather well at preserving individual buildings and set-pieces in the urban scene, did not, argued members of local amenity groups, seem to understand the importance of areas of character, stretches of townscape or the wholeness of the visual qualities of the Bristol scene of which they professed themselves proud. Such complaints were made with equal validity against the planning outlook in many other provincial cities. In Bristol's case, the fears expressed were amply justified in early 1971 by the Avon Gorge case, of which more presently.

In London, the local planning authorities (the thirty-two London boroughs plus the City of London) got off on the whole to a good start. Greenwich was first off the mark, and followed its initial conservation area—the historic riverside Naval College/park complex—with some interesting and varied choices, including the Progress Estate at Eltham, built for munitions workers in 1914-16 and notable less for any architectural quality than for a street layout and standard of housing and environmental provision in advance of its time.

London boroughs which made designations did not always seem to understand what they were about, and sometimes by their actions in practice appeared to betray the whole spirit of conservation. The affair of the Bedford Park trees, which we come to in a moment, was a case in point. But the biggest disappointment in London was the City Corporation: tardy to designate considering its resources and the potential, and disappointing when it did because of the 'pocket-handkerchief' restrictiveness of almost all the areas chosen, which contained little more than key buildings and their immediate surroundings.

There are, one concedes, special problems in the City. The commercial pressures generated by the astronomic cost of land in the Square Mile are intense. But to argue this so far is surely to miss the point of conservation areas —that they are there to protect the distinctive character of not only individual buildings and small groups of buildings, but also of the local scene and atmosphere. Moreover they do so not by preventing all change, but by seeking to ensure that change is not inimical to what exists. Nor does the apparent attitude of owners and developers in the Bow Lane conservation area—liked by City workers because of its Victorian intimacy of scale and neighbourhood atmosphere—give much grounds for hoping that, in any conflict between development profits and conservation in the City the Civic Amenities Act will make much difference.*

* The City later took courage and placed a group Building Preservation Notice on the Bow Lane buildings.

The main criticism, however, which the Civic Trust was inclined to make of planning authorities' treatment of conservation areas was not of late or restrictive designation, but of failure to follow up with what Ian Nairn in his weekly *Sunday Times* column called 'improvement'. What this means is imaginative adaptation and new uses bringing fresh life to old buildings and decaying localities without destroying the visual and social qualities which the conservation area procedure is designed to protect. It also means deflecting, guiding and controlling pressures generated by economic success or popularity rather than decay, and seeing that they do not destroy in a place the very qualities that attract them.

One example of the way in which designation can be followed up with action relevant in this latter type of problem was provided by East Sussex County Council at Alfriston, an attractive old village in the Cuckmere Valley, in the midst of the South Downs and only a few miles from the sea. Alfriston is extremely popular with holidaymakers and day-out excursionists in summer, and one of its problems has been the resulting traffic and car parking.

Alfriston's narrow village street was substantially freed of congestion and parked cars by new parking regulations and the provision of an unobtrusive off-street car park. The Ministry of Transport was persuaded in this instance to modify their normal no-waiting signs and yellow-lining. The 'No waiting 8 a.m. to 7 p.m.' signs were fixed to walls instead of kerbside posts; the single yellow line was, by special dispensation, three inches instead of four inches wide—and that inch does make a difference!

Moreover, Trust Houses, who own the fifteenth-century Star Inn in the high street, agreed to remove their proliferating hotel name, AA and RAC signs and substitute a specially designed sign incorporating all three; and Hailsham rural council secured the removal of other obtrusive and out-of-keeping signs and other visual clutter. Possibly all this sounds like detailed but minor improvement; in fact it can—and in this instance did—add up to a remarkable transformation of a place. Twentieth-century signscape and wirescape spread like cobwebs across the face of our streets. It is only when there is a determined clean-up and they go that we realise how much difference they made.

## The Bedford Park trees affair

My other example is of follow-up of the wrong kind: an object lesson of how not to preserve the character of a conservation area. Bedford Park, earliest of planned garden suburbs laid out by Norman Shaw from 1875 onwards, is a conservation area which straddles the boundary between two London boroughs, Hounslow and Ealing. The houses are tall, three-storey affairs by Shaw himself and a number of other architects, including some of his followers, but they are all very much of a style. Pevsner describes them as characteristically having 'Dutch gables or tile-hung gables, much use of decorative tiles, white window casements, white little oriels, cosy porches etc'; and he stresses what as long ago as 1880 William Morris commented on—the preservation of the tall, mature forest trees.

Shaw in fact aligned all but three of Bedford Park's roads to allow the preservation of the trees—mostly planes, horse chestnuts and sycamores—and these spacious leafy avenues are as much a part of Bedford Park as the architecture or the street plan.

The impression had been gained that Hounslow council had decided that broad-leaved forest trees were a nuisance and a liability. The borough seemed to have adopted a blanket policy of progressively replacing them with smaller ornamental trees like flowering cherries, which whatever their aesthetic or other merits are totally inappropriate to Bedford Park or any locality like it. Its plans involved felling some several thousand mature forest trees throughout the borough and replacing them with what it regarded as the more manageable ornamental species.

This plan was strongly resisted by a local amenity group, the Bedford Park Society, with considerable help from a loosely organised but remarkably effective organisation called Women on the Move, of which the formidably articulate 'coordinator' Mrs Irene Coates happened to be a Bedford Park resident. The society called in a landscape architect and tree expert, Philip Hicks. He was tree consultant to a London borough, Islington, which was so little of Hounslow's mind that it was planting forest trees: clearly the right choice for a district of tall Victorian houses, just as it was for Shaw's houses in the more spacious, tranquil Bedford Park.

Shaw's suburb, insisted Mr Hicks, had a character of its own in contrast to the anonymity of surrounding suburbs. 'The council's replanting policy,' he complained, 'is going to make it just like any other bit of London.' 'This,' he added, 'is after all what conservation is about—where an area has something special, you don't just throw it away. If you plant the same size trees everywhere, you end up with everywhere looking alike.' Hounslow had amended its planting scheme to try to appease the protesters, but it was a very slight gesture with little real departure from the original scheme. The trees listed in it were still, said Mr Hicks, 'out of character with the existing quality and character of the area. These are garden trees, not town trees.'

The Bedford Park Society also enlisted the support of the Victorian Society's architectural adviser, David Lloyd, who wrote to the town clerk stressing that replanting should be in scale with the houses if the conservation area's visual character was not to suffer 'grave impairment'; and polled residents with a 75 per cent response, of which 95 per cent were against the ousting of tall forest trees. Ironically the then chairman of the council's management committee who approved finance for the scheme was a Councillor Woodman who lived in Woodstock Road right in the heart of leafy Bedford Park. He seems not to have realised how strongly most of his neighbours felt about their trees. There had apparently been some complaints from householders about large trees blocking their light, and the council chose to interpret these as support for its replanting policy. The society argued that such complaints were few, and did not anyway imply support for wholesale felling, but rather a wish for judicious tree surgery.

Hounslow's mistakes in this matter can broadly be listed as follows. (1) The council sought to apply to the whole borough a blanket felling and replanting policy, which treated forest trees as 'unsuitable', without noticing that the policy did not fit Bedford Park. (2) Though it recognised that the area was special and worth designating as a conservation area, no one in authority seems to have noticed what made it special—houses, landscape and trees all in scale. (3) It had consultations with Ealing (which is responsible for the other half of Bedford Park) and the G L C. but nonetheless appears to have been ready to fell and replant up to its boundary irrespective of what happened beyond it. (4) Its 'consultation' with residents seems to have consisted in explaining what it meant to do only *after* the effective decision (and budgeting commitments) had already been made.

Finally (5) the council seems to have been guilty of an odd kind of double-think. In August 1970 householders with fine mature trees in their gardens received notice of tree preservation orders which the council proposed to make on them. This 'residential area of unique charm and character', asserted the letters, written by Hounslow's town clerk Mr Mathieson, 'is greatly enhanced by the presence of many fine trees within it, and it is therefore expedient to retain as many of these trees as possible in the interests of the visual amenity of the area.' 'Exactly,' said the residents. 'But, physician, why do you not take your own prescription?' In private gardens the council took steps to preserve mature forest trees; on its streets it proposed to fell them.

## New uses for old buildings

We have seen that the successful application of conservation area policies often involves, for the planning authority, maintaining a precarious balance between preservation of individual buildings and overall character and avoiding choking the life out of a place by excessive opposition to change and renewal. One factor of great and increasing importance in achieving this balance is the search for new and vital uses for old buildings—uses to which they can be adapted reasonably economically yet without disastrous alterations in their individual appearance or the character of the surrounding scene. Let us now look at two cases of attractive old buildings, in very different circumstances, which both underline this lesson that a living, adaptive use is better than either death for the building or a dead, 'museum' use.

The first is set in Bristol, where an earlier—and quite enlightened—policy of preservation by the city fathers had kept, for Bristolians and visitors alike to enjoy, an almost complete eighteenth-century street redolent of the city's great period of mercantile prosperity—King Street—between the city centre and the old enclosed dock system called the Floating Harbour. It contained some buildings with community uses: among them the Theatre Royal, home of the Bristol Old Vic company, and the seventeenth-century timbered and gabled Llandoger Trow, which now serves steaks as well as ales in four times as many bars as it had fifteen years ago.

But one building which the city had preserved was used only for storing vegetables and presented little more than a dead though beautiful façade to the street. This was the eighteenth-century Coopers Hall. A ministry Grade II listed building, it could scarcely be demolished, but lacked any economic use to support it. Then the Bristol Old Vic Company—whose headquarters, the Grade I Theatre Royal, was next door, produced plans to incorporate it into their theatre complex as foyer for the existing auditorium and a new second auditorium they were building there. They planned a straightforward external restoration but—as is all too often the case—discovered that quite extensive structural repairs were needed too.

How could a theatre trust, already pulling out all the stops to raise £800,000 for their new theatre complex, cope with this unexpected extra expense? This is the perennial penalty of those who bravely choose to adapt fine old buildings rather than put up new ones. Useful help can often be obtained—though to cover only a part of the cost—from the Historical Buildings Council (there are separate councils for England, Scotland and Wales); and in this case the H B C for England chipped in with a £5,000 grant.

The Coopers Hall would, it may be noticed, almost certainly have been preserved at least in external appearance, though the inside might have become a crumbling, unused shell. How much better to keep it and use it: part of an exercise in lively conservation.

## The Rainham grainstore

My second case of a new use for an old building is one which would not have survived without a new use. In most respects very different, it comes from Rainham, Kent, on the eastern edge of the Medway towns (and not to be confused with its Essex namesake). Commuter country of the fastest growing kind, Rainham had come in thirteen years from a village of 7,000 people on the edge of Gillingham to a suburb of 35,000.

In other places such growth would have ranked official new town status, with community halls and youth centre provided automatically. Instead Rainham's community association and youth club made do for years with the increasingly inadequate and unsuitable Victorian former school building which had served the old village. A project to provide new facilities could, however, count on some public money and a great deal of local fund-raising effort. The idea of a completely new building was considered, but the two bodies eventually decided to buy, restore and convert a large Victorian grain store and two oast-houses which adjoined it. These mid-nineteenth-century buildings would, their architects and surveyors advised them, provide very roomy and suitable facilities for their activities; and they had the advantage of being near the centre of Rainham and—a point of no small importance in a commuter area—right next door to the railway station.

Wakeley Brothers' old hop and grain store was a four-storey brick building, with painted wooden heads to hoists projecting from the top storey, and the distinctive cone-shaped tops of the oasts reaching up from behind. A comfortable, handsome building it seemed—even in dereliction. But the dereliction, fortunately, was superficial—windows broken and the like—and the building structurally sound. The floors, indeed, were built to take 300 tons, so could support even quite boisterous youth club or community association activities! It would provide the joint committee of association and youth club with 12,500 sq. ft. of floor space, which on a total cost for purchase (£12,500) and restoration (£22,500) of £35,000, meant it was costing under £3 per sq. ft.

What were they getting for it? On the ground floor of the main grain store building they would have a lounge, canteen and committee rooms; at first floor level rooms for group activities ranging from drama and bridge to Darby and Joan. The two top floors knocked into one gave a large hall for theatre, cinema or games. A large outbuilding with another 1,500 sq. ft. was suitable for conversion to a dance hall. The oasts themselves were happily almost exactly squash court dimensions—Rainham lacked squash courts—and at second floor level provided one large or two small extra rooms. A row of nondescript cottages on one side of the long, thin railwayside site would be mostly demolished to make room for a bowling-green (another lack in this mushroom commuter village), but the largest of them would be refurbished to house a resident warden or manager.

The money aspect of the Rainham project is interesting because it shows how conservation can attract public funds other than those earmarked for conservation purposes. The total cost, as we have seen, was £35,000. Of this, £10,000 was promised by Gillingham Council as its contribution to youth club and community centre facilities; a maximum grant of £10,000 from the D O E was expected for the project; and an appeal locally and from firms in the City of London with which the Community Association's chairman had contacts pulled in £2,000 in its first nine months. Obviously an appeal to save the building as a building or even as a local landmark would have been lucky to raise a fraction of this. An appeal to save and convert it into youth and social centre premises commanded very wide support.

The Rainham project struck me, when I looked at it in February 1971, as doubly worthwhile. It promised to provide in an interesting as well as economical way and in a central position facilities which could otherwise only have been built more expensively on a less convenient site. And it made possible the retention of a building of character in a district where the £5,000 semi had been eating up the acres and demanding demolition of many other distinctive older buildings.

This was not a listed building, nor would have been very likely to rank for listing. Yet in local terms the value that is put on an old building may be relatively greater where distinctive older buildings—those familiar landmarks that give a place its character—are thin on the ground. Where historic buildings abound, one might not grieve over the loss of such a structure as Wakeleys' grain and hop store. In Rainham one would. And this highlights again a key conservation issue: not persuading people that given buildings are worth preserving, but finding economic uses which justify retention—uses which serve living community needs.

## The case of the Charlton stables

The way in which local authorities and others sometimes take pains, very commendably, to restore a historic building but without first working out fully whether it can be put to some worthwhile use was illustrated recently by the London Borough of Greenwich, a council generally speaking enlightened in these matters. Next door to Charlton House—a Jacobean manor house which Pevsner ranks after Holland House as London's best—is a seventeenth-century stable block. The council, with the help of a historic buildings grant, restored the stables at a total cost of £38,000, then wondered exactly what to do with them.

Its housing committee then put in a bid to turn one of the two separate restored buildings into a district housing office for rent collection and other purposes. Its arts and recreation committee wanted to have it as an extension of the library and community centre activities carried on in Charlton House itself; and a campaign for some such social use was carried on by the young but lively Charlton Society. It argued that the ground floors of the two wings would make admirable studios and workshops for arts and crafts groups, while the upper floors would serve well as galleries for exhibitions.

The society's secretary, Mrs Cicely Denny, pointed out that the upper floors at least could not be used as offices without expensive and difficult conversion (this on top of the cost of restoration, which had not been carried out with office use in view) and would even then probably not be very good offices. Mrs Denny added that a traditional Horn Fair had been held at Charlton village from about 1300 until 1880. 'What about reviving it in the stable courtyard?' she suggested. Charlton House and the stables were still very much at the centre of the local community. True, replied the housing committee. That is why we want our rent office, for our large adjacent council estate, in the building.

Eventually, it seemed there would be a compromise: a rent office and art group facilities. With all due respect to the Charlton Society, this was surely no bad thing. It promised to make more council tenants who came to pay their rent aware of the activities going on there. In economic terms this solution was less attractive than one originally entertained by the council, which involved renting one block to a firm of architects. In social terms it was much to be preferred. A fine old building on whose restoration public funds had been spent—as local people would no doubt opine, lavishly—was being put to maximum public use.

There is additionally the psychological point that a building preserved as a museum or a museum piece is something that most people regard—consciously or unconsciously —as something set apart, separate from themselves. They may respect it, but mostly their feelings towards it are not warm. But if they use it daily, weekly, or even monthly—go in and out of its doors—it becomes familiar and subconsciously they probably develop some affection for it. One hopes, also, that some sense of elegance and spaciousness—even from a building like a stable block— will rub off on young minds and help in some small measure to strengthen the æsthetic revolution which is part of the battle for the environment.

## Islington: four conservation area case studies

These last few buildings we have been discussing were ones with no obvious present-day purpose where ingenuity and imagination as well as a good deal of extra money were needed to give them a new living use. With houses the problems are different. The use is there: there is no shortage of home-seekers. The problems are those of making interiors comfortable and acceptable by modern standards while preserving the exterior; of converting too large or too small houses into acceptably sized units without destroying the external character; and of reconciling the higher level of cost needed to achieve all this with the normal economics of public or private housing.

In the local authority field, Islington—for so long dedicated to the clear-and-build-flats principle in its council housing—became in the late sixties converted to the twin principles of rehabilitation and conservation. I want to look at four different ways in which the Borough Architect

Alfred Head applied these principles in two of Islington's conservation areas. They illustrate the too-often ignored truth that there is no single answer to the problems of conservation area policy, and that different solutions fit different sites and surroundings.

The first example is Colinsdale: a salutary reminder that even in a conservation area, conservation does not necessarily mean preservation. Colinsdale is a new block of council flats in a sensitive position with one face on the elegant eighteenth-century Colebrooke Row, the other to the now-famous Camden Passage, both of which in their ways have become smarter and more highly regarded as part of the Islington renaissance discussed earlier. Colinsdale, to its credit, makes no attempt to ape its eighteenth- or nineteenth-century neighbours, but Mr Head went to great trouble to ensure that it was in sympathy with them.

One problem with this kind of exercise is that modern local authority housing tends to be on the horizontal—flats —whereas neighbouring Victorian and Georgian terraces are both functionally and visually vertical. On the Colebrooke Row side the architect has broken the elevation into narrow vertical strips by recessing it. The device is more than just an æsthetic one, however. He has used the recesses to hide the doors to cupboards holding those jumbo refuse bins on wheels these days demanded in flats by council refuse departments, and the vents for gas water heaters; and he also tucks away his bathroom windows, which are smaller than the others, in these same recesses.

On the Camden Passage side, where the development made possible a road closure which had the effect of further extending the pedestrian shopping street, railings salvaged from a demolished Victorian house elsewhere in the borough give the grass in front of the flats an elegance and sense of place. The road closure also allowed a pub, the Camden Head, newly 'done up' to a scheme by the Victorian Society's architect, to make itself a pleasant sitting-out place. The scheme provided fifty much needed council flats; its effect is altogether that not of the new aping the old, but being a thoughtful good neigbour to it. Buildings don't need to be old to be good-mannered.

Islington's second example is an L-shaped block of terrace houses at the corner of Queen's Head Street and Cruden Street, dating from the 1850s and early 1860s. They are also in the borough's No 3 conservation area and a valuable part of the townscape if not in themselves so very special. But they were in a run-down condition, and their neighbours in Queen's Head Street had been demolished to provide new council flats. Happily the council then became more conservation-conscious and decided that this corner—a key one visually—was too good to pull down.

Instead they converted the block to provide four three-bedroom houses, one two-bedroom house, two one-bedroom flats and two two-bedroom maisonettes—nine homes in all. The block lost its corner shop, but this had been empty for some years, and in view of its proximity to the area's main shopping street, Upper Street, it would have been excessively romantic to pretend that it was a viable part of this handsome, comfortable townscape. The scheme attracted a housing grant towards the contract price of £31,822, and resulting weekly rents ranged from £3.60 to £6.60. Alfred Head warns, however, that in rehabilitation schemes of this kind costs always run out higher than you originally think. Walls crumble as you put in new wiring: a repair here uncovers work needed elsewhere. His council, fortunately, was committed to preserving wherever possible the attractive townscape of residential—even artisan residential—Islington.

Further south in what used to be Finsbury borough is Islington's No 2 conservation area—round Wilmington Square. Its late Georgian/early Victorian terraces were attractive even in decay—decay which is not always just superficial. Nos 38 and 39 Wilmington Square, on the corner of Attneave Street (our third example) had been condemned as structurally unsafe and were in very poor shape inside. But from a townscape point of view, their position was a key one.

So here Islington resorted to demolition and rebuilding —not just with something in sympathy, but a house which matched in all essential external details (windows, doors, railings, mouldings)—the corner frontages of the old building. Inside, however, floor levels were changed and instead of two houses there are seven one-bedroom flats and one bedsitter. From the service yard at the back you can see that inside this is a new, purpose-built block of flats. From the front—especially since one of the tenants collects Victoriana—it looks an authentic, well-cared-for part of the original square. The cost—£30,000—scarcely seems in the circumstances excessive.

Our fourth example is in Yardley Street, just out of Wilmington Square but in the same line of buildings as Nos 38 and 39. Here the case was rather different: a terrace of 1860s houses, some of them already demolished as slum clearance, others in a condition which made their retention impracticable. The site was not a key one like the Wilmington Square corner, but an unsympathetic building would have marred the conservation area.

What Mr Head's department did here is no doubt regarded by purists as a fraud. They have in effect put a modern, horizontally arranged block of fourteen old people's flats, with standard local authority rear access balconies, behind a new Victorian-style façade. The elevations don't quite line up with neighbouring buildings, but a set-back of a few feet disguises this. The windows from inside are sometimes a bit low on the room walls—modern ceiling heights don't match Victorian ones, even of artisan dwelling standards!—but outside, with railings cast from a recovered mould, the overall effect is very much in sympathy with its neighbours. Matching gates to a plain square entrance arch are an important extra detail. The contract price for this building (£51,000) was only about £1,900 more than the plain, unvarnished modern block would have cost. Mr Head's comment: 'We have paid our respects to our neighbours. What we have put back is meant to have a matching effect with the square, not to match it in every detail.'

The lessons one can draw from these four very different conservation exercises are perhaps these: (1) 'conservation' is not preservation of outworn uses but sympathetic, ingenious finding of new uses. (2) There is no one single, simple conservation answer. You have to play it by ear—or rather by eye—taking into account what is economically and politically practicable. (3) Rehabilitation as against rebuilding can be a very expensive process, and has a habit of exceeding initial cost estimates. And (4)—the message of Colinsdale—you can, in the inner city areas, build sympathetically within the tight ministry cost yardsticks, because, says Head, low-rise high-density housing attracts the more generous yardstick geared to high-rise flats. But high-rise would have ruined that corner of Islington and made nonsense of its designation as a conservation area. Instead, we have Colinsdale, which is new, but feels as well as looks part of tight-knit, low-terraced, urban Islington.

## New Walk, Leicester

These are individual solutions to the problems of retaining or harmoniously repairing a damaged or threatened townscape. My final conservation case study goes further than this. It is the imaginative and stylish restoration of a grand idea. New Walk in Leicester is a Georgian pedestrian promenade stretching three-quarters of a mile from near the city centre out to one of the main municipal parks. It was a splendid piece of town planning or, as the current jargon has it, 'high-grade environment'. Yet when Leicester's colourful and controversial planning officer, Konrad Smigielski, came to the city in 1962, New Walk was neglected, in decay. 'Clutter, litter and vandalism' were what he found there.

At the end nearest the city centre, vandalism had taken its heaviest toll—partly, thinks Mr Smigelski, reacting to a drab squalid townscape. When the elegant Victorian 'Paris' style lamp-posts were damaged, they had been replaced by 'shocking concrete ones'. Tarmac covered the ground area right up to the trunks of trees. A sorry assortment of 'No cycling' notices proliferated. The houses were ill-cared for and what passed for gardens worse cared for. And cars had all but invaded the actual pedestrian walk. No one used it with pleasure, few respected it any longer. 'It was a degraded environment. When I first came to see it, I was really depressed,' recalls Mr Smigielski. The process of decay, aided by plans then current for an inner ring road cutting right through the Walk, had snowballed and looked irreversible.

But Leicester's city planner managed against the odds to kill the ring road, and his efforts to curb the encroachment on the inner city of the commuter car were successful enough for Mrs Castle, when Transport Minister, to dub

Leicester 'Smigielskiville'. Perhaps the abandonment of the ring road was the turning point for New Walk, but it was still uphill work.

Part of the trouble was the sad decay and drabness of the houses along the Walk. 'I sent out 100 letters to the owners. No response.' So Smigelski adopted shock tactics. He 'talked against the rules'—made a very rude speech on prosperous Leicester's lack of concern about its 'dilapidated, shabby, dirty, chaotic' environment. He gave them angry home truths about the chicken wire strung round what had been beautiful de Montfort Square. The city council was now putting up money for improvements, he said, yet 'town planning cannot be done by one man, but by a conscious and co-operative effort of the whole society.'

That was five years ago. The angry outburst and well-judged encouragement by example did the trick. New Walk today is a different place. The city's expenditure was, for what it had achieved, surprisingly modest: £25,000 spent judiciously on putting down a replacement for the grim sea of asphalt—new red tarmac broken by lateral strips of paving; repairing and replacing the Victorian street lamps and railings; getting rid of vandal-proof but ugly, tank-like concrete seats, chicken wire and broken-down hedges and fences; and planting trees and grass.

In addition, the three 'squares' which punctuate and enliven New Walk—Museum Square, de Montfort Square, and the Oval—have been opened up, cleared of clutter and mess and upgraded in the same way as the actual promenade. The museum itself has not only had its fine portico repainted with flair and fine effect, but a piazza created in front of it instead of the previous tangle of walls, hedges and parked cars. New seats and litter baskets tread a tightrope between elegance and resistance to vandalism, and the railings of the Oval, a delightful small green open space at the further end of the Walk, once broken and unremarkable, are now repaired and painted elegantly in white and gold.

All this, plus the lifting of ring road blight, has acted as a catalyst. Owners of properties fronting the Walk have responded by restoring and repainting them in the city's suggested colour schemes; gardens and garden walls have been repaired and tidied up; and one developer has found it worthwhile to convert (to an agreed design) two Victorian houses into self-contained flats. The process of decline has been pushed into reverse.

More significant still, the public now use and enjoy New Walk as it was meant to be. On any fine day at lunchtime, it is full of strolling groups and couples. They come and sit and eat their lunch, or just use it as a pleasant, traffic-free route through town. Vandalism continues, but much abated. There are more people around, and anyway elegant, attractive surroundings command a certain respect—just as run-down surroundings invite abuse.

The museum building, floodlit at night, is a worthy setting for official and semi-official functions; de Montfort Square (rid of the redundant meteorological station which Smigelski once observed 'looked like a miniature concentration camp') is once again a usable open space. New Walk, Leicester, so nearly one of conservation's defeats, stands out today as a victory and an object lesson. It not only looks good, but people use it and enjoy doing so.

## Chapter Ten

# BATTLE FOR THE COUNTRYSIDE

*Threats to the countryside*

Many people would regard the threat to ecological balance posed by modern farming methods—and especially chemical fertilisers and pesticides—as *the* main threat to the countryside. But that will not be the main theme of the present chapter, partly because the subject has been dealt with expertly by others with a far more detailed understanding than I have of it, and their discussion of it is readily accessible (for instance, Dr Mellanby's *Pesticides and Pollution*); partly because there is a major threat to the countryside which has not been so frequently or fully discussed and which is probably as great: the threat posed to the British countryside by the mobile, leisured townsman descending on it in great numbers. The chief question to be posed here is, quite simply, can it survive this mass curiosity or mass admiration? Need the townsman (usually with the countryman buried in him only three or four generations deep, but with his countryman's good instincts withered away)—need he destroy the rural qualities he professed to admire? If destruction can be avoided, then how?

That is perhaps this chapter's main theme, but let us look first at one or two ecological and other factors which affect the quality of the countryside under the threat from that leisure invasion. The first is what the ecologists call 'loss of cover'—cover being the basic vegetation which supports other forms of wildlife and upon which, because of the chain of ecological interdependence, much of the pattern of nature in an area may depend.

We are most of us, of course, influenced by a great romantic fallacy about the countryside: that the landscape is 'natural' as distinct from the elements that go to make it up. Most of the landscape of England (as distinct from that of Scotland) is man-made, large parts of it within the last two or three centuries. The great East Anglian drainage and planting schemes of the seventeenth century, for instance, both made economic grain growing possible there and changed the countryside from desolate fen to arable land with woods, spinneys, tree belts and, above all, hedgerows dividing and protecting the newly created field system.

## Loss of cover

That is just, as it were, to set the record straight. It does not imply that the result is any less countryside, or any less worth preserving. But in fact the countryside which many of us have come to regard as the classic English rural landscape—with fields bordered by flowering hedgerows and punctuated by woodlands of predominantly deciduous trees rather than conifers or other evergreens—has been slowly, silently but steadily disappearing from large parts of England in recent years. And disappearing with the encouragement and fiscal support of one of its official guardians, the Ministry of Agriculture.

In a paper presented at a Nature Conservancy symposium in November 1968, Dr Max Hooper of the Conservancy's Monks Wood research station produced the results of a survey which suggested that hedges were being removed from the English countryside at a rate of something between 7,000 and 14,000 miles a year. Even if the lower rate continued, theoretically we could expect to see 'the last hedge in England grubbed up by A D 2049'. He added that this extrapolation was, of course, not to be taken too seriously; but it did indicate the scale and rate of denuding.

This figure for hedgerow removal disguised great variations between different parts of the country, and between arable and non-arable lands. It tallied neither with the Ministry's figures (lower) nor those of the British Trust for Ornithology (higher). Yet whichever figure is adopted, it represents a disturbing rate of change. How did it come about, and what are the implications?

The main reason for hedgerow removal is an economic one. With larger field units, mechanised agriculture can be more efficient and thoroughgoing. But the hope that once hedgerow removal and filling in of ditches (both encouraged by Ministry grants) would slow down once optimum field sizes had been achieved has been shown to be illusory. Again cost is the reason.

The published report of the Monks Wood symposium

quoted above includes a comparison of erection and maintenance costs of hedges and fences. It contrasts an initial cost of 30p to 50p per yard for the cheaper wire fences with 60p a yard for hawthorn hedge. When maintenance costs were taken into account, together with the fact that well-maintained hedges last indefinitely, the authors of the comparison reached the conclusion that 'all new boundaries are likely to be fences rather than hedges in the interests of flexibility of management. Only if one can be sure the boundary will still be required in forty years time is planting a hedge justified in terms of direct costs.'

Dr Hooper's paper also made it clear that, though the Ministry was aiding and abetting this destruction of hedgerows by paying grants to farmers to destroy them, this was only reinforcement to a process which would anyway have been dictated by farm economics; and that where a landowner was interested in game or wildlife (and especially wildlife), he was very much more likely to preserve his hedgerows, judging the economic penalty this imposed money well spent.

Two main effects, broadly, are feared: (1) that loss of windbreak will cause or contribute to a weakening and impoverishment of soil structure, leading to dustbowl conditions such as occurred in Oklahoma and Texas in the 1920s and 1930s (though some ecologists argue that excessive use of chemical rather than organic fertilisers is bringing about this impoverishment rather than hedgerow removal); (2) loss of cover to animal and plant life, disturbing the balance of nature, because species which form a link in an ecological chain, performing some useful purpose by feeding or feeding on others, are driven out when they have nowhere to live.

The Ministry of Agriculture's attitude has been at least until recently, that the ecological lobby were being alarmist and greatly exaggerating the damage caused, which it argued was small enough to be an acceptable price for more efficient and economic food production. Lately, there have been signs that they are inclined to treat loss of cover, and possibly soil impoverishment, fears more seriously. This has not yet, however, prevented them from continuing to pay grants for destruction of hedgerows and filling in of ditches.

One difficulty here is that the grant system and the statute permitting it assume a sort of blind even-handedness in paying out. There is little or no scope under present legislation for the Ministry to distinguish between situations where field rationalisation sensibly dictates hedgerow removal and those where there is little sense and the action occasions definite ecological and scenic damage.

Ultimately if substitution of intensive for traditional animal husbandry, and of synthetic foods for natural ones, continues to grow, at the same time as increasing public demand for the preservation of the country as it is, for the townsman's enjoyment, the logical solution will surely be to pay farmers grants explicitly for maintenance of landscape, as distinct from subsidies for food production or rural community support. Applied in a thoroughgoing way, this would demand landscape maintenance, preservation and management as the price of the grant. Income from food production within those constraints might then in some cases become almost incidental.

### Wildlife's flight to the suburbs

The destruction of cover sometimes encourages animal life to move unexpectedly from the countryside into the suburbs of towns. The organisers of the *London Atlas of Birds* have discovered a remarkable range of species previously not found in London penetrating along the green cuttings and embankments of some railway lines, and thence into parks and people's gardens. Cleaner air resulting from smokeless zones may also have had something to do with this; but the same can hardly be said for the foxes now commonly found in the leafier London suburbs. Names like Foxes Dale or, for that matter, Woodpecker Lane, are now often no longer dryly historical in their associations.

One outstanding case of flight to the suburbs from a habitat rendered hostile by countryside change has been engaging the attention of another Monks Wood researcher Dr Arnold Cooke. The common frog, he has shown, is a particularly hard-hit victim of those grant-aided bulldozers, tractors and dragline excavators. Ditches are disappearing with hedgerows, or where they are retained are mechanically maintained so that their profile is V-shaped, not the gentle U-shape agreeable to the frog and the toad.

Tentative results from surveys undertaken for Monks Wood by school biology classes show frog populations decreasing in the countryside wherever ponds and ditches are filled in—whether by farmers or builders on the fringes of towns and villages—and increasing in the suburbs. 'My advice to any self-respecting, prudent common frog,' Dr Cooke told me, 'would be to take himself off to some nice, large, green suburban garden with a pond in it, and stay put there.'

## Power lines and amenity

Another set of threats to the countryside comes from the various kinds of man-made development which assail it: housing, industry, roads, power stations, pylons, radio masts and the like. And whereas most conservation battles come down sooner or later to weighing a qualitative factor—like, for instance, good residential environment—against economics, in the countryside there is very frequently the choice to be made between conflicting amenity interests.

Take the choice of route for the Central Electricity Generating Board's 400kV electricity supply 'Supergrid', which frequently raises this sort of question. 'Do we take it across a beautiful landscape where no one lives, or through less beautiful countryside where the standard 165 ft pylons will be close to and visible from several villages?' Council for the Protection of Rural England officials complain that the CEGB's wayleave officers tend to go for the open country route, however great its scenic value, because where there are people they can expect protest and delay.

And as a political fact, well-organised and eloquent though the CPRE and other rural amenity bodies may be, it is usually the resident protest, with its pressure through parish and rural councils, that is likely to make trouble. Yet the CPRE is surely right: in many cases the loss of fine landscape should weigh more heavily—if only because it is for everyone who goes that way—than marginal change in the indifferent view out of a dozen cottage windows.

The ordinary citizen's reaction, when threatened with a power line near his home or through a favourite landscape, is often: 'Why don't they put it underground?' Unfortunately this solution is only rarely available because of its colossal cost. Currently it works out at something like £1 million a mile for a main 400kV grid line—sixteen to seventeen times as much as the overhead equivalent. The reasons for this are the difficulty and expense of effective insulation and cooling systems with this voltage of current.

## CPRE view on power lines

In European Conservation Year (1970), the CPRE set up a number of working parties, one of which studied this problem of transmission lines. Their conclusions are worth looking at. They wanted professional landscape advice to be obligatory on both the CEGB and the area boards, whose distribution lines and pylons are smaller but more numerous. And they wanted mandatory consultation with all the local authorities whose areas might be affected before a route was planned. As with road schemes, so with power lines, objectors have too often frustratingly found that piecemeal consultation left little room for manœuvre: by the time the section of route affecting them was canvassed, stretches on either side had already been settled.

The working party noted that electricity boards, like many other statutory undertakings, have written into their empowering legislation a specific duty to have regard to the landscape. But, they pointed out, this is so generalised a duty as to be virtually meaningless in any given case. Their suggested answer was to have a fixed proportion of electricity board budgets reserved for landscape care—an amenity fund, as it were, which the boards could spend as they thought fit on landscaping and visual improvement, but could spend on nothing else.

As for the lower voltage distribution lines, they pointed out that these, though the impact of any individual line is likely to be less, can have along with other forms of 'wire-scape', a considerable erosive effect on the countryside or country village scene. Some boards have in recent years been making a real effort to clear up the worst eyesores, either by undergrounding—relatively less expensive for lower voltages, because the difficulty and cost of thermal insulation grows disproportionately with increase in voltage—or by rationalising wirescapes built up haphazardly in the past. But records differ from board to board. In European Conservation Year, for instance, the South Western Electricity Board earmarked £50,000 for such work, the Eastern Board £125,000 but the Southern Board nothing.

The C P R E working party also urged that more money and effort should be devoted to design of equipment, which is often crudely functional and designed without apparent regard for appearance and that, more radically, the training of engineers should be revised 'to include some elementary education in the principles of applied design and the understanding of æthetic values'! There should be more experiment with fresh designs, with reaction on them sought from landscape architects, planners and conservationists, they urged. And electricity regulations, which in their view tended to lay a dead hand on experiment and variation, should be revised 'to set standards rather than impose restrictions.'

They wanted more low voltage lines undergrounded, and a *prima facie* assumption that they would be in conservation areas. High voltage lines should, they urged, avoid National Parks and Areas of Outstanding Natural Beauty wherever possible. Where they could not, then very much more stringent standards for routing and design should apply. Moreover they urged that an annual sum should be set aside for remedying the worst visual atrocities from the past either by undergrounding or using new and less obtrusive types of pylon.

Other recommendations of the working party were devoted to the planning process—they wanted statutory undertakings put on the same footing as any other developer where the present obligations on them were less stringent; and argued that the siting of electricity sub-stations as well as generating stations should be considered not in isolation but along with the powerlines which would have to connect with them.

But their most radical—and for the power men most controversial—recommendation was one which said, in effect: 'Let's try to cut the growth of electricity transmission. It is cheaper and less damaging to the countryside to send gas or oil through pipelines than electricity on pylons. The next grid, if growth in demand for power goes on as it has in the past, doubling every decade or so, will in all logic have to be 750kV or something like it, and will need higher pylons still. Let oil compete on equal terms with indigenous fuels. It may cut electricity's growth and obviate the need for more and bigger transmission lines.'

This sounds like economic heresy—although the counter-argument that oil as an imported fuel should be discriminated against is by no means clear-cut, because of the overseas earnings of British oil companies. Environmentally, however, it has considerable attractions. Electricity's rival natural gas could well fuel localised power stations, or even 'power pack' generators for individual commercial premises and households, leaving a minimal electricity grid as standby. The notion is anathema to the electricity engineers.

One of its weaknesses as far as they are concerned is that the industry can cater for baseload demand fairly cheaply; it is meeting the peaks that costs big money. A standby role for the CEGB to firms and even householders with their own generators would be peaky without the supporting profitable base. There is also the big question mark of how long North Sea natural gas supplies will last, and how reliable international oil supplies are going to be in a decade or two.

Nuclear energy is a clean, non-polluting way of generating electricity, but it can only be used economically in large units—and large units mean more transmission lines. So the working party's policy for limiting growth of power lines in this way could—if gas or oil supplies dwindled in the 1980s—imply a very high price indeed for amenity. Their suggestion in any case runs counter to the whole history of events in that, by substituting local power generation, it reverses the trend to capitalising on economy of scale. One cannot really see it happening.

So we are left with palliatives, but palliatives which add up to quite a lot; better use of landscaping skills, better design of pylons and equipment; more attention to visual amenity, ensured by earmarked finance; and, above all, more effort and money put into research on undergrounding— not because money necessarily buys success, but because the chance of a breakthrough on this intractable technical problem should not be missed for want of a little extra cash and resources. The environmental pay-off on, say, cutting undergrounding costs by half justifies backing what is, in research terms, an outsider.

*Other visual damage*

Pylons and transmission lines have, it should be noted, one negative virtue. Unlike most of the other detritus of industry's incursions into the countryside, they are relatively easily removable if and when they become redundant. This is not true of other industrial installations—including the power station which after a twenty or thirty year life becomes, in spite of having repaid its capital costs, uneconomic to run.

Nor for that matter is it true of natural gas installations. Incredibly, one discovers, there is no commitment by the Gas Council to reinstate the site at their Bacton North Sea gas terminal in Norfolk, once the reserves run out in perhaps thirty, perhaps twenty years' time. Nor is there apparently any legal obligation on them to dismantle their tanks, pipes and treatment plant buildings except to the extent of removing any obvious safety hazards. A vigorous stand by the local representative of the Ministry of Agriculture, backed by the planning authority, has, however, obliged them to accept a commitment to reinstate completely the site of their Lincolnshire terminal whenever it is no longer needed.

And rightly. Britain's countryside and coasts have suffered too long from the attentions (or inattentions) of government departments and statutory bodies who assumed they could take, use, and then abandon—without clearing up the mess after them. The biggest offenders in this respect have been the defence departments, who also indulge the companion vice of clinging possessively to large tracts of land which they no longer really use or need.

Mr Heath's government, the D O E, and the Countryside Commission which persuaded them to it, deserve full marks for setting up a review committee to look at the Defence Department's real needs and consider which areas ought to be released. And it was reassuring that the committee's membership included non-military members such as John

Cripps, Chairman of the Countryside Commission and former editor of *The Countryman*.

## Roads and the countryside

Other big inroads into the countryside are made by industry (which we shall look at in Chapter 12), roads, and housing. Roads are considered by many to be the greatest despoiler, and, in terms of acreage, in the real countryside they certainly take a huge toll. Visually it need not always be so. That depends on the particular countryside, what kind of road is inserted into it, and how. One has only to contrast the grey monotony of Britain's earliest stretch of motorway, the southern section of the M1, with its ugly stumpy bridges, prosaic routing and lack of any but very superficial landscape work, with the dramatic, attractively landscaped qualities of some of the later motorways like the M6, with its elegant bridge structures, and attention to the character of the terrain through which it passes, to be convinced of this. Though this view is perhaps heretical, one is driven to the conclusion that, visually at any rate, some stretches of our countryside actually gain by the insertion into them of a well-designed motorway, just as others do by the flooding of valleys to make reservoirs or by afforestation with conifers.

In practice, however, arguments about visual loss or gain cannot be separated from resistance to change based on other reasons: noise, disturbance, financial loss, disruption of communities and severance of their local roads and footpaths and, not least, plain abhorrence of any tampering with the familiar. Distrust of the road builders in the countryside is partly the result of the same kinds of apparent insensitivity to community and conservation values as is evident in urban motorway building. Partly it stems from the unwillingness in the last resort of most defenders of field and hill to admit that the route they are opposing might just possibly be the least damaging of the practicable alternatives. Defenders of the countryside are as a rule united in their opposition to the Ministry route of the moment, but rarely in their priorities on what ought to be saved and what may have to be sacrificed.

Thus the long and valiant fight of the Chiltern Society to alter the route of the M40 across the Chiltern escarpment —in which the Ramblers' Association's national secretary Christopher Hall, an ex-chief information officer of the Ministry of Transport, played a leading and skilful role— eventually foundered because they failed to convince successive ministers, and some independent people of influence, that the official route was more damaging than the alternative they proposed.

The DOE, and a late convert to their cause, Peter Shepheard, then president of the Royal Institute of British Architects, were convinced by photographic mock-ups of the official route and the alternative suggested by landscape architect Geoffrey Jellicoe and engineer Ove Arup, that the Jellicoe/Arup route would do even more violence to the Chiltern landscape than the Ministry one. Shepheard, a landscape architect went to the DOE with a deputation to argue for feasibility studies on the Jellicoe/Arup route, but when he saw the two lines superimposed on photographs of that landscape, had the courage to change his mind and to admit it.

That, of course, was on a visual appreciation of the two routes (though it is arguable that the more serious complaint against the Ministry was its reluctance to allow the alternative to be fully examined). The opponents of the MOT route were, however, not just concerned with appearance from a series of viewing points at a distance. They were also concerned with the fabric, the texture of the actual three-dimensional countryside they knew from living in and walking through it, and with—for it contained a nature reserve—the damage to flora, fauna and, as it were, 'ecological micro-climate'. Peter Shepheard (and the DOE) was probably right to prefer the official route in landscape terms. But visual quality is not the only quality at risk to rural motorway construction.

## Motorways as destroyers of communities

This point was very vividly made by a couple of controversial routings which came to my attention during 1970 and 1971. The first was at Claydon in Suffolk, where apparently simply to cut cost a motorway was planned to slice through the village, demolishing houses, severing the daily and intricate patterns of movement in the community, and foisting a monstrous flyover on a country village which need not have been damaged by it at all.

A well-routed motorway would not only have avoided the village, but promised some relief from the lesser traffic noise and nuisance at its existing trunk road crossroads. This is what the D O E's 'total environment' approach is supposed to be about, and one can only hope that routings like the Claydon one which take account of construction cost and journey time, but apparently not of social/environmental costs, will in future not even be canvassed by the ministry's road construction units.

In an attractive rural landscape between Southampton and Winchester, the Hampshire village Rownhams had long known that the M27 south coast motorway would pass it close. What none of the 600 villagers realised until too late was just how close. The official route runs through the village, demolishing several houses and passing, albeit in cutting a matter of 20 ft or 30 ft from others.

The villagers fought strenuously to have it moved half a mile further north through open country; but the Ministry's south-eastern road construction unit said at a public inquiry that that would be more difficult and expensive, and convinced the inspector and the Minister that its route was on balance to be preferred.

The plan included stopping up and diverting Rownham's Lane, a north-south road through the village, leaving seventeen homes stranded on the other side of the six-lane motorway. The men from the Ministry accepted that it was regrettable, but argued that their diverted route was substantially cheaper because its bridge crossed the motorway at right angles. The existing road would have to cross it on a long diagonal. Again the inspector and the Minister accepted that on balance the officials were right, the residents wrong.

Then came a bigger shock. Plans to site a service area astride the motorway at Great Copse, scarcely 100 yards from the eastern edge of the village, were disclosed. It would have petrol pumps, breakdown facilities, restaurants and snack bars, and all the other impedimenta of such places, including 24ft-high lamp standards.

Because this key stretch of the M27 provides a link between London and both the New Forest and Southampton docks, it will carry heavy summer holiday traffic. The villagers' fear, according to Mr Jack Parker, chairman of Rownhams' residents' association and a rural councillor, is that they will be subjected to motoring noises at all hours and to transistor radios and unwittingly loud voices wafted on the warm summer air through open bedroom windows.

The village, of course, objected. The parish council objected. The rural council objected. But it seems that the Minister, while obliged to hold an inquiry into actual routing, if objections are substantial, has, under the 1959 Highways Act, complete discretion so far as service areas are concerned to inquire publicly or not to inquire publicly. He chose not to.

The local people resent this decision. They argue that the need for a service area there is doubtful because it is so near Southampton and within ten to twelve miles of other proposed service areas on the M27 and the Chandlers Ford north-south by-pass.

Had the inspector at the original route inquiry been told of the proposed service area site, that might have tipped the balance in favour of their alternative route, they say. The nuisance of motorway plus service area is clearly very much greater.

The ministry men reply that they had not then decided which of several sites to choose. But Hampshire's planning committee, which—rather reluctantly, it seems—accepts the official proposals, has told the Ministry bluntly: 'In future let us see your proposals for service areas at the same time as the motorway route.'

Rownhams' sister village, Nursling, stands to suffer because a feeder road—called, in no wise to its satisfaction, 'the Nursling link'—leaves the motorway further west to run towards Southampton docks. It cuts country roads, causing long diversions between homes, shops and schools.

This is one of the two main kinds of damage a rural motorway can inflict on unsuspecting country communities. It is as if a mechanical trench cutter severed half the root system of a mature tree and the driver expressed surprise when the tree began to wither.

The other kind of damage is noise and visual intrusion;

more here from the service area than the actual road. As Mr Parker puts it, people moved to the village, put their savings into houses, because they wanted rural tranquillity and the green views across that pleasant landscape to Tanner's Brook. If the road comes, he says, the residents most affected 'might just as well take up residence at Waterloo Station'.

The proposals were substantially formulated while the department responsible was still the Ministry of Transport. It is now part of the D O E; unfortunately a change of name does not of itself transform road planning processes. Yet if ministers really meant what they say about ensuring that motorways are made 'environmentally acceptable', this should apply to a village of 600 just as much as to Hampstead or Blackheath.

This village, if present proposals stand, will become a rural Westway in muted form, and with no such justification of 'necessity'. One hopes that D O E ministers will look more carefully in future at the impact of motorways on villages like Rownhams and Claydon.

*Housing and green belts*

The impact of housing development on the countryside makes itself felt most sharply in two main circumstances—new towns and development proposals in 'green belt' areas on the fringes of our towns and cities. Green belts, originally in the case of London the product of an inter-war initiative by the L C C and the home counties and extended to other large and sometimes not so large towns (e.g. Gloucester/Cheltenham) under the Town and Country Planning Acts, are sometimes misunderstood and have of late come in for some criticism. The original purpose was to prevent the sort of urban sprawl to which much of the old county of Middlesex had by then succumbed.

Green belts throw a cordon round the built-up areas and in effect tell the developer: 'Thus far and no farther.' They do not, however, as such do anything to ensure or facilitate public access or recreational use of land so restricted, though they often include large open spaces which are traditionally or as a result of acquisition open to public use, as well as public footpath systems. From the farmer's or land-owner's point of view, however, green belt designation may be far from a blessing. He may have to cope with the trespass, damage and hooliganism which tends to occur in farmland near a town's edges, without being able to sell up and reap the benefit of development values.

Another weakness of the green belt is that development tends to leapfrog to the country towns beyond, leading to more mass, long-distance commuting, which it may be argued is undesirable socially in terms of individual working and family lives, and economically in so far as imbalance of railway operation and demand for extra road provision result.

Broadly, however, green belts have served their prime purpose of limiting sprawl and providing an attractive and healthy setting for many of the post-war new towns, and politicians and civil servants at the D O E show every intention of continuing to uphold them, even in the face of acute demand for building land. They are not, however, inflexible; and it is in a way a testimony to green belt status and reputation that whenever a minister decides to remove a few acres from this designation and allows homes to be built there, there is a great outcry—even if the plot concerned is of indifferent amenity value and appearance and was originally made 'green belt' almost by accident.

Recent decisions from Peter Walker have mostly upheld green belt status, saying to prospective developers: 'No. The extra housing that is needed can be achieved by infilling of "back-garden" land in the more spacious suburbs on the town side of the green belt concerned.' This line of argument has probably come out more clearly for Greater London than for Birmingham and other conurbations. Even a salient of open green-belt land into the built-up area, such as a local amenity group strongly defended at Riddlesdown, Croydon, in 1970, can be a valuable breathing space from bricks and mortar—indeed, the more so because enclosed on its other sides by houses—and the very amenity that led many residents to settle there. It should not be—and is not —lightly snuffed out by the Ministry.

Rather the aim should be more towards an attacking strategy, seeking wherever possible to extend such green wedges, for example by purchase as playing fields and public open space, so as to link them to pockets of 'urban countryside' further into the city. The need for these links is the greater today as an increasing weight of motor traffic makes roads difficult to cross on foot and leaves fewer and fewer places to wander along.

## New towns and rural acres

As for new towns, the single-minded preservationist remains appalled at the way in which they eat up the rural acres. The argument of the supposed irreplaceability of good agricultural land apart, country lovers must regret the disappearance of any pleasant, unpeopled landscape and notice with disquiet that the conventional new town like Stevenage (6,256 acres, and eventually 80.000 people) is being followed by much larger scale 'new cities' like Milton Keynes (22,000 acres, with an eventual 250,000 people).

That is regrettable, and the *Architectural Review*'s recent issue devoted to showing how a civilised, high-density modern city could be created out of derelict industrial land ('Civilia', *Architectural Review*, June 1971) shows vividly that there are sometimes ways of avoiding it. But it is not always or even usually an option. And most people looking at the social and environmental gains of providing good housing and social facilities in pleasant surroundings at what are currently regarded as acceptable population densities to replace substandard, overcrowded housing in the older large cities, conclude that the price in lost countryside is on balance worth paying.

The question: 'Why new towns in beautiful countryside eating up rich farmland and fine views? Why not on the sites of nineteenth-century dereliction in our older industrial areas, or even more dramatically among, for instance, the wilds of the Yorkshire Moors?' needs to be put if only to show the limitations of the answer implicit in it.

Leaving aside for a moment the question of whether a new city in a national park would be less a crime against the countryside than taking 17,000 acres of pleasant but unspectacular Buckinghamshire farmland, the real answer is this. In a reasonably free society, new towns and cities have to be built in areas where their potential inhabitants are willing or can be persuaded to live, and where industry and commerce are willing to put their factories, warehouses and offices.

Economic carrots can be, and have been, useful in persuading firms and families alike to go where official regional and decentralisation policies suggest would be in the national interest. But post-war experience has shown that most people are not as mobile as was once thought. They want to be within easy reach of families and friends, or in a community with the same social outlook as their present one. And there is no virtue in planning and starting to build a town which will stay only half complete because people prefer to remain in near slum conditions they know rather than move 200 miles into, for them, the alien and unfamiliar. Milton Keynes' 17,000 acres of farmland (the city area also includes several small existing towns) may not be the ideal solution, but it provides a practicable one.

On the other hand, one must not be too fatalistic about this. If only the economic ground rules could be altered to reflect cost and benefit to the nation less narrowly, then a Civilia-type answer will become a real possibility. Within the present planning and cost constraints it could not be done imaginatively and attractively enough to make its very high population densities acceptable.

But if population growth and demand for housing increases as we expect in the coming decades, then Britain will need Civilias (high-density, high-amenity new cities on reclaimed sites) to complement, if not necessarily to supersede, its Milton Keyneses (low-density, polycentric new cities). The debate is unfortunately complicated by an element of planning politics: on the one hand those like the Town and Country Planning Association, who basically believe that high housing densities are barbaric and that everyone should live in as near to garden city conditions as possible; and the opposite camp (represented by the *Architectural Review*'s 'Civilia' issue) which dismisses the TCPA approach as 'prairie planning' and preaches that urban sprawl, however high its standard of individual dwellings, creates far more problems than it solves.

From a countryside preservation point of view, all one can say with certainty is that a large-scale, generously-financed experiment on Civilia lines ought to be undertaken because, if successful, it would (a) demonstrate that attractive urban living conditions can be provided without eating up huge areas of countryside where they will be most needed for recreation by the leisured townsman of coming decades; and (b) if really excitingly attractive in the concentration of amenity it provided on a small site, could create a counter-magnet to draw people away from the West Midlands and the South-east, where the countryside will be particularly under pressure as housing demand rises.

## People as rural polluters

This argument about the impact of new towns on the countryside brings me naturally to the main theme of this chapter: the threat posed to the countryside by the leisured, mobile townsman. Before the age of mass motoring, this threat scarcely existed. The townsman's penetration in numbers was limited to where the scheduled train or bus or tram would take him; and he could be, and usually was, catered for in those places. His numbers were limited and predictable, and the minority who went further, on foot or cycle, presented no great problem to rural conservation.

There is, moreover, I think, a psychological difference between arriving in the countryside by public transport and arriving in your own car. Those who arrived by bus and train, however alien and 'townee' countrymen might find them, did have to make some effort to readjust; to some extent they took the country on its own terms. One suspects that the family that gets out of its own car is less apt to make this adjustment unless it is positively encouraged to.

There are, as has already been suggested, two main ingredients to the threat posed by a mass leisure invasion of the countryside. One is that people have much more free time, and more money than ever to spend on it; the other is that they are mobile, with their own cars, motor caravans and the like. There are two facets to this growing mobility, however, which—together with the certainty of a four-day week as the norm within the next decade or so—give it a particularly explosive quality. One is the actual number of extra cars: another 9 million are forecast by 1980. The other is the effect of the motorway system in cutting down journey times and therefore making the potential choice of destination for the week-end, day or afternoon out so much wider. Fears have been expressed, for instance, about the effect of the completed M6 bringing the Manchester and Liverpool conurbations (with a combined population of 4 million) within not much more than an hour's travelling time of the Lake District.

This, together with the effect of the mass media, tends to give a volatility and concentration to leisure journeys——like quicksilver which can suddenly and very rapidly run all to one point in even quite a complex pattern of available channels. Suppose, for instance, television features in its new programmes one Friday evening an attractive corner of a National Park—perhaps for some reason unconnected with its beauty, like a murder or the fact that a pop star has been staying nearby. Suppose, next morning being fine, only half a per cent of the, say, five million people within an hour or so's driving time decide to go and have a look.

That could be 25,000 people in probably 9,000 to 10,000 cars all heading in the same direction. Suppose again three-quarters of them fail to arrive—lose their way, or are discouraged by traffic jams—, that still means something like 2,000 to 3,000 cars funnelling into narrow country lanes, parking on grass verges; some of their occupants perhaps breaking down a hedge or fence in search of a non-existent footpath, others in default of inadequate or non-existent lavatories.

Perhaps a frustrated driver, trying to go where his better judgement tells him he had better not, punctures an oil sump. An old crock stuck on a hill has its radiator run dry and is abandoned by the roadside. Even if most of the visitors are well-behaved, a minority will light fires and a minority leave paper bags, plastic bottles and broken glass about. Frustration and disappointment that the unspoiled spot they have come to see is wrecked by numbers makes some people even less inclined to respect it in other ways. This is concentrated pollution by people. Does it need to be like that?

FIGURE 7. Conservation areas in England and Wales. (*Based on a map prepared by the Countryside Commission.*)

## The Goyt Valley experiment

The answer of the countryside planner is that it does not need to be and must not be. And he can point to some rather encouraging experiments. One such was at the Goyt Valley in the Peak District National Park. This is an attractive, uninhabited valley a few miles west of Buxton in Derbyshire. Access to it from two nearby main routes— the A537 and the A5002—is difficult because of the narrow tortuous nature of the approach roads which climb down from above the 1,000 ft contour (see Figure 7). Until a few years ago it had few visitors.

Then the Stockport and District Water Board built a reservoir in the valley which won a Civic Trust Award for its sensitive treatment of the landscape. After that the fine summer week-ends brought cars in their hundreds, rising to a peak of 1,500 in one day. I am not saying Goyt at that time was like my imaginary bit of national park, but the park authorities were worried on two scores. One of the roads at least was dangerous under such conditions; and the congestion which resulted, as well as the influx of cars itself, was tending to destroy the very tranquillity and beauty these motorised invaders presumably sought.

1970 was different. With the encouragement and financial support of the Countryside Commission, the park planning board made a bold experiment. Between 10 a.m. and 6 p.m. at week-ends and on Bank holidays, visitors' cars got no further than the approaches to the valley. There they found a new system of expanded car parks, tactful wardens handing out leaflets explaining what was afoot and why, and free white minibuses to carry them on into the actual valley.

The questions the park planners were seeking to answer were: is the week-end motorist in the countryside willing, if asked politely, to leave his car for the sake of the countryside he is visiting? And, once separated from it, does he stay fretting near it, a victim at once of some sort of rural agoraphobia and to the loss of an accustomed artificial limb? Or does he find himself enjoying a new found sense of liberation—actually walking off into the country and enjoying it?

Right from the start the response was most encouraging.

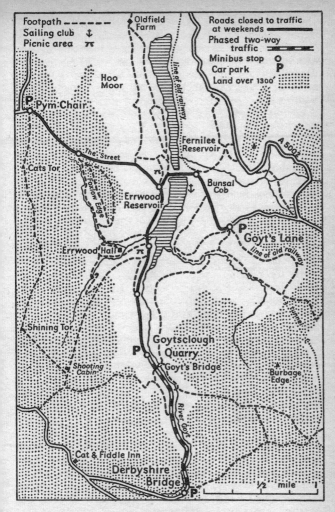

FIGURE 8. The Goyt Valley experiment. (*Based on a map prepared by the Peak Park Planning Board.*)

The Peak Park Director, Theo Burrell, found that few motorists showed any signs of bad temper, and those who did only initially because they assumed that this was yet another case of persecution of the long-suffering motorist. Almost all, once they understood what was going on, accepted it and expressed approval of the purpose of the experiment.

But what was even more encouraging was how they acted once they left their cars. 'They are beginning to walk and realise how much more they enjoy the countryside when they're walking,' Mr Burrell told me. 'And they're beginning to produce prams and pushchairs you just haven't seen on these roads before.' Comparative counts at the Goytsclough Quarry car park at the southern edge of the valley showed that, before the experiment, only about 10 per cent of those who parked there went away from the actual car park area. After a few months of the Goyt experiment, Theo Burrell was able to say: 'I have a very strong impression from my personal observation that many more are walking considerably further afield.' And field work confirmed this: 52 to 66 per cent were walking on roads closed to traffic; 38 to 45 per cent following nature trials; and 43 to 52 per cent other paths.

Now the big point to stress about Goyt was that the Peak Park did not just resort, as others had elsewhere, to the negative policy of banning cars. They spent quite a lot of money in a positive approach both to the provision of facilities—bigger car parks and more and better lavatories—and on informing, explaining and helping the public to make the most of the new arrangements. The explanatory leaflet they issued did not just explain why cars were banned and leave it at that. (Cars carrying handicapped people were, incidentally, an exception.) It told them about the valley and its history, what there was to be seen there, and what walks they could take. And those walks it way-marked with coloured arrows—a practice widely followed in the Alpine countries such as Switzerland and Austria, but not to any great extent yet here—though it is now beginning to happen in some areas.

Perhaps guidance of this kind was one reason why more people began to move further from their cars. They were made to feel welcome, and not outsiders there on sufferance.

Tell a man he cannot drive on, but make no clear suggestions where he may walk, and he may well sit tight and read the Sunday papers, or camp in the car park on bargain offer tubular garden furniture. The great virtue of the Goyt experiment was that it did not just say: 'Cars, keep out!' It said, 'You're welcome to park, and ride in our free minibus if you want to. While you're here you might be interested in this walk through the wood, or that one by the lake.'

### 'Managing' people in the country

All this, of course, implies management—management of cars and people in the countryside. And this raises considerable psychological barriers. For a great many countrylovers, getting out into the countryside is, consciously or unconsciously, an escape from being organised. *Arcadia ruri*, their whole instincts tells them, is not meant to be tampered with in this way. Discreet forestry and maintenance of paths—all right. But management of people and activities, no!

This, very possibly, was one of the reasons why during 1970 a number of schemes for country parks which had the backing of the Countryside Commission and the county councils concerned ran into opposition. One detects two main currents of hostility. The first says, 'Country parks are a good idea in principle, but this one—which happens to be near the rather high-class commuter village to which I moved for its rustic tranquillity five years ago—is demonstrably badly sited, with inadequate roads and not the kind of attractions that the urban proletariat really want when they come gawping in their Ford Cortinas.'

The second, which I respect more though I think it is equally wrong-headed, says: 'People have enjoyed this beauty spot for years without the need to call it a country park and build car parks and lavatory blocks' (for some reason countrylovers are supposed not to need lavatories). Part of the opposition derives from the fact that the label 'country park', under which the Countryside Commission can give grants for such work, covers a whole range of schemes from the simple provision of a discreetly screened car park and public lavatories at the entrance to a well-known beauty spot, right to the other extreme of a Woburn or Beaulieu type operation with attractions to keep the kids happy—though the Commission is a little choosy about the kind of sideshows it considers rural in character. Speedway tracks or go-cart racing are out.

So when a proposal comes up like that of the East Sussex County Planning Officer, Leslie Jay, to buy land along the Seven Sisters coastline near Beachy Head and make it into a country park, there is an understandable but mistaken tendency to imagine the worst. In fact the East Sussex proposals for the Seven Sisters seem to have had two main purposes: to acquire land which might otherwise have been used in ways not compatible with the conservation of this ancient stretch of downland (the plan included reinstatement to downland of land which had been ploughed under); and provision of the means to absorb and cope more effectively with car-borne visitors *who would come there anyway.*

That to my mind is the fundamental fallacy in arguments against management of visitors to the countryside: to assume that the choice is between people so catered for and no people. It is not. The real choice will generally be between an ever-rising tide of visitors catered for and guided to places and activities where they will by their presence and numbers do least damage, and the same rising tide running where it will.

Other pioneers among the counties in country park provision include Derbyshire, whose Elverstone Castle was a trail-blazer in this field, and Hampshire, which has very strong reasons for wanting to create new countryside attraction. The fear of the county planners there is that, with one million more people in the South Hampshire area as a result of the planned expansion of employment and housing between and around Portsmouth and Southampton, the already intense recreational pressure on the New Forest will become so great as to erode its still unspoiled quality.

## Honeypots: Butser/Queen Elizabeth

They have therefore thought in terms of creating counter-attractions or 'honeypots' which will lure the urban swarms away before they get within range of the New Forest. One of these honeypots, put forward by Hampshire's County Planning Officer, Gerald Smart, and its County Land Agent, Colin Bonsey, was a skilful amalgam of two existing attractions on either side of the A3 trunk road between Portsmouth and Petersfield. One was the established and popular beauty spot, Butser Hill—885 ft above sea level, open, windswept and already under threat from an unmanaged car invasion. By 1970 it was already getting 150,000 visitors a year, and when more than a few dozen cars crawled up the narrow road from the A3 and parked on top, the beauty spot was already eroded in quality.

What Hampshire's countryside committee proposed was a merger of Butser Hill's 525 acres with 620 acres of the adjacent Queen Elizabeth Forest, joined by an underpass which would in any case have to be provided when the A3 was widened and improved at this point. From the main road visitors would be able either to drive along specially planned scenic routes through the forest, with informal and scattered picnic areas; or they could park and follow walks and nature trails through the forest; or ride along bridle ways, or go grass-skiing on the slopes of the hill. Hampshire council and the Countryside Commission were also working out the feasibility of installing a monorail or some tracked vehicle to take visitors from the car park up to the top of the hill. The car park, discreetly hidden in a dip, would also have near it an information centre with a snack bar and a lecture theatre for nature study talks, films and the like.

All this really set the hackles rising among some country lovers. What, scenic drives! grass-skiing! a monorail! Yet again the true contrast is with what would otherwise happen. Screened rural drives with scattered, screened car parks —or motorists stopping on verges or driving through field gates. One silent, fairly unobtrusive monorail, or 200 cars struggling up the narrow lane to cover the hillside. Grass-skiing here, or too many youngsters from Portsmouth invading the New Forest or at a loss what to do on Pompey island.

Unfortunately psychological barriers begin to go up at the very mention of anything like 'monorail'. And notions of 'management' and 'recreational provision' run counter to a sort of deep-rooted pathetic fallacy which ignores the fact that most of our countryside is only what it is because of management. Few people in Switzerland or Austria suggest that mountain railways or cable cars really spoil the landscape or its tranquillity. Nor need that monorail. But 250 cars on Butser certainly do.

An added psychological tripwire to the Queen Elizabeth/ Butser scheme was that it entailed (oh, heinous crime!) charging people who drove into the place at the rate of 15p per car. Some people might say, especially in view of the £113,000 being spent on the scheme, that this was a modest price to pay for the parking and other facilities—indeed Colin Bonsey's researches suggested that fewer than 10 per cent of Butser users would jib at this. Probably with Goyt-type explanations and leaflets the proportion would be much less. But there is a very strongly-rooted objection in some quarters to anything that looks like charging for access to or use of the countryside. It is our heritage, runs the argument. It should be free.

## Country park policies

As one who disliked in principle and for its practical effects the introduction of museum charges, I have a certain respect for this view, but I think the argument is a muddled one. What countryside planners sometimes suggest charging for is not access to or use of the countryside but the provision of some facility which would otherwise be absent. For Butser the 15p charge proposed was for use of the car park—anyone who entered the park on foot or horseback would do so free. There was no provision for charging them.

In congested towns people pay to park because (among other reasons) unrestricted parking causes danger and damage to the environment. There is no reason why these considerations should not apply in a popular and therefore potentially congested bit of countryside. No one, as far as I know, has suggested erecting a fence round the North Yorks Moors or Dartmoor and levying a toll on the rucksack-laden hiker for entry. Yet to judge from the reactions of some rural conservationists, one would imagine that something like this was proposed.

There is, however, just a hint of justification in all this. There is a danger that, because people accept a charge towards the provision of specific facilities, it might be assumed by some in central or local government that no public money is needed. In fact, if our countryside policies are going to be effective, very much larger sums to support many more imaginative schemes are going to be needed. At the moment it is probably awareness of the need and the potential that is lacking, and not, in general, the cash. In 1971 the Countryside Commission was actually lamenting that private land-owners (to whom it also has power to make grants towards country park provision) had not taken up the earmarked money. But the climate will change, and when it does very much bigger sums from the taxpayers' money will be needed.

Part of the change will be a matter of public education. People will come to understand that there is nothing sinister about the word 'management' in the countryside context, and that people can be guided to do the things least harmful to the countryside by clever management without any need to resort to coercion. The countryside planner like Colin Bonsey needs to be both a bit of a landscape designer and a bit of a psychologist. He needs not only to know how to construct car parks whose surfaces look grassy but have a kind of vestigial hard standing underneath; but about 'edge effect' (see Figure 9)—the fact that motorists tend in a big open car park to cluster along the edges, while in an irregularly shaped, broken up area they will spread out into the corners. (There is, by the way, a continuing need for country parks for the carless, linked to the cities and towns they serve by good, frequent bus or train services.)

The skilled country park planner and manager takes this psychological approach further, and it governs the whole policy of siting different amenities and attractions. There is a mobility factor to visitor penetration inside parks, just as there is in the countryside as a whole. Thus countryside planners who have visited Kenne Merduinen, a large country park on the Dutch north-east coast, or the Bos on the Dutch coast near The Hague, are much impressed by the way in which these parks absorb large numbers of visitors but, because of their internal arrangement, the siting of paths and landscaping, and the positioning of attractions like picnic spots, boating lakes and bathing places near the

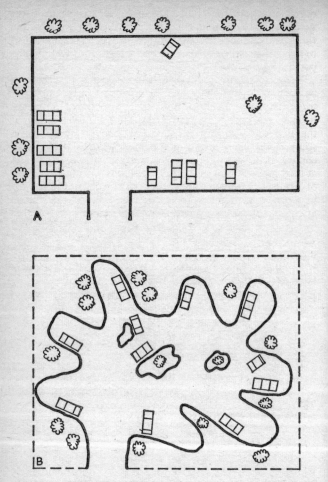

FIGURE 9. Car parks: avoiding the 'edge' effect. (*a*) Regular car park. Drivers tend to bunch. Visual effect is of massed vehicles. (*b*) Irregular car park with glades. Drivers tend to go into recesses. Pleasanter picnicking. Visual effect dispersed.

entrances, the majority of visitors do not penetrate to the wilder parts, and the quality of the real countryside within their boundaries is left for those who will make the effort to reach it to enjoy. It is, in a sense, a sort of internal honey-pot strategy at work.

This principle of persuasive management and persuasive positioning of attractions and facilities may in fact turn out to be the key to many of our rural conservation problems. It does not completely answer the dangers posed earlier of the extreme volatility of car-borne trippers, but careful study of the likely penetration of the countryside by week-end exodus from conurbations and other large towns would at least give the possibility of intercepting a high percentage of casual trippers in places where they can be catered for in terms of road space, car parks, refreshments and recreational opportunity. Honeypots on the nearer approaches to the Lake District, for instance, may be a sacrifice well worth making to preserve the other 95 per cent of the area uncrowded for those who live there, and for the minority who cherish a more intimate acquaintance with the lonely fells and the sky.

# PART V

# Industrial Pollution and other Key Battles

*Chapter Eleven*

## POLLUTION BY INDUSTRY

The subject of this chapter of course itself merits a whole book—or even a series of books. The present examination can be no more than an attempt to analyse the size and nature of the broad problem and illustrate it by one or two examples.

Pollution by industry is of several kinds: pollution of the air by harmful or unpleasant gases; and pollution of water, whether salt or fresh, and whether by land-based industry or by ships; pollution of the land, whether by the products of industry or by dereliction. These three—pollution by air, water and land, are perhaps the types of pollution most commonly associated with industry. But I would like also to mention two others: noise pollution; and—a cross category—what I will call visual pollution.

None of these is new. Ecologically speaking, as Sir Frank Fraser Darling pointed out in his 1969 Reith Lectures, Bronze-Age man had begun to pollute his environment and raid his stock of unrenewable resources when he burned wood to smelt copper and tin. In Britain the first really big impact came with the Industrial Revolution, and the growth of the nineteenth-century *laisser-faire* industrialism saw also a single-minded exploitation of technology with little regard for environmental considerations. Today in Britain, though we still—particularly in the north—suffer the legacy of industrial dereliction, firms know that both planning law and public opinion will continue to impose ever more exacting standards—at least on air, water, land and visual pollution. And yet . . . And yet pollution is today out of all proportion a more serious problem than it was in the nineteenth century. Why? There are, I think, three fundamental reasons: scale of operation, complexity of the processes involved, and pace of change.

Let me give examples of change in scale. First, steel production. In the immediate post-war period, Britain's largest steel-works produced about 700,000 tons a year. The largest operational British steel-works today is at Port Talbot with an annual output of $3\frac{1}{4}$ million tons; but the Japanese and the Russians have units capable of producing 8 to 10 million tons with expansion plans which will bring them up to 20 million tons by the early eighties. In Britain British Steel Corporation plan two works of 10 million tons. Modern steel-works both use less land and have more efficient anti-pollution devices for both air and water. But, despite the improvements made possible by the change from 'open hearth' to 'basic oxygen' production, control methods are far from perfect; and the increase in scale itself (though concentration of production makes cleaning up easier) means that there is more in the way of fumes and effluent to clean up.

Another example of increase in scale. When Bankside power station in the centre of London was built in the late forties despite much opposition, it was the biggest and most modern power station Britain had ever had. It had an initial capacity of 180 MW. Now there are several coal-fired stations of 2,000 MW and a 3,300 MW oil-fired power station is being built at the Isle of Grain on the Thames estuary. Chimneys are taller, the smoke that comes out of them looks cleaner (they contain even more efficient 'washing' devices). But fumes do blow away into the atmosphere, and more and more of them. We have only a very imperfect idea of where they go and in practice industry is less interested in their destination and effect when they cease to be traceable. That, however, does not mean they do no harm. National boundaries rarely look more out of date than in the context of atmospheric pollution. The Swedes complain convincingly that their atmosphere is polluted by both the Norwegians and the Germans. The only answer at present is international agreement on control at source, and that was one reason for calling the 1972 Stockholm Conference. But multi-national agreements are even more difficult and slower to achieve than domestic legislation with an overcrowded parliamentary timetable. And if enforcement remains with the different national authorities, international control may well turn out to be only as effective as its weakest link.

Water pollution illustrates the linked factors of complexity of industrial process and rate of technological change. A Confederation of British Industry pollution expert cited to me recently the case of a north London factory which accidentally let a minute trace of the chemical pentachlorphenol go down the drain into the local sewer. It was present in the waste, the Water Pollution Research Establishment later concluded, only in the proportion of around 0.00001 parts per million. Yet because of the nature of modern biological sewage treatment processes, that chemical put a whole large sewage works out of action for several days.

Though the C B I man was no doubt right when he said: 'I don't think anyone could have expected that result,' concentration of production does make monitoring, control and tracing after the event easier. In Britain we have the contrast in the field of water pollution between a Thames cleaner now than it has been for a century, and rivers like the Mersey and the Tame, which are used as a drain by scores of firms large and small for the discharge of their industrial effluents. In the Mersey, the quality of river water is now such, incidentally, that not only is swimming very definitely not recommended, but victims of involuntary immersion are routinely given injections against tetanus and a number of other infections (producing that ecological sick joke, 'The quality of Mersey is not strained'). It has not yet reached the plight of the River Cuyahoga in Cleveland, which is so full of chemical effluents that it is classified a fire risk. Nonetheless the Mersey in its present state is a standing affront to a supposedly civilised society, and an indictment of the price we have been prepared unthinkingly to pay for the conveniences of industrial and economic growth.

In the longer term, the answer may lie in concentrating new chemical and other effluent-producing industry where its waste products can be dealt with in bulk. This solution has been adopted in one instance in Germany where a 'sealed stream' collects liquid wastes from a number of Rhineland industrial plants and carries them to a single treatment works.

Existing industry is the problem. Some experts say the powers are adequate, but their application is a delicate balancing act with economics and public opinion. Suppose the Mersey and Weaver River Authority suddenly got tough with half the works discharging waste into the Mersey, instead of applying pressure where it seemed realistic to demand improvement. What would happen? Some of the firms would either instal better anti-pollution equipment or move. Some would go out of business, either because they could not pay the cost of improvement or because in practical terms improvement was not feasible on that site. Others would judge that their competitiveness—especially international competitiveness—would not survive the expense, and choose to go out of production. Result: loss of jobs and local prosperity, and—in a region where there is considerable unemployment still—very possibly a hostile reaction from public opinion and politically to anti-pollution measures generally.

So this aspect of any campaign against pollution falls down because of lack of public comprehension. People understand what lost jobs mean: that is 'for real'. So, in a minor way, is 5p on the price of a packet of detergent. The possible 'death' of a river or lake is not. Yet it has happened. Incidentally, one misconception which colours talk of water pollution is the notion of 'dirtiness'. Dirt is not the same thing as pollution. A river can be very dirty after heavy rain without being seriously polluted. Conversely, a river can look very clean and yet be quite seriously polluted. The measure generally adopted is 'B O D'—biological or biochemical oxygen demand. This is what makes a river live. When the B O D falls too low eutrophication follows, and a river or lake 'dies' as Lake Erie in North America has done. It is choked with algae, the only plant life it can support. No fish, no insects, no other plants. It is a blank, dead space in the complex of ecological cycles which keep our world alive, productive and habitable—and as such a frightening warning of what might happen on a wider scale.

The field of marine pollution presents an even more

worrying example of public mis-assumptions. People are of course worried about oil tankers breaking up at sea. They know oil is nasty messy stuff because little Sarah sat in some on the beach last summer, and then trod another lump into the car seat. They have also been told that it can do serious damage to marine life. But what they usually do not appreciate is how vulnerable marine life is. They think of the oceans as limitless, and assume that what lives in it is somehow inexhaustible. The truth is, marine biologists tell us, that some 90 per cent of that richness is concentrated in something like 1 per cent of ocean areas—those nearest our coasts. And those are the areas most vulnerable to oil spillage, partly because those are the likeliest collision areas, partly because floating oil tends to end up there. Because of the relative tidelessness of the Mediterranean, and the recklessness with which some nations tip all manner of waste and untreated effluent into it, the Mediterranean has suffered worst from this. There are signs that its coastal strip, once so rich in marine life, is already dying, and it may already be too late to save large parts of the Mediterranean from becoming literally a 'dead sea'.

The only really safe solution to the problem of oil pollution is not to ship oil on—or for that matter under—the sea. Until we have developed a fuel as convenient and cheap however, that is in practical terms no solution. We have instead to look for palliatives: safer sea lanes and shipping practices, better salvage arrangements when accidents do occur, and better techniques for dealing with oil as floating slicks and, in the last resort, on the beaches. Britain is a lot better prepared now than at the time of the *Torrey Canyon* affair, but technically we are still by no means well prepared. Many scientists doubt, for instance, whether we should go on using detergents (products, incidentally, of the same industry which spills the oil) rather than mechanical means to clear up the mess. In 1969 a Swansea shipping consultant Michael Spencer-Davies developed a craft called the Sea Mantis, a catamaran towing dracones (or huge floating sacks) of 1,000 tons each and with long booms which would be linked to tugs. The Sea Mantis has a fair turn of speed, and its strategy is to get to the slick fast, contain it with the booms, and suck the oil into the dracones. Government scientists dubbed it 'the best oil clearing system we have yet seen'. Oil company experts have examined Sea Mantis but at the time of writing nothing seems to have come of it, though the principle is undoubtedly sound. It is difficult to believe that if the international oil world faced the option of either developing an effective means of coping with slicks or closing down, it would not have leapt on this and any other promising solution and poured money and effort into developing it.

The truth is that industry needs generally to be pushed into expensive action either by governments or exceptionally strong public opinion; governments and administrators also need to feel the spur of public opinion; and public opinion has to be made aware of the true costs and dangers of pollution, either by a slow and steady process of education or by the salutary lesson of catastrophe. All one can hope is that catastrophes when they come will be just big enough to drive home the lesson, and no bigger. Here again concentration of resources and the modern law of economy of scale both allow better control and reduction of pollution risks, yet at the same time offer the bleak prospect that when, inevitably, an accident occurs, the mess will be bigger and its possible ecological chain reaction that much more serious.

Natural gas has, rightly, been heralded as environmentally the most acceptable fuel we have. Its only snag from that point of view seems to be the network of masts necessary for telemetered remote control of flows. The same will not necessarily be so if North Sea oil is brought ashore by pipeline. The pollution caused by oil escape off the California coast at Santa Barbara in 1969 was the writing on the wall for that kind of exercise. The North Sea bed is not geologically so stable nor its waters so free of storms that we can afford to take such a warning lightly. There is, of course, an element of risk in any technological advance, and decisions whether to go ahead or not will usually depend on the best assessment possible of that risk. But when the environmental penalty of things going wrong is huge and the risk assessment a shaky process involving many unknowns, then arguments about the need for economic growth should not be allowed to weigh too heavily.

## Unknown consequences of new technology

What I find most worrying in all the detailed arguments about pollution dangers and control is the frequency with which, if you really press the point, the experts will admit: 'We do not know for certain what the effect of this will be. No one knows. We are only making the best assessment we can of what we think its effects will be.' Thus some scientists predict that general adoption by the world's airlines of supersonic aircraft would result in damage to the earth's atmosphere which could quite possibly be fatal to life on earth. Others say this is unlikely. Their arguments are respectable, but no one knows. In the Cleveland Potash mining affair which I shall examine later from other points of view, the company said they were sure that a mile-long pipeline out to sea would ensure harmless dispersal of powdery waste solids from the potash production process; the minister said he thought it would, but wanted the option of stopping production if it were shown to be otherwise; and marine biologists from the nearby Wellcome Laboratory at Robin Hood's Bay said there was just a chance that the waste, if it were carried back in sufficiently heavy concentrations towards the shore, might clog and suffocate marine life of certain kinds and seriously damage the ecological balance But no one really knew. They were only beginning to understand the factors involved.

This sense of the smallness of scientific knowledge of areas into which technology is single-mindedly breaking is, to me, frightening. Of course science works on the basis of probabilities, but science works in limited, controlled situations. Technology moves in on a mass-production scale, with big money involved and prosperity mortgaged to its success. In his 1969 Reith Lectures, Sir Frank Fraser Darling warned against the danger of technology's working up an irresistible momentum—and indeed this almost happened, and may still happen, with the supersonic airliner. The danger is that so many jobs, so many people's prosperity may come to depend upon a project that it is its own justification. Perhaps you point out that the S S T gets a few thousand people across the Atlantic an hour or two quicker while making life unpleasant for hundreds of thousands who live near airports or on flight paths (leaving aside the possible bashing it gives to the earth's atmosphere) and that this is too high a price to pay. 'Ah!' say the technologists, 'but you cannot stand in the way of "progress".' This is akin to the argument that men must risk climbing mountains because they're there. Fair enough. But when the costs to the community of rescue operations grows too high, steps may have to be taken to limit the numbers licensed to risk their own and others' safety.

What I am arguing, I think, is this. That politically and socially we need to fit better brakes to the powerful sports car of technology; we need to spend much more on the scientific research which enables its driver to see where he is really going; and we need to take the environmental corners rather more slowly and carefully than we do at present. Thalidomide was a warning of this which has to some extent been heeded. I talked in an earlier chapter of 'engineers' tunnel vision'—their tendency to solve the practical problem in hand without too much thought for environmental niceties. Commercial technology tends to suffer from a similar failing. The community as a whole needs to put very much more money and skilled resources into a wide variety of research which can alert it if technology seems to be taking a dangerous road, and can warn convincingly from really detailed, thorough knowledge.

## The fight against visual pollution

After the frightening imponderables of murdered marine life and damaged atmosphere, 'visual pollution' appears as a relatively simple problem. It has basically two varieties: one is the wanton creation of industrial dereliction such as colliery spoil heaps or abandoned works—largely the product of the single-minded industrialism of the past. The other is the more conscious and calculated variety which says: 'We accept that this installation spoils your view, but the gains to the community or the nation outweigh the loss, which we will try to keep to the minimum.'

The assault on derelict land has at last, in recent years, really begun to make some impact. There are, I think, three reasons for this. One is a more critical, impatient public, placing a higher value on 'good environment' and affronted by the needless squalor of messes not even justified by continuing industrial activity. Second is the means—great new earth-moving machines doing in days what would previously have taken months, and in months what would before have seemed impossible. And here the Coal Board, through its Opencast Executive, is atoning to some extent for the past sins of its industry. Third is Aberfan—again tragedy as a catalyst to action. Wales needed Aberfan to concentrate its mind on what was possible and desirable.

In recent years the Welsh Office's Derelict Land Unit, a similarly expert unit set up by district councils in Monmouthshire, and individual local authorities, have been transforming in a positive way the environment of numerous communities in the mining valleys of South Wales. This has not just been a matter of removing dangerous or oppressive slag heaps towering over people's homes. It has created, in narrow valley bottoms where space has always been short, new flat areas both for housing and recreation, and for building factories to provide jobs to replace those lost in colliery closures. Government grants provide 85 per cent of the net cost of approved schemes in a development area, and rate equalisation grants often take the true proportion higher. Even so, it is argued, a small local authority with a low rateable value may find it difficult to meet even that proportion. That may be so. One or two small urban councils, however, have actually managed after selling land to industry to make a profit on derelict land clearance.

In England an outstanding example of what can be done is provided by the city of Stoke-on-Trent—winner in 1971 of *The Times*/Royal Institution of Chartered Surveyors Awards for land reclamation. The award-winning project was a 128-acre site containing the long-standing dereliction of huge, unsightly colliery spoil heaps and pottery marl holes. This has now been transformed into a natural-seeming, hilly and wooded landscape with special paths and trails for walkers, cyclists and horse-riders, football pitches, a pitch-and-putt course, and a lake for boating.

Almost the sole reminder of its past is the retention of the colliery pit-head gear, both as a dramatic piece of industrial archæology and as a viewing platform looking over the city. Central Forest Park is being linked to other reclamation areas in Stoke-on-Trent by a system of 'greenways' landscaped out of the disused railway lines of which the city has a profusion, which used to link them as live industrial sites, and which lost their viability at the time of the colliery closures of the late 1950s and early 1960s.

The project was conceived in 1967 by a London firm of landscape architects, Land Use Consultants, and in particular by its partner Clifford Tandy, later president of the Institute of Landscape Architects. It has been very much a joint endeavour by them, the National Coal Board's Opencast Executive and Stoke's planning and parks departments —though *The Times*/R I C S judges criticised the Coal Board for the high price it charged for land sold to the city.

The attitudes of mind which create dereliction almost unthinkingly still, however, persist. British Rail is one of the worst offenders. I travelled recently on a branch line where colour light signalling had some time ago been installed. The signal columns were neat enough in themselves, but British Rail's method of dealing with the redundant signal boxes had been to immobilise them. There they stood, every mile or two, smashed up and derelict. Whether British Rail did most of the smashing, or vandals is not the point. It should be axiomatic, and enforceable at law, that if any industrial or commercial concern no longer uses a building or structure, it must either keep it in good order or demolish it and remove the debris. Just as the law provides ways of dealing with an unsafe structure, or a 'nuisance' which affronts the nose or ears, so it should provide remedies for 'visual nuisance'.

## Pollution and potash mining in Yorkshire

Now let me state in some detail a case—that of potash mining in the North Yorks Moors—which has elements in it of three different kinds of pollution: air, water and visual, all of which the industry concerned has made considerable efforts to limit, with varying degrees of success.

The visitor arriving at Cleveland Potash's mine at Boulby, near Staithes along the coast from Tees-side, could well find it difficult to understand what all the fuss was about potash mining in North Yorkshire. The mine, jointly owned by I C I and the mining giant Charter Consolidated, and with an eventual planned output of 1.5 million tons a year, is in the North Yorks Moor National Park and does have some tall chimneys and large industrial buildings.

From a siting point of view, however, it has the advantage of being in a dish-shaped valley on the edge of the moors. A paper study of map contours led North Riding county planners to the conclusion that it would be visible from about 6,000 acres of the national park, as compared with 17,000 acres for the proposed Shell (Whitby Potash project. Neither of these was even building at the time of writing, though both had planning permission. If in the event the state of the world potash market means that only one mine is viable, it is as well from the visual point of view that I C I/Charter got off the ground first.

There are four different kinds of objection that can be raised against the Cleveland mine: visual spoliation of countryside so beautiful that it has been designated a national park; possible air pollution; pollution of the sea and beaches by effluent; and the disturbance caused by transporting out the finished product.

On the first, it can be argued that the visual invasion of any national park by large-scale industrial buildings is a contradiction of our whole countryside policy and to be resisted. It is harder to argue in that way when one knows that, in an area with some 10 per cent unemployed to which it has proved exceedingly difficult to attract new jobs, the mine will employ 600 to 800 people, a good proportion of them local. Countryside preservation may be something in a vacuum to some preservationists, but neither the North Riding County Council nor the Countryside Commission felt able, in these circumstances, to oppose this project. Each was content to watch for snags and shortcomings in detailed implementation. North Riding county planners indeed say frankly that they regard Sir Frederick Gibberd and Partners' design and landscaping of the Boulby works as no more than making the best of a bad job. It is, they say, the price to be paid for jobs and prosperity. Yet given that starting point, I think such an assessment fails to do justice to a fine and positive job. The two tall chimneys, 289 feet high, have a certain elegance, and both Gibberd's materials and their roof angles—which 'rhyme' with the angles of the ramps needed by the mechanical scrapers which move the ore—do better than merely aim at being unobtrusive. The roofline of the minehead building between its two stumpy concrete shafts catches the excitement of nineteenth-century pit-head buildings without their grimness; and the woodframed raw ore silo is, inside, almost cathedral-like—or rather like the interior of an eighteenth- or nineteenth-century barn but a dozen times bigger. In landscaping few pains have been spared. The firm has moved 350,000 cubic yards of earth into a bank to mask the bulk of its silos from certain angles, and has planted 20,000 trees.

The significant thing about the potash affair—and it applies also to the two other (unstarted) mine projects—is that they went further than merely promising 'cosmetic' treatment. In their efforts to allay public anxiety and obtain planning permission, all three called in landscape architects early in the day—Derek Lovejoy and Partners in the case of both R T Z and Shell—and allowed them to influence siting as well as basic design of installations. It may still amount to making the best of a bad job, but it is the right way to use a landscape architect, who should not be—but often is—just a tidier-up of other people's messes.

The second objection was atmospheric pollution: the reason for those tall and widely visible stacks. Rightly or wrongly, everyone seemed convinced that they would effectively disperse the fumes. The price was that the tops of the chimneys are visible over a wider area.

The third objection—marine pollution—was the most difficult for Cleveland and the planners to deal with, and the subject of a delayed-action and very stringently tied up planning consent from the D O E. Cleveland tackled the problem by building a mile-long tunnel out under the rock floor which extends in front of Boulby cliff, and to get their permission had to agree to waive any claim for compensation if the Minister ordered them to stop discharging effluent because it was causing marine pollution.

The fourth objection was met by reopening, at considerable expense, an abandoned railway line from Tees-side. Pollution by heavy lorry was thus, in this instance, avoided.

There is a fifth objection implicit in the argument about the Boulby mine: that, though relatively unobjectionable in itself, it represented a wedge in the door. Where once industry penetrates a national park, whether in North Yorkshire or Snowdonia, it is difficult to parry further thrusts, and the character of these areas is thus in danger of being steadily eroded. The Shell and R T Z mines, which were generally regarded as more objectionable than the Boulby one, are only on paper at present. But if the world potash market changes and they become a tempting proposition, both firms have planning permissions with a seven-year life.

On the face of it, the most serious pollution danger at Boulby—marine—attracted the most stringent control and safeguard. The minister, as we have seen, made the company carry the risk that its expensive mile-long pipeline would not be effective. I hope I will be forgiven for a certain scepticism. Let us look at what would be likely to happen in practice. Suppose that Robin Hood's Bay laboratory had reason to suspect damage to marine life and the crab fisheries. They would want to be as sure of themselves as possible before acting. And then opinions might well differ between the laboratory's scientists and Cleveland Potash's experts as to the existence or seriousness of the damage.

Suppose, however, that everyone was convinced that some damage was occurring. The minister or the government would then have to weigh that damage against the damage caused to the economy and local unemployment levels of closing down, temporarily or permanently, Britain's only big potash mine. Crab fishermen could, no doubt, be compensated, but you cannot compensate the community for killing of marine life on, say, a five mile stretch of coast. You can only weigh one kind of damage against another. My guess is that a minister might make fierce noises, order urgent investigations in the hope of finding some remedial modification to the effluent system, but let the mine go on working and save the jobs. Which rather goes to illustrate a sort of environmental 'nine points of the law'. It is easier to be tough with a potential polluter before he has his planning permission and started up than after he has gone into production. All this is, in the case of Cleveland Potash, it must be stressed, hypothetical. The chances are that the pipeline will do the trick, and everyone

—including the crab fishermen—will stay happy. I certainly hope so.

The right 'long-term', ecological answer is, of course, recycling: using industry's waste products—liquid, solid and gaseous—to create new products or useful energy. Industry has done it again and again in two sets of circumstances—when it perceived an unfilled commercial market for a potential product of recycling: and when the discharge of a product in the ordinary way became too difficult or unpopular. We need to reinforce both these motives: not only by pointing the way through research to what is technically possible, but by favouring those who recycle and progressively more stringently penalising those who do not. What is needed is a fiscal policy which will make it worthwhile for industry to search out every opportunity for recycling. The negative system of penalising the polluter is not enough. Public opinion disapproving of the apparent and visible manifestations of pollution is not enough. We need to translate into cash terms the black and red of the ecological balance sheet. And this must somehow be achieved on an international basis (the Common Market should be a helpmate not a hindrance) and quickly: for the long term is now not so long. Serious ecological damage on a scale that will make us rue our technological recklessness may well be just round the corner.

*Chapter Twelve*

# SOME KEY ENVIRONMENTAL BATTLES

The battlegrounds of the 'environmentalist' are legion. This chapter deals with eight or nine more of them which I consider crucial at one level or another—some in terms of a threatened amenity for future generations in Britain, others involving possibly the very survival of the human race or large sections of it. They all seem to me, however, to be battles very well worth fighting. The first is concerned with :

## INLAND WATERWAYS

This title includes rivers and river navigations, but the battle is mainly concerned with the British canal system. This has to a large extent been a Cinderella ever since the railway companies began buying up canals in the 1850s. Railway company tactics to do down the canals ranged from degrees of neglect consistent with statutory duty to actions verging on sabotage. The Shropshire Union Canal which, as we have seen in Chapter 3, the Welsh Office proposed to destroy as an amenity to the town of Welshpool in order to save itself marginal extra cost on a so-called 'by-pass', was long ago severed from the Llangollen Canal by 1930s embankment collapse. This, canal adherents darkly mutter, was a very sinister incident. Maybe the railway company had nothing to do with the collapse, but their exaggerated protestations about the cost of repairing it were characteristic of an undertaking which had no enthusiasm for the canal system at all.

And that has been the trouble. Until the end of the 1960s at least, public opinion regarded canals as a pleasant anachronism; and those officially responsible for them, including a series of nationalised bodies, as a cross to be borne. Attitudes were defensive. Traffic was dwindling; the general assumption was that carriage and freight by inland waterway, because less modern and less speedy than rail or lorry, was less efficient—an assumption which, in spite of lack of capital investment in the system, was often the reverse of true.

Some parts of the canal system, though owned by the railways, were not in direct competition with them. The 150 miles or so of the Birmingham Canal Navigation, for instance, throve until the late 1950s when their staple, the coal trade, was hit by colliery rationalisation and closures; thereafter the decline of its freight traffic was rapid.

For long the main defenders of the canals against neglect and closure were a small band of enthusiasts—recreational boaters with the stamina to explore the little used cut and work the rusty lock-gate—and industrial archæologists who appreciated the grandeur of tunnels and aqueducts by Brindley, Telford or Brunel. But gradually it began to be recognised more generally that, in an age bracing itself for the leisure explosion which always seemed to be just on the point of detonation, and in a country with relatively little space to accommodate it, this Cinderella system of canals and river navigations provided recreational opportunities the nation should not lightly snuff out. The system ran tranquil past the neglected backs of towns and cities, tunnelled quietly under their roadworks and traffic jams, gave unexpectedly green routes from the drabbest urban areas into the countryside—not just for the lucky or energetic with boats, but for walkers and anglers too.

And so, when the 1968 Transport Bill came before Parliament, its canals section provided for continued maintenance of two categories of canals—those still commercially viable, and 'cruiseways', which the government and the British Waterways Board judged would earn their keep from recreational use. For a third category, 'remainder waterways', the future looked bleak. But there was a strong feeling abroad that many of these canals—including for instance the central section of the Kennet and Avon. linking the Thames at Reading to the Bristol Avon at Bath—were assets too precious to allow to decay. And in a sense the bitter party political battle over other clauses of the Transport Bill saved the day. Rather than have the measure further delayed, the government gave the remainder waterways a reprieve—or rather put them under suspended sentence. In a statement in the Lords in September 1968, Lord Gardiner (then Lord Chancellor) repeated and added the government's authority to a Waterways Board pledge not to do anything to prejudice the future of these canals for a period of three years so as to give the Board, the local authorities concerned and the canal preservation societies an opportunity to work out ways and means of keeping them alive.

In those three years, the canal enthusiasts, buoyed up by increasing public interest in and use of canals generally, made tremendous efforts to demonstrate what could be done with the neglected sections of the system on which commercial trade was dying. Gangs of volunteers spent weekends thigh-deep in rubbish and silt clearing blocked locks and pounds. The Inland Waterways Association and individual canal preservation societies raised thousands of pounds to repair lock-gates which most people would have assumed it was the Board's duty to repair. And rallies of boats served the dual purpose of keeping overgrown stretches of waterway open and demonstrating the strength of recreational potential.

But as the three years of the Lord Chancellor's guarantee drew to a close, the preservationists became worried. Certainly the climate had changed and recreational potential was more widely appreciated. But hard agreements for maintenance of the remainder waterways too often seemed to be held up by hard bargaining between local authorities with tight budgets who did not rate canals very high priority, and the Board, which felt itself impelled by statutory duty to shift that burden to other shoulders. Moreover, though sympathetic noises came from some quarters in the DOE, other agents of the Department, as well as of county highway departments, were quite prepared to prevent navigation for ever on crucial link stretches of canal if lower bridges would save them money or structural complications.

At the time of writing, some extension of the guarantee period was still being sought. Hopeful signs were twofold. First the British Waterways Board was making reassuring noises about not chopping canals summarily, and was playing a much more positive role in promoting recreational use and the sort of transformation of canal banks which had won Birmingham City Council a Civic Trust Award at Farmer's Bridge, minutes away from the city centre. Secondly, the lesson seemed to be going home that it would usually cost considerably more to get rid of canals than to keep them.

This point was made by a report on the Birmingham Canal Navigation system published with considerable publicity by the Board in August 1971. It represented the efforts of a working party representing canal groups and local councils as well as B W B officials, and argued that the cost of filling in B C N remainder waterways would have to include a replacement land drainage system and would therefore total around £22 million as compared with only some £45,000 for reinstatement of all the main sections of canal. The preservationists on that working party detected a remarkable 'change of gear' between two successive meetings of that working party, with its official members doubting at the first whether it had power to recommend action, and at the second backing firm recommendations for the upgrading of the bulk of the B C N to cruiseway status and strongly backing action for reinstatement and development. One interpretation put on this is that the Board's Chairman, Sir Frank Price, sometime leader of Birmingham City Council, decided that there must be positive action if the recreational opportunity the system offered the West Midlands conurbation was not to be lost. Previously Sir Frank and his fellow board members had often seemed to I W A A C —the Minister's Inland Waterways Amenity Advisory Committee, chaired successively by a fiery Welsh schoolmaster and Labour politician Illtyd Harrington, and a soldier of Suez fame and no less determination where canals were concerned, General Sir Hugh Stockwell—to be backpedalling. More recently, with more positive backing from the top, the board's officials have become almost evangelical about keeping the canals open.

Perhaps the Cinderella image is fading, the vicious circle of low regard breeding vandalism and rubbish reversed. The sad irony has in the past been that those ill-favoured urban areas for which canals offered relatively the most valuable opportunities have most abused them. The cut was a drain and a rubbish dump. It needs courage and determination to reverse this. And it was therefore immensely encouraging to have the B W B's recreational services manager, Allan Blenkarn, publicly preaching the gospel of repeated re-instatement as an answer to vandalism. 'Vandals smash a place up at the weekend. Repair it first thing on Monday morning. They come again next weekend. Repair it again. The third weekend they probably won't come back.' Psychologically sound over a much wider area than canals, but a very difficult principle for public authorities to apply, or cost-conscious public officials to believe in. Their usual re-action is to fence it off or close it down. Our canals need to be opened up, so that the public may know and respect them—not just chuck old prams into them over any convenient bridge.

## PEDESTRIAN STREETS

In theory public opinion is in favour, in practice people find all sorts of reasons for not excluding traffic in particular cases. The traders of Bond Street believe they will suffer from loss of the 'carriage trade.' Similar 'quality' shopping streets in continental cities know that the reverse is true. Shoppers making luxury purchases spend more time and money if they are not belaboured by car noise, pinned on to narrow pavements and impeded from wandering from one side of the street to the other.

Shopkeepers in Norwich's London Street found this out when road repairs temporarily closed the road. It has never been reopened. Damage by heavy traffic to Windsor Bridge caused its sudden closure to vehicles in 1970. Eton on the farther bank felt its umbilical cord had been severed. The panic reaction was: 'Rebuild the bridge quickly!' But this was impossible. It would take two years at least. And then many shopkeepers found their trade was improving. House-holders and masters at Eton College could use rooms over-looking the High Street and hear themselves speak; shoppers could cross the road safely for the first time in decades. Opinion swung round. Eton likes being a vehicular cul-de-sac. The bridge seems likely to remain pedestrian only.

But in Britain we are often curiously inflexible about our pedestrian streets. We tend to say 'All or nothing.' And the total ban on vehicles makes unnecessary enemies. A more flexible approach, which achieves the spirit of pedestrianisation and 90 per cent of its effect without its irksome restrictiveness, has been working successfully in many continental cities for years. This seems to be what Leeds has adopted for some of its paved shopping streets between Headrow and Boar Lane. The odd van moving at 5 m.p.h. and kept to that speed by deliberately speed-restricting surfaces is no real threat either to the shopper's safety or pleasant shopping conditions. A stream of vehicles, even with raised and railed pavements, is.

## AIRCRAFT AND AIRPORTS

Short of banning all flying over populated districts, there are only two tolerably effective ways of dealing with aircraft noise: by building aircraft with very much quieter engines; and by siting airports where few people will be disturbed by them. Both these solutions are being attempted, and should eventually benefit Britons affected by the problem. Both are unfortunately lengthy and expensive processes.

It may be said that there are two reasons for the increase of aircraft noise: growth of civil airline traffic, swollen of late years by the package-tour explosion; and the jet engine. Historically the difficulty with jets has been that the ordinary engine silencer, such as in a car or a propeller-driven aircraft, would not work.

The exhaust—the source of most of the noise—on a jet aircraft was also the means of propulsion. The very considerable success that research on quietening engines has had to date has worked on the 'shape' of the jet and its interaction with surrounding still air, since the interaction of these two is what produces the characteristic jet roar.

One says 'success' with some diffidence. Householders near Heathrow and Gatwick airports, for instance, are apt not to concede any success. Yet but for the noise-suppressors fitted to present-generation jet airliners (which generally work by use of a corrugated jet nozzle or by splitting the jet into a number of smaller ones) their plight would be even less bearable than it is. However, one source of more real improvement is likely to be the new type of engine, which works basically by producing a broader, slower exhaust jet, thus giving the same thrust with much less noise.

The government's choice of Foulness as the third London airport is, of course, the most striking testimony to the environmental factors in airport siting—though there are many people in north Kent and south-east Essex who would say this is more symbolic than real. Just how many existing householders on Sheerness island, say, or in the eastern fringes of Southend, are burdened with really bad aircraft noise and how many escape it depends on the siting of runways.

The Roskill alignment of runways, chosen partly to give Foulness the most favourable economic rating for that site, was probably worse than it need be now that Foulness has been selected. Some people have suggested that there should be a sort of rapid mini-Roskill on which runway alignment will do least noise damage.

If, however, we accept for the moment that coastal sites of this kind, with skilful arrangement of runways and flight paths not unduly constrained by narrow economic considerations, can minimise 'noise shadow' even for heavily populated countries like Britain, there are still problems. Huge capital investment at existing airports makes it unthinkable for any government, at least in the present political climate, to write them off or even substantially run them down.

Present government policy is to steer the noisier aircraft to Foulness when it is built, allowing only the quieter ones to land at Heathrow and Gatwick if, in spite of differential landing charges and the glamour and attractions of the third airport, they find it worthwhile to do so. This will be part of a stick-and-carrot policy.

The noise certification scheme introduced in 1971 by the Board of Trade under an International Civil Aviation Organisation decision of the previous year (Britain was the pioneer in implementing it) will bite increasingly as the new aircraft to which it applies replace the old, to which it does not apply.

But Foulness's first runway will not be in action until, at earliest, the late 1970s, and some of the existing noisy aircraft have a remarkably long life. There are means technically available of quietening them—at a cost. Britain, France and the United States have spearheaded the attack on this problem, and the pressure on airline operators to fit 'hush kits'—silencing outfits packaged in rather the same way as gas boards have kits to convert gas cookers to North Sea gas—can be available if operators are willing to pay for them.

But silencing is expensive, both in terms of initial cost and less efficient operation. Why should Sudan or the United Arab Republic national airlines spend hundreds of thousands of pounds to produce a silenced aircraft which will largely 'waste its sweetness on the desert air', just for one trip a week to Paris or London? In practice, in many cases it is cheaper to write off the old aircraft and buy a newer, quieter one—hard for the operators, but better for the people on the ground.

Short of quieter engines and environmentally better airport siting, pretty well all other answers are palliatives of limited effectiveness and with substantial drawbacks. They range from grant-assisted double-glazing of homes and giant mufflers for ground testing of aircraft engines, to juggling with flight paths and take-off and landing routes, and the device now employed for take-offs at Heathrow: cutback of engine power once a safe height has been reached, postponing further noisy climbing until the aircraft has cleared the most densely populated districts.

Double-glazing is clearly essential as long as, for example, districts under the take-off path need primary schools. Teaching without it is impossible. The use made of grants for residential double-glazing has, however, been disappointing. This is partly because the maximum grant does not go far enough towards meeting real costs; partly perhaps because people do not like to seal themselves into their houses, thereby accentuating the contrast when they go out into their gardens; and partly because many of them do not much care.

Surveys indicate that about 30 per cent of people are not too greatly pained or disturbed by aircraft noise, and the proportion near Heathrow who are supposedly insensitive to it has risen over the years (though it can be assumed that, in a population with a high rate of change, many who were most disturbed have moved away).

The device of cutting back power at about 1,000 ft, the first safe moment, then climbing more gradually and quietly until the built-up area has been cleared, is one which is enforced at Heathrow despite opposition from some pilots. It is, however, justifiable only where a heavily populated area is in the take-off path. Its disadvantages—that the noise produced by the extended climb is spread over a longer path, and the postponed climb under full power is at somebody else's expense—make it unjustifiable at, for instance, Gatwick.

This is the flaw with almost all such palliatives—it is as if, in trying to rid yourself of kitchen fumes, you turned on your extractor fan, only to waft them in through your neighbour's window. Even the restrictions placed on numbers of night flights, and now extended to Gatwick as well as Heathrow, are of limited value. One jet flying—perhaps by mistake, perhaps unavoidably—lower or more noisily than normal, probably does more to disturb sleeping householders than twice the number of aircraft flying as prescribed.

One device which has been under examination does, however, provide some hope of considerable noise abatement without any great environmental side-effect, though the economic penalty is certainly there. This is the concept of the two-angle approach or 'double-segment glide-slope', as the Department of Trade and Industry noise control officials call it.

It calls for an initially quite steep approach followed at about 1,000 ft or less by a shallower landing angle. The engine thrust demanded to bring the aircraft on to this shallower path for the final two miles of landing is no noisier, it seems, than otherwise, but the steepness of the previous seven miles of approach cuts noise levels by up to ten perceived noise decibels.

The main cost would be provision of a duplicate set of landing equipment both in aircraft and on the ground, and it would require international agreement. Probably, here, as elsewhere, the political difficulties are greater than the economic ones. In practice, quieter engines and remoter airports may take effect almost as soon.

One worrying development—and it is an illustration of what Sir Frank Fraser Darling has called 'the technological exponential'—is the S S T phenomenon. It seems to me perfectly clear that on any sane assessment supersonic passenger aircraft in any numbers will cost the human race much more than they benefit us. This would, I think, even if there were no noise consideration, be, as argued in the previous chapter, one of those cases where technology should go a little slower until science has plotted the surrounding area more thoroughly.

But the argument is fudged by this 'technological exponential' of which Sir Frank spoke in his Reith Lectures. In other words, technological advance (I avoid begging the question by calling it 'progress') builds up a head of steam of its own. So many millions are poured into projects, so many thousands of jobs come to be, directly or indirectly, at stake, that the responsibility of stopping such a project is a heavy one. Cancellation or refusal to support continuation may precipitate a Rolls-Royce situation, in which failure of a prestigious national company rocks the economy. Opponents of such a technologically superb achievement as the Concorde are accused of being (a) Luddites trying to hold up inevitable progress, and (b) unpatriotic. Yet the strength of the environmental lobby in America has blocked the s s t there, and if many more countries refuse to permit supersonic overflying, then it may well cease to be viable anyway. If it could be demonstrated than an s s t does not cause damage to the earth's atmosphere and if one were certain that it could and would be operated really quietly at subsonic speeds over and near land, much of the objection would disappear—though it would still seem to many of us a very dubious use of huge resources in a world which has so many more urgent claims on technology.


NOISE

Noise in general is one of the most ubiquitous forms of pollution, and one of the most difficult for the law to control. It does not need Parliament to do as it did with aircraft noise and cancel the citizen's right to recover damages for the nuisance. Everywhere he is surrounded by noise in its other forms, and the same thread runs through it all. Convenience and cheapness to one man is bought at the expense of his neighbour's tranquillity. I cut the grass more easily and quickly with a cheap mains electric lawnmower sold for £9 or £10 with fifty feet of flex, and risk spoiling any or all of half-a-dozen near neighbours' deckchair repose! This may sound trivial, but it is very largely the aggregation of trivial noises which goes to make up what is often a gross affront to the environment. Noise has come to be accepted as a part of modern living, yet even where it is accepted that does not mean it is acceptable. Doctors have become worried because the level of noise from amplifiers in discotheques is often such as to inflict permanent damage to hearing on the teenagers exposed to it. An even more serious danger apprehended by some psychologists is that constant exposure to noise, though most people appear to adapt to it, may impose mental strains leading to urban neuroses with incalculable effects. The Association of Public Health Inspectors has suggested noise zoning—on the analogy of clean air zones—with varying maximum levels enforced to suit local circumstances. There would seem to be four areas where action could and should be taken on noise: (a) more research into its effects; (b) a more comprehensive legal framework for its control; (c) more effective methods of enforcement; and (d) above all more education to produce public awareness that, though noise may not be tangible, it can be harmful to people and is damaging to their environment.

## COASTS

The seaside holiday is the traditional English family holiday—so traditional that we may be forgiven for forgetting that this popularity is really not more than 150 years old. In recent times it has thrown immense pressures on the more accessible parts of the British coastline, and urbanised whole stretches. Others have been taken over by industry. Two trends have been increasing these pressures: more mobility and money for holidays, and more holiday or week-end homes; and the increasing need of modern industry for large supplies of water for cooling and other industrial processes and to dilute and disperse their wastes.

The Countryside Commission, in two reports, *The Planning of the Coastline* and *The Coastal Heritage*, set out a strategy for taking the pressure off our best unspoiled stretches of coastline and concentrating development in a limited number of places. Thus, it urged grouping of new seaside holiday facilities largely around existing resorts, which were to be made more attractive to the new and more sophisticated holidaymaker, and the designation of regional parks in coastal areas with the greatest potential for recreation, as 'honeypots' to preserve areas of special scenic or scientific interest from being swamped.

As for industry, *The Planning of the Coastline* adopted the notion of Maritime and Industrial Development Areas (M I D A) as a device to concentrate industry and ports in a few locations rather than permitting them to pro-liferate round the coasts. The second report, *The Coastal Heritage*, listed thirty-four sections of coast for special pro-tective designation. It thought present planning techniques to protect the coastline inadequate, and called for clearer planning and sharper controls. The commission's philosophy should not, however, be thought one of control and re-pression. It was urging: you must tell people much more clearly where they can do what. It is no good just saying, 'No noisy water-skiing off this bird reserve; no ice-cream vans on the South Downs.' You must show people who want to water-ski or have a continual supply of ice-lollies —or for that matter open light industrial concerns—good and acceptable places to do these things. Only that way can you keep the beautiful, unspoiled stretches of coastline still unspoiled.

## LITTER, CIGARETTES AND OTHER RUBBISH

If the litter problem in Britain is becoming worse, then two main factors are to blame: lack of environmental edu-cation, and the economics of modern packaging and con-tainers. At a conference of plastics manufacturers in London in 1970, Mr Peter Walker appeared to accept their argument that biodegradable plastics—which have an ad-ditive that cause them to decay like paper, wood and other vegetable substances after a specified life-span—were not the right answer, and that educating the public into being less anti-social about how it disposed of them was.

This view is surely sadly mistaken. This aspect of en-vironmental education does, of course, need much more effort. But even supposing that 99 per cent of us, 99 per cent of the time, did the right thing with our rubbish and put it in litter bins or took it home, that would still leave the other 1 per cent—and forgetfulness and accidents. When the object of their forgetfulness lasts virtually for ever, that rubbish can mount up. There are serious reservations about building in limited life with foodstuff containers, but this safety factor can surely be taken care of by some colour coding which marks the container and the food if they have begun to deteriorate. It is to be hoped the minister and the industry will have second thoughts on this.

Similar arguments about education and putting temptation in the way of the litterbug apply to non-returnable, no-deposit bottles, over which a lively correspondence was waged in *The Times* during the summer of 1971. Because of higher labour and distribution costs and concentration of manufacturing in fewer centres, the old returnable bottle has become less economic for manufacturers of soft drinks and other beverages. There are two objections to no-deposit bottles: the manufacturers hand the cost of collection and recycling to the refuse services, and thus to their customers as ratepayers; and they provide more excuse for the lazy or careless customer to leave them about on beaches, in the countryside and elsewhere as unsightly litter and a danger to the unwary. Public opinion has in certain circumstances forced companies to revert to returnable bottles carrying a deposit. I doubt whether it is strong enough always or even usually to overcome the economic disadvantages, and suggest that a small environmental tax to remove the attractions to manufacturers of non-returnable bottles (or at least help pay for their collection by the public service) may ultimately be the only answer.

As for litter in general, an improvement requires three things: steady education; good example; and more people ready to show disapproval publicly of the individual offender. Without this last, Parliament can go blue in the face prescribing penalties for spreading litter. They are likely to be as little enforced as the present law on the subject, which is almost a dead letter.

Something of the same public show of displeasure is needed to bring about better manners in smokers. I do not here go into the argument against smoking on health grounds, but only the erosion of the non-smoker's environment caused by the thoughtless or selfish smoker. It is essentially, like litter, a matter of environmental good manners.

I remember a colleague with the horror story of a special celebration meal at an expensive restaurant virtually ruined by a boorish fellow who smoked cigars constantly at a neighbouring table; and recall myself entertaining a man I was interviewing for *The Times* to a lunch which he picked at desultorily and spoiled for me by smoking a pipe the whole time. Like smoking in non-smoking carriages, these practices should be beyond the pale and their perpetrators should be quickly and sharply made aware that they are giving offence. Non-smokers who have previously smoked tend to feel most strongly about this, and might form a spearhead in the battle—though I do not necessarily recommend my own reaction on one occasion when, having chased along a station platform to find a vacant seat in a non-smoker, I discovered to my fury that the man sitting next to me had lit a cigarette and declined to put it out on the grounds that this would be an infringement of individual liberty. I opened the carriage window to look for a guard or other railwayman. No one in sight. I found myself strangely shaking with fury, reflecting angrily that £25 penalties were useless if no one was around to enforce them. Should I pull the communication cord? Then suddenly with a recklessness that afterwards made me shudder, I simply seized this rather tough character's cigarette and dropped it out of the window. We were both so astounded that neither said a word for the rest of the journey, though some of our fellow passengers expressed an unseemly merriment. I don't think I'd ever do it again—but I wish more people would. I also wish that someone would develop the idea put forward by that champion of the non-smokers' interests, the Rev Hubert Little, of a small battery-fan for blowing smoke back on the smoker—just as a hint! A limited range suppressor to jam portable transistor radios played in parks or on beaches would also be most welcome.

## PACKAGE TOUR POLLUTION

The growth of leisure, mobility and wealth can, as we have seen, threaten ecological or urban balance. One of their most concentrated expressions is international travel by 'package tour', as a G L C discussion paper published in the spring of 1971 most vividly demonstrated. It quoted the estimates produced by Sir George Young, a G L C member who spent two years studying the subject as a research fellow at Surrey University. Demand for hotel accommodation in London could rise from 91 million 'bednights' in 1967 to 208 million by 1980, he thought, producing a theoretical demand for 220,000 extra hotel rooms, of which almost 100,000 were then already at some stage of development—stimulated to a large extent by grants under the Development of Tourism Act which were available until March 1971.

Those figures and what they imply are indeed daunting; hundreds of jumbo jets disgorging tens of thousands of budget holiday-makers daily into thousands of air-conditioned coaches to jam the barbarically narrow elevated section of the M4 on their way to hundreds of alien, box-like concrete and glass hotels which dwarf and blight the residential districts of Kensington and Hammersmith. This in truth amounts to pollution by package tour, and has its damaging side-effects too. How, for instance, do we cope with the fact that probably half the visitors demanding all those 'bednights' will want at some time during their stay to see Westminster Abbey, the Changing of the Guard, or the Tower of London?

And, because of the nature of package tours, they will expect to be taken to within a short tourist waddle of these places in some of the same large, long, air-conditioned, fifty-seat blunderbuses. The coach drivers all try to get near Buckingham Palace at the time of the Changing of the Guard. It is their job. And the danger is that as this vast army of earnest or curious tourists mills in and around, say, the Abbey, at some point it destroys the value of what it comes to see. We cannot duplicate Westminster Abbey—though it would be quite feasible to arrange counter-attractions to such London set-pieces as the Changing of the Guard. It could well be that by 1980 tourist visits to the Abbey will have to be by appointment or ticket only, limited in number, with those turned away encouraged to visit St Paul's instead, or better still some beautiful but little known Wren church in the City.

Pollution by package tour also hurts the cities it fastens on to : hotels, whether new or converted, eat up homes for the natives, or spaces which are potentially homes for the natives; and new hotels wreck the look of the place—in London by bringing alien scale and alien materials into sensitive townscapes. In social and community terms, moreover, the package tour hotel tends to be an encapsulated affair, sealed off from the surrounding residential neighbourhood. Its guests arrive in sealed coach, sally forth to see the sights in sealed coach, and largely find the services they need within the capsule. They are an alien presence within the community.

One way to save London from the worst effects of package tour pollution is to spread its effects. This is to some extent beginning to happen. The G L C's 'green' (discussion) paper mentioned earlier wanted more medium-price hotels downriver and in suburban centres. Foulness airport should help that process. But dilution is not enough. We need to integrate the tourist, get him out of the package tour capsule. Much more should be done to get him to travel by bus and underground (in off-peak hours, of course) or by taxi, rather than in coach parties or private car. A congestion tax specifically on tourist coaches in the centre might be considered for this purpose, or a very heavy 'black box' weighting if metering is adopted. And, rather than build more and more necessarily rather too expensive hotels, why not mount a campaign for private householders to offer bed-and-breakfast to tourists. A few do, but the potential has never been really exploited. In terms of more economic use of available resources, as well as for the protection of the urban environment, it would be worth some future Chancellor of the Exchequer offering tempting tax incentives to those who did so, at least in areas where massive new hotel building is the alternative.

## POLLUTION BY POPULATION

In a sense, however, too many tourists in London is just a rather trivial symptom of the most serious form of pollution of them all—pollution by overpopulation. The present acuteness of the problem is the result of that old phenomenon, man's material skills outstripping his social and political skills. Modern medicine following in the wake of Second World War armies controlled disease, but failed until too late to take sufficiently seriously the control of population. And for many of the peoples for whom increasing numbers now threaten even subsistence, let alone good environment, birth control runs counter to the instincts of generation on generation. They always needed large families to survive. Now they need to have small families to survive. Accepting this involves a psychological wrenching up of roots of the first order. No wonder then that Western urgings to implement birth control programmes are sometimes represented in Africa and Asia as a European plot to keep ex-colonial peoples down.

In Britain the results of rising population are, of course, less severe. We are not very likely in the foreseeable future to go hungry because there are too many of us. But even to the extent that housing is eating up land, and our citizens becoming ever more mobile and voracious in their recreational and other demands on a small country, population increase does limit environmental quality. Moreover, exhortations to the rest of the world to have fewer children sound distinctly less convincing when our own population is still growing rapidly.

In principle Britain accepts that its citizens should be given every encouragement and aid to effective family planning. Yet it is only recently that hospitals began as a matter of routine to give advice to mothers of already large families in hospital for the birth of an obviously unplanned and undesired additional child. With abortion law reform and contraceptive advice for unmarrieds, the climate is obviously changing, but there are still anomalies. A mother of a family of three or four can be sterilised free on the National Health Service. The operation is quite a serious and complicated one, and it and the ensuing extended stay in hospital costly to the N H S in financial terms. Male sterilisation by vasectomy is a relatively simple operation. The husband can be out the same day and simply convalesce for a couple of days at home; and there are unlikely to be any psychological, let alone physical, after-effects. In real terms it is much cheaper, and in almost every other way more satisfactory. But it is not normally obtainable on the N H S. A husband's sterilisation will cost a couple who, even for medical reasons, wish to avoid the risk of another child, something like £35 to £40. The wife's sterilisation (which is much less desirable) is free. Surely the Conservation Society's president, Tory M P Sir David Renton, was right when he urged that society, in its own interests, should provide both free. Even in the narrow economics of family allowances and possible supplementary benefits it would make sense. The realisation is at last dawning that if we do not do everything we can to make it easy for people to limit their families voluntarily, then, by default, we may eventually be driven to contemplating some element of compulsory family limitation.

## CONSERVATION AND CLASS

This heading is shorthand for a tendency which has been growing more and more evident in conservationist battles: for those who oppose a particular conservationist position to label its adherents selfish defenders of vested interest. This happened during the Roskill inquiry, when a fifth column appeared behind the embattled defenders of Cublington proclaiming that resistance to a third airport in Buckinghamshire was not genuine grass-roots opposition, but simply an articulate and influential middle-class minority seeking to maintain their own privileged tranquillity even though working people in the area could do with the jobs and the prosperity the airport would bring there. This view did not in fact have much support in the area, and in wider terms was suspect because vacant jobs greatly exceeded unemployment in the area, while the reverse was true of the Southend area which badly needed the jobs Foulness would generate. But it was significant as one of the first signs of the 'Conservation is selfish' argument.

It was brought into fresh relief in the autumn of 1970 by public exchanges between Peter Scott, the wildlife conservationist of Slimbridge fame, and Anthony Crosland. Mr Scott, talking in the context of ecological interdependence, urged that economic growth was the enemy of conservation, and that more cars and more television sets did not make people any happier. Mr Crosland, speaking at Coenco (the Committee for Environmental Conservation, formed as a co-ordinating body to carry on the efforts of the Countryside in 1970 conference) warned conservationists not to oppose all economic growth, because this amounted to the comfortably off 'pulling up the ladder behind them'. In a gathering which represented the car-and-comfortable-cottage owning countryman rather than the cloth-cap countryman, Mr Crosland said he could accept neither the proposition that economic growth was all-important nor the opposite extreme that there was no need for it. He was an enthusiastic and dedicated conservationist, but the argument he had often heard as a minister that you must on no account have reservoirs or potash mines in national parks was fundamentally an anti-growth one which he believed to be extraordinarily dangerous. 'When we have very substantial poverty, slum hospitals, slum primary schools, desperately overcrowded housing, and a heavy backlog of most urgent social demand—so long as this backlog exists, we cannot be antigrowth,' he told them. And, as we have already seen, his opposite number, the new minister, was thinking in strikingly similar terms.

Of course, there is a conflict in priorities between conservation of existing good environment and the growth and development needed to power efforts to improve substandard environment. This is even truer when ecologically conservationist policies are urged on underdeveloped peoples with subsistence and below-subsistence standards of living, than when the middle classes from Surrey and Sussex appear to be arguing for limitation of industrial growth or car ownership. As Mr Crosland put it, 'My constituents in Grimsby will not accept that—and I ought not to expect them to.' The same words could, in principle, have come from Mr Kenyatta.

There are, however, some distinctions to be made. In an

increasing number of cases, the 'selfish', 'middle-class' accusation seems to be thrown in simply to bolster anti-conservation arguments which are themselves selfish and sectional. This is unfortunate because it obscures the real issues and tends to devalue the language of conservation. There is a real problem here as to how far we need to, or indeed can, curb economic growth without destroying our ability to cope with the environmental problems we have. The economic machine run-down could arguably leave us in a worse position to cope than when it is running rather too fast and marginally out of control. It must be a matter of balance—though one would feel more confident that the balancing act will be a success if there were fewer unknowns.

As to the conflict between those who already enjoy the good life and want to keep it that way, and those who aspire to it, but threaten to destroy as they climb, this is to some extent inevitable. Two kinds of effort can mitigate it: more and better environmental education; and environmental good example. The first is beginning to happen. It needs to be backed—whether in terms of nations refraining from polluting the seas and skies, or individuals not dropping litter—by the persuasive weight of our practising what we preach.

# PART VI

# Planning and the Public

---

## Chapter Thirteen

## PLANNING BY INQUIRY

In this and the next chapter I want to take a fairly wide-ranging look at the whole process by which the public—as distinct from their elected representatives—are involved in the process of town and country planning control which to a large extent governs whether and how our environment is changed. The public inquiry and the ministerial decision which follows it are aspects which receive most public attention, but quantitatively they are a very small part of the process, since they usually represent only the most contentious cases or those involving a large scale and radical change in land use which may mean more or less drastic changes in people's environment. Cases coming to public inquiry can be placed into four broad categories:

(*a*) Appeals against a planning authority's refusal to give planning permission for an individual scheme, or against conditions attached to its permission.

(*b*) Local authority 'development' or 'structure' plans. These are the framework to which the local planning authority will relate individual planning decisions. They have to be approved by the minister and, if objected to, are submitted to 'trial by public inquiry'.

(*c*) Road schemes (including motorways) and associated works. The distinguishing feature of these is that they are proposed by a public authority (often the ministry) which is also to a greater or lesser extent the body sitting in judgement on them.

(*d*) Special inquiries, like the Roskill Commission on the Third London Airport, set up by the government to deal with specially large, difficult planning problems, and usually with more wide-ranging terms of reference than local inquiries.

Category (a), though by far the most common kind of public inquiry and numbering about 8,000 in 1970, is only the tip of an extremely large planning iceberg. A not untypical county planning office, Kent, deals with some 14,500 planning applications every year, ranging from permission sought to add a projecting porch to an ordinary semi-detached house to redevelopment proposals involving millions of pounds and sites of 100 acres or more.

The vast majority of these applications, it should be remembered, do not come to appeal. Either they are allowed, often with modifications agreed between the planners and the applicant; or they are refused and the 'developer' does not think it worth his while to take the case to appeal. Instead he will very often—and this will, for example, frequently be the case with the smallish speculative builder wanting to put up ten to fifty houses on a suitably zoned housing site—go away and rethink the scheme to bring it more into line with what the local planning committee and its officers seem likely to accept.

If he does appeal, then the DOE (or previously the Ministry of Housing and Local Government) will send one of its inspectors—normally men or women with professional planning, engineering, surveying, legal or other relevant qualifications—to hold an inquiry in the actual locality. Finding a suitable hall or other building can, sometimes, cause difficulty. When the inquiry into Rio Tinto-Zinc's appeal against Merioneth County Council's refusal of permission to mine in the Snowdonia National Park opened at Assize Court in Dolgellau in December 1970, it was perfectly clear that the county council had underestimated the number of people who would wish to attend, and the facilities that would be needed. The transcript records that a 'representative of the Press' complained to the inspector at the inconvenience and discomfort of having to report the case from the dock. But in a town of only 3,000 population, the centre of a sparsely populated area, they were in some difficulty to offer any alternative. On the second day, however, the Press were moved to different seats. Nonetheless, the principle governing the location of inquiries—that the inspector should travel to the nearest suitable centre to the site in question, for the convenience of the parties, and be able easily to visit it—is so obviously sound that we have now come to take it for granted.

In straightforward planning appeals of this kind, it is sometimes asked whether the judicialised form of the public local inquiry with the rules providing for examination, cross-examination and re-examination of witnesses as in a court of law, is not rather formal and heavy—a legalistic steam-hammer to crack a planning walnut? Would not something more like the informality of a rent tribunal be more suitable?

Relations between the legal and planning professions are complex and fraught with professional resentments and vested interests, as we shall see later. But on this particular question, one needs to remember two important points. One is that adherence to a well-tried method of testing evidence and ensuring fair play (sympathetic questions; critical questions; clarification by sympathetic questioner) need not, and generally does not, import court-room atmosphere or the style of questioning found in a criminal trial. When it does, that will generally not be the fault of the procedure, but of an untypical individual.

The second point is that the present balance between informality and fairness was the result of procedures in some public tribunals becoming so loose and informal in the early 1950s as to be unfair to the parties on occasion. The present measure of formality is largely the direct result of recommendations by the 1955 Franks Committee, and is designed to ensure basically a right of reply to or comment on every factor put to the inspector or which he takes into account.

This sometimes stretches further than one might expect. For instance, in at least one case the minister submitted to a High Court judgement where the grounds of challenge were that the decision had turned on factors noticed by the inspector during inspection of the site, but which the appellants had no chance to comment on. Inspectors these days are more careful whether their site visits are 'accompanied'—with representatives of the parties making or noting all the points he gathers there—or 'unaccompanied'. In either case any new information must be referred back to the appellants.

There still remains some truth in the criticism that the extent to which an inquiry is formalised creates inevitably a sense of confrontation, hardens attitudes and reduces any chance of compromise. The answer, it seems to me, is not to change the nature of the inquiry—it is doing the job it was designed for: hearing and advising the minister on the conflicting arguments of the planners and the planned. Rather it is to maximise the opportunities for constructive examination of the issue before it reaches the stage of appeal or public inquiry.

In some cases an initiative is taken by the local planning authority, either in terms of a plan for an area or because it is itself—often in partnership with a commercial firm—undertaking development. Here the doctrine of public participation, which we shall be examining in more detail (Chapter 14), is designed to ensure that plans (ideally involving alternative approaches to redevelopment) are brought out in the open and discussed before attitudes have hardened. This interplay of different views and interests which this allows and stimulates is healthy and beneficial even if no inquiry follows.

But what of the individual developer, face to face with his local planning authority? Though most planning officers in principle seek to clarify apparently unacceptable proposals and their reasons for rejecting them, and to suggest alternative solutions, there remains plenty of scope for misunderstandings, and they do quite frequently occur. Thus Miss Pamela Payne a former M H L G decision officer—one of the skilled band who examine inspectors' inquiry reports and 'advise' the minister which way to rule (he personally sees the papers only in a minority of cases)—recently quoted in the Town Planning Institute Journal the following reply from a disappointed appellant:

'Although the minister's decision is a matter of regret for Mr X and myself, this sentiment is very much overshadowed by the knowledge we now have that so much time, trouble, correspondence and public expense would have been saved *had the clear and simple reason in your letter been given by the county council in the first instance*' (my italics). She cites this as testimony to the thoroughness and fairness of her fellow decision officers, but it also indicates a failure in communication on the part of local planners.

Leslie Lane, sometime L C C chief planner and, more recently, a director of the Civic Trust, goes so far as to say that simple misunderstanding or lack of communication is at the root of the majority of appeals. These consequently produce a large number of unnecessary inquiries—unnecessary because based on a misconception by either the local planners of the developer's real purpose or intention, or by the developers of the planners' objections, or both.

Mr Lane's suggested answer is a planning conciliation service, operated by a staff of skilled D O E officials in much the same way as the Ministry of Labour (now the Department of Employment) has for years operated an industrial conciliation service for labour disputes.

It would, he suggests, become compulsory before an appeal could be made to the minister, for the parties to the dispute to meet, albeit informally, under the chairmanship of one of these planning conciliation officers, to thrash out the real points of difference, if any, and discover whether any alternative or compromise solution could be agreed that satisfied both the developer and the planning principles insisted on by the local authority. A certificate that the conciliation procedure had been exhausted would be needed in order to appeal. Mr Lane believes that this procedure, properly applied, could lead to a great reduction in appeals and inquiries—especially those in which much public and private time and money are wasted because the parties have never really understood each other on one or more quite vital points.

Planning law does in fact allow one form of appeal not by public inquiry—the so-called 'written representation' procedure, which can be a boon to the party who wishes to appeal, wants to conduct his own case, but is shy about doing so in public. It also has the advantage that he can study the documents and the planning authority's case in the quiet of his own home and not under the pressure of concentrated public hearing. An M H L G circular in 1965 set out a timetable for such exchanges, and if the parties keep to this the system can be very speedy. Some professional advisers prefer it for that reason.

But it has its limitations. If the timetable is not kept to, exchanges can become very protracted: it is not suitable for all kinds of case—if technical data are likely to be the subject of argument, for instance, or where they are likely to be complex and unwieldy. But the most severe limitation is probably that of third party interest. Sometimes the local authority is asked, when the written representation procedure is used, to circulate neighbours inviting their views. Ministry officials have erred on the side of giving opportunity for third parties to comment since the Parliamentary Commissioner criticised lack of this in a case at Solihull.

This procedure is, of course, a substitute for the public inquiry in the simpler, disputed cases; not, as Mr. Lane's conciliation procedure would be, a means of avoiding formal dispute by clarification and compromise before the appeal stage has been reached. It does, however, point a warning. Agreement between a developer and a planning authority, whether with the proposed conciliator's help or not, should not lessen the need to consult third parties who may be affected—whether they are neighbours or a wider public.

As to the system of public inquiries itself, it might be said that there are two opposing views currently held—the complacent and the despairing. This was brought home to me very forcibly on the fine spring evening of April 26, 1971, the day after the government's announcement that, in spite of the Roskill Commission's two-and-a-half years painstaking hard labour, the third London airport was to be at Foulness, not Cublington. The Royal Institute of British Architects and the Town and Country Planning Association had, with remarkable but fortuitous timing, advertised a discussion meeting on what they called 'Planning by Judicial Inquiry?' and, when it became plain that the Roskill decision would be out the day before, and members of the Commission freed from their self-denying vow of silence, asked Colin Buchanan along to take part. The meeting began at six, at RIBA's headquarters in Portland Place.

I remember that evening for the three very interesting, but very different, contributions made by the three speakers I did manage to hear—though above all for Buchanan's. The opener was Professor Peter Self, who had recently been finding the GLDP inquiry exercise a frustrating and, at the witness table, bruising experience. He argued that the normal public inquiry procedure, with its barristers and court-room rules of procedure, its sense of confrontation and accusation, was a profoundly inappropriate forum for a certain category of cases for which it was used. All right, he suggested, for detailed, run-of-the-mill planning applications, to build a block of flats here, compulsorily acquire this and that strip of garden for road widening. But on questions of broad policy, it was hopeless. Long before such a forensic confrontation, with its examination, cross-examination and re-examination, attitudes had hardened, committed positions been taken up. It was a debate, with points made and even scored, not a discussion. Everyone came to it to defend or attack positions already taken up, not to hear, learn and sensibly decide.

For such questions of broad policy, he wished to substitute a statutory conference,* held early in the day, at which the parties came together in a spirit of open-minded willingness to learn, ready to be persuaded by sound and convincing arguments. After this, the planners—that is, the elected representatives and their officials—would go away to produce final policy, and it would be for the detailed implementation of that to be tested at conventional planning inquiries.

If Professor Self in the R I B A / T C P A discussion epitomised despair with the existing system and a wish to make radical, formal alterations to it, then the next speaker, barrister-engineer-town-planner Mr E. A. Vaughan-Neil, undoubtedly seemed to many of the gathering to embody the complacent vested interest which they, planners and architects, had always suspected to pervade the lawyers' stranglehold on 'their' business. A somewhat formal, ornate turn of phrase and more than a slight tendency to circumlocution contributed to this impression.

But what this barrister-planner had to say, however much wrapped up, included some points worth repeating. First, he pointed out, planning inquiries in Britain were not 'judicial', either technically or in reality. If they had lawyers taking part, that was because parties thought the trained advocate was the best man to represent him. If they had rules of procedure which somewhat resembled those

* The D O E included provision for a statutory conference of selected objectors, to debate the broad principles and strategy of structure plans, in its Town and Country Planning (Amendment) Bill published in November, 1971.

of the court of law, that was because this was the accepted and fair way of conducting an argument. In the early days of post-war planning law, he reminded his listeners, informality had gone to extremes, and it had taken the Franks Committee on administrative tribunals to point out too much informality could lead to injustice if it adversely affected a party's right to make his case or reply to points raised by another. But he also made the basic point—so obvious that it may sometimes escape notice—that even an inquiry with a judge in the chair and QCs briefed by the local authority and the objectors is radically different from a court of law because it gives no verdict. It only hears the evidence, notes it, states the facts and the arguments to the minister and makes a recommendation. Ministers can—and frequently do—decide differently. That point could scarcely fail to go home, even to an unsympathetic and impatient audience, on the day after the government's Foulness verdict.

Then came Buchanan, saying he had no wish to be indiscreet, yet betrayed by his characteristic frankness into something rather like indiscretion. He began by saying that, for most kinds of planning cases, the British public local inquiry was about as good an instrument for securing just and sensible decisions as you could have. Ministry inspectors were pretty good at getting down to the essential issues, and he did not think they were generally taken in or impressed—rather the reverse—by the sharp practice or bullying tactics of the occasional misguided lawyer.

But Buchanan's undoubted admiration for and loyalty to his chairman on the Third London Airport Commission, Mr Justice Roskill, did not stop him from doubting the wisdom of having lawyers or judges as chairmen of important inquiries. 'I don't think a judge is absolutely necessary,' he said. His own long experience of planning cases suggested that 'non-legal people can perfectly well handle the semi-court room procedures which are involved, deal with quite complex cases—and can handle awkward barristers.' Perhaps, he added, a judge in the chair did 'tend to inspire very much the judicial atmosphere of a court, that a verdict has to be given and must be based on the evidence.' And then he came out with a statement which must have seemed like heresy of the first order to any lawyers in the audience, though some of us had begun to suspect it a while before. 'I hate to say it, but I think I reached my conclusion not on the evidence at all, but on the basis of my experience in land use planning.'

Although he had not previously said this quite as explicitly before, he had told me in an interview on the Foulness decision, published in *The Times* the day before, that once the size of the airport site and the likely locations were known so that he had been able to look at them on the ground, 'A great red warning light came on in my mind.' All his planning experience told him that the inland sites were bad in environmental and planning terms and, what was more, that public opinion was unlikely to accept them. Politically he smelt trouble. Some planning decisions were ones that would run with public opinion, or the public would run with. An inland site, whatever its economic merits, was not one of these. Experience told him it could only be implemented with the utmost difficulty, and he thought it not just legitimate, but no more than commonsense, to take account of that.

But his colleagues on the Roskill Commission did not, and would not, work that way. Theirs was the typically judicial view—a verdict on the evidence, without fear or favour. To be influenced by strength of public opinion would have been improper. Nonetheless, Professor Buchanan still thought there was no real alternative open to a government confronted with what he called the occasional 'knotty problems' of planning but to appoint a 'group of reasonably intelligent men' and let them thrash it out. He did, however, make several significant reservations. Membership and terms of reference of a commission were often a crucial factor. Commissions should not work in a vacuum, but should feel free, like consultants, to go back to their client, the minister, report interim findings and ask for fresh instructions. They should not thrash on endlessly to reach a single firm verdict regardless of circumstances. It should be open to them to present several alternative options, with the costs and implications clearly shown, instead of *the* answer. And a commission and its chairman should not feel bound to follow exhaustively and exhaustingly all the tortuous meanderings of every line of reasoning. It should be possible for them in suitable cases to cut proceedings short, to say: 'We have heard enough to reach a sensible conclusion.' All of which are departures from judicialised procedure, and against the instincts of lawyers, but make good sense in lengthy cases where, for several reasons, protracted proceedings tend to be counter-productive.

Referring specifically to his Roskill experience, from which these ideas substantially derived, Buchanan thought that the commission had probably got off on the wrong foot right from the circumstances of its appointment. Though 'this was a planning matter if ever there was one', the commission had been set up under the umbrella of the then Board of Trade, the ministry responsible for airports, and not by the planning ministry, Housing and Local Government. It therefore turned out, through no fault of its members, to be 'heavily weighted on the economic side, and that led to the research team being heavily weighted in the same direction.' His fellow commissioners, he thought, had looked at the third airport question as an economic problem to which there was an important planning side, whereas his own view was that it was par excellence a planning question, with an important economic aspect. This I find a penetrating remark, and, assuming it is correct, it goes a long way to explain Roskill's political reversal. For the political and public opinion tide was running against narrowly or even dominantly economic criteria; the D O E was an expression of that tide; and the big battalions of the Cabinet, including the Minister of Trade and Industry, John Davies, who announced and defended the choice of Foulness, were heavily influenced by, and probably largely shared, these changing attitudes.

Buchanan himself was at some pains to defend his Roskill colleagues' integrity and to refute allegations that they were 'philistines'. They had taken account of environmental factors, he said, but simply given them a different and lower weighting than he had. At the R I B A / T C P A meeting he argued that the Roskill exercise was in no way proof that such commissions of inquiry were a bad method of seeking a solution for the big planning questions, adding with not altogether unconscious humour: 'The fact is that this went wrong in respect of one of the three recommendations it made. It just got this small matter of the site wrong!'

## The cost-benefit approach

He might have added that the fact that Roskill's elaborate cost-benefit exercise by a skilled and dedicatedly objective research team produced what was judged, in environmental terms, a bad answer, did not prove that cost-benefit analysis was a bad or unsuitable technique for such cases. There was, many people felt, a danger after Roskill (and even more after the government's decision in favour of Foulness) that cost-benefit techniques would be given a bad name by the public and politically somewhat discredited. Although some (on the face of it) devastating criticisms have been made of the team's methods by academics and others competent to judge them, as journalists or members of the public cannot be, for example by Professor Peter Hall, *New Society*, April 1971, the real fault, it seems to me, was in the commission, or rather the commission's methods.

Ever since cost-benefit analysis was used to rescue the Victoria Line's Brixton extension from harsher economic tests, there has been no shortage of people who saw its usefulness in redressing the imbalance of existing objective criteria for capital projects. Christopher Foster's Brixton exercise, which persuaded Mrs Castle when Transport Minister to sanction the scheme (or possibly rather gave her an excuse to do so), has since been rather pooh-poohed by many of the growing band of practitioners in cost-benefit techniques. Foster, they tend to argue, threw everything bar the kitchen sink in in favour of the Brixton project and just managed to produce the right result. 'That may have been all right in cost-benefit's infant days,' they say. 'Now we aspire to something more objectively scientific.'

The danger of this, however, is that it may give them, as a character in a Rattigan play puts it, *'Idées au dessus de sa gare.'* They want to provide a complete answer, to oust the final element of value judgement or at least reduce its operation to the minimum. And this seems to have been the approach that the Roskill majority, at least implicitly, accepted. There were some values, obviously, which were not amenable to the technique, but wherever cost-benefit analysis could make some plausible attempt at writing a price-tag, that price-tag should be preferred to adding that element to the list of factors for which the judgement of informed men's common sense was the only form of evaluation to hand.

There are several dangers to this. One is that, instead of being regarded as a useful and adaptable tool which can be used as an aid to substituting analysis and objective valuation for prejudiced hunch, cost-benefit begins to take on some of the attributes of a religious faith. Either you accept it, and regard it as very nearly a complete answer to the shortcomings of physical planning, stretching it by near-theological argument to fit factors which it is ill-suited to measure, or you are an unbeliever—or worse, a heretic. Thus (probably the most-quoted example) a patently derisory price-tag of £51,000 was put on Stewkley church with its Norman tower rather than leave yet another item to the chance of overall value judgement.

A second danger, of which Professor Buchanan was all too aware during the inquiry proceedings, was that cost-benefit techniques would get such a grip on proceedings that, instead of serving as a tool, they became almost the commission's master. He told me after the government's decision had been announced how the cost-benefit exercise had come out as twenty-five separate calculations, not added together until almost the end of the commission's deliberations. In many cases experts had been produced to give conflicting cost-benefit answers to those of the commission's own team, and he had been far from certain—despite their integrity and objectivity—that the team were always right. And then, right at the end, came the final sum, and a result which he had felt in his bones was awry, without being able adequately to challenge the separate parts. The Roskill proceedings at that stage had taken on an almost mechanistic quality. Cost-benefit as interpreted by the team had taken over. Most of the commissioners sat tight, trusting it would take them in the right direction. Colin Buchanan felt like shouting out: 'Stop! We're no longer in control. I want to get off.'

One has great sympathy for the Roskill research team because of the burden of ill-informed abuse which it had to bear, and the widespread lack of public understanding of what it was about and the value of its efforts. But the public reaction of one or two members of the team to the final decision (for example, Mr A. F. D. Flowerdew in *The Times* of April 29, 1970) scarcely did the cause of cost-benefit much good in public eyes. The burden of Mr Flowerdew's letter was that sordid political pressure had overturned the scrupulous findings of the best and most objective methodology available to government. What could be done to prevent this in future cases? And this was, not unexpectedly, represented by later correspondents as a conspiracy of experts to keep the public and democracy in its (subservient) place. It would have been tactful for an exponent of the relatively undeveloped art and science of cost-benefit to argue its virtues with a greater air of (if necessary, false) modesty.

It is, however, a revealing attitude, and indicative of a quite common fear among experts in the planning field who honour democracy as a system of government but distrust its likely results as applied to their field. This fear is, quite simply, that in an increasingly complex world, the public —and even quite intelligent members of the public—will not be able to understand. Thus, I have heard it argued by senior G L C road planners, that the case for the construction of certain urban motorways which they believed to be essential to the future well-being of the metropolis, might fail to convince, because no one without an understanding of quite sophisticated mathematical techniques could follow or appreciate the projections of demand which led to these schemes being proposed.

I think this is a mistaken argument. It arises partly because the expert—whether engineer or mathematician—is hurt when people do not believe that his calculations, and the solutions he bases on them, are objective. Yet in the contentious cases of which we are thinking, what else can they be but sceptical when they see other experts—as far as they are concerned, equally learned and abstruse—produced to refute both calculations and conclusions. A notable example is again the G L D P inquiry's examination of the Ringways, where a substantial part of the London Motorway Action Group's case against was devoted to economist Mr Michael Thomson's efforts to demolish the validity of the traffic projections on which the case for the Ringways was based.

At the point when a major policy is questioned, and the calculations on which it is based, an important psychological transmutation occurs which public officials are not always sufficiently aware of. They are from that moment no longer regarded as the impartial, objective professionals, but as parties to the dispute—and by some as the arch villains. There are two levels to this. One is the emotional and practical need to see a planning controversy in black-and-white terms: the need to have villains as well as knights in shining armour, and not to credit the villains with any saving qualities at all. The other is the commonsense reaction of the ordinary citizen, who, without understanding the detailed argument, sees two sets of experts at loggerheads. The answer provided by the authorities is questioned, and is therefore suspect until the contrary is proved—and on the whole he will be (healthily, many would say) anti-authority. There is no complete cure for this disease. Decision by the minister advised by inquiry panel or inspector is in our system a partial let-out, though the officials worried by this problem can with justice point out that what they regard as mistaken political pressures may sometimes be strong enough (a) to distort the minister's decision or (b) force withdrawal of sound and necessary proposals in advance of a public inquiry.

These fears are real ones—but I think in part the outcome feared is a product of the fear itself. If you do not trust the public to understand, your efforts to explain may be less thorough-going and very likely less resourceful and imaginative. Planners and politicians, moreover, not infrequently adopt the course of justifying actions with reasons other than the ones which chiefly led them to those actions. A central area shopping development may be publicly justified almost entirely in terms of providing better facilities to townsfolk and a better environment, whereas the dominant political reason (scarcely mentioned) may be additional rateable value to keep municipal finances healthy. A by-pass may be publicly justified in terms of reducing environmental damage to the area by-passed, whereas the dominant motive in the minds of the road planners (again scarcely mentioned) is to build a vital link in a through route. Both these ulterior purposes may be perfectly legitimate, but they have not been fairly stated. And sooner or later, opponents of some feature of the proposal are likely to smell a rat. 'Why,' their reasoning runs, 'if the planners really believed this was a justifiable purpose, did they keep so quiet about it?'

## Independent consultants

In a case where the issues are really complex, so that neither the intelligent layman nor the resourceful local society can really be expected to master the calculations on which a recommended course of action is based, but the suspicion has grown up that the official planners are engaging in some kind of technical sleight of hand, one answer which may be resorted to is to engage independent consultants. The advantages of this course, in local government as in commercial concerns, is threefold. They should have the time and detachment which employees inevitably lack to stand back from the detail; they are not committed to making the best of past mistakes, and can contemplate more easily the jettisoning of plans on which months and years of money and scarce skilled resources may have been expended; and if the machinery of public participation is well used (consultants are sometimes very good at consulting, as distinct from being consulted) they can win for themselves a considerable degree of public confidence that they are genuinely independent. The achievement of the Buchanan Greenwich/Blackheath team is a remarkable example of this. When Buchanan and Partners were first appointed, the choice of consultant was roundly condemned by spokesmen of at least one local amenity group. The firm were already consultants to the G L C on the Ringways and could not possibly be independent, was the complaint.

Within six months this attitude had disappeared. Members of the team, led by Nigel Moor, had spent a great deal of time talking not only to G L C officials and Greenwich borough planners but to local groups. They were seen to take seriously alternative road solutions which the G L C had dismissed out of hand. They not only listened sympathetically, but showed that they understood the nature of the objections. By the end of the study period, though local groups did not know what the Buchanan team would propose, they did know that this was far from being a whitewash operation. The consideration of alternatives was real and meaningful, not just a charade performed to keep the natives from becoming too restive.

In the GLC's defence, it should be added that, if they were beginning their gargantuan development plan exercise again, they would do it differently. One of its troubles is that it was largely put together in the pre-Skeffington era before the present doctrine of public participation had been officially established, but had to meet trial by inquiry in a full-bloodedly post-Skeffington climate. The criticism remains valid, however, that GLC planners gave the impression that they were reluctant to give away too much publicly about their intentions, and this boomeranged on them in a massive build-up of mistrust and hostility—especially over the Ringway programme.

Nowadays innovations in GLC policy are cautiously canvassed in Government-style 'green papers' issued to promote discussion and in principle not committing the council to the possibilities they canvass. This allows a genuine rather than a paper debate, and also is a cannier course politically. But one fears it will require many, many green papers and some real (rather than tactical) changes of course seen to result from discussion of them, before the GLC lives down its 'play the cards close to our chests until all the tricks are lined up' reputation. Besides, old habits die hard.

## The public inquiry

If the recommendations and the reasonings of local planners are frequently called into question, and the ultimate ruling of the minister not immune from criticism, the institution of the public inquiry and resulting inspector's report to the minister commands for the most part an impressive degree of confidence and respect. It is a curious apparatus, for what goes into it is acknowledged to be (and rightly so) political, and the person who is theoretically the ultimate decision-taker at the other end, the minister, is acknowledged to be an essentially political animal (though his decisions are most frequently labelled 'political' in a pejorative sense when he overturns his inspector's recommendation). Yet in the middle comes this quasi-judicial sieve, the public inquiry.

Well over 10,000 inquiries are held each year in England

and Wales, and they range from the half-day affair over the local planning committee's refusal to allow extension of a private house to the monster G L D P inquiry, lasting well over a year, involving dozens of counsel, hundreds of witnesses, literally tons of documents, and which has before it some 22,000 objections. We have seen that there is resistance in some quarters to the alleged formality of the proceedings and, more commonly, to the part played in them by lawyers. The complaint is sometimes heard that objectors who cannot afford legal representation are handicapped. I doubt whether this is so in the ordinary, relatively simple inquiry into a fairly clear-cut issue. Pamela Payne in the T P I Journal article already quoted mentions a case where a seventeen-year-old boy 'presented his own case and was congratulated by both the [planning] authority and the inspector on the way in which he did it.' My own more limited experience of public inquiries in action suggests that inspectors deliberately lean towards giving laymen every chance to make their objections, even to the point of tolerating clear irrelevance and political and social polemic. Miss Payne, on the other hand, is worried about the tendency of some lawyers to turn an inquiry into a court room. In a quite simple appeal about development on a five-acre garden site which turned on densities and access, she was, she recalls, horrified to find on arrival 'that the appellant, the authority, neighbours to the east and neighbours to the west, were all represented by counsel, who behaved throughout as though they were engaged in criminal proceedings. The two younger ones even prefaced most of their questions with "Would you mind telling the court . . . ?"'

The atmosphere, she goes on, 'was so tense, with counsel competing to ask witnesses the most penetrating or discomforting questions, that I for one could not have risen to my feet to speak.' And yet, as she rightly adds, public inquiries ought not to have an atmosphere which ordinary folk find intimidating, and they should be conducted in such a way that any party who understands his case should feel able to present it personally if he wants to.

Miss Payne contrasts this case of ordeal by inquiry with an earlier hearing she had attended where the atmosphere was quiet and relaxed, and 'the predominant feature was the obvious search for essential facts in favour of or against the proposal. The deputy town clerk and a solicitor put their cases directly and we all went home by lunch-time.' That obviously is the style to aim at with the ordinary, straightforward appeal. Difficulties need not arise, stresses Miss Payne, if barristers 'leave their courtroom manner behind with their wig and gown'.

But once broader issues of public dispute come into an inquiry, once it takes on a political content (not necessarily party political), and—dare a journalist say it—once the Press are present in force, then there may be a tendency for some barristers to go after the headlines with provocative, needling or even savage questioning in cross-examination. They are less likely to hand out this treatment to the helpless layman, because such a course tends to lose both the public's and the inspector's sympathy. A more frequent target is the expert witness or the professional planner who, it may be said, is paid to argue the toss. Indeed the outside expert witness, paid to attend and lend his weight to a client's argument, is perhaps fair game. He has been able to choose whether he joined the fray or not, and can scarcely complain if he gets a bloody nose. Certainly the expert witness who takes a fat fee from a developer to argue his case on planning and aesthetic grounds is—even allowing he sincerely believes what he says—unlikely to receive much sympathy from anyone if he is made to look foolish by counsel appearing, sometimes without fee, for an objecting amenity society.

The case of the city or county planning officer who, because of temperament, finds presenting his council's development plan at an inquiry a well-nigh unbearable ordeal, and suffers agonies of apprehension as the hour for cross-examination approaches, is rather different. Some people may retort that that is all part of the job he is paid to do, and that most professional posts have their element of ordeal which a professional has to put up with. The logical implication, though, is that that most talented planner should eschew top postings in local government if he fears he will not be a robust witness should fate confront him with a beastly, bullying barrister. A further argument I have heard is that fear of such cross-examination, once a planner has been 'put in the dock' by really rough handling from a lawyer and 'made to feel like a criminal', may warp all he does for the next couple of years as a planner. He may play safe when he should be bold, take the neutral alternative rather than face justifiable risk. One cannot be sure. Planners after all should be accountable to the public as well as to their political masters.

Perhaps the answer is to be found in the demonstrable fact that the skilful advocate can. and generally does, get his results without bludgeoning. bullying or melodrama—certainly when it is a planning inspector, not a jury, he has to convince. Questions put in a deceptively mild manner are frequently the more effective for that. A solution may lie simply in realisation by those members of the legal profession apt to err in this respect that anything like a bullying manner is not good manners at a public inquiry. Bad cases seem to be rare, but that does not mean no problem exists. While there are bad cases, public inquiries will continue to have a bad name among those who have come across such instances. It is, of course, difficult to curb such practices by making rules, but some guidance from the Bar Council and the Law Society might help to lessen even further the number of black sheep, while perhaps inspectors might be briefed to deal firmly with such forensic failings. Words like : 'Mr A., please remember this is a public inquiry, not the Old Bailey' might on occasion have a salutary effect, especially if they stirred echoes of recent advice to the same effect from the professional body concerned. Generally speaking, however, lawyers—and particularly those specialising in planning matters—do an efficient job, their worst fault is often long-windedness, and their cross-examinations are probing rather than wounding. Planning inquiries could not do without them.

On the other hand, it could do with others besides them. One change which ought to be seriously considered is the reversal of that strange ruling of the (now Royal) Town Planning Institute that its members should not take on the role of advocate at public inquiries. Virtually everyone else, it seems, including laymen quite unversed in either planning law and practice or inquiry procedure, is permitted to present a case to a public inquiry and examine witnesses—but not the professional planner. Lawyers have frequently been zealous in upholding this rule of another professional body, sometimes by threatening not to appear if a chartered planner does; more often by promising to report the defaulter to the Institute.

Now lawyers clearly have a vested interest in helping to enforce a rule which keeps their main potential rivals as planning advocates out of that role (though they are happy to have them in the arena as expert witnesses). It is very much harder to see why the planning profession itself denies its members this opportunity. The reasoning is, as one understands it, that conflict may arise between the roles of advocate and planning professional. Not by any means all R T P I members agree, however, that this blanket prohibition is the right answer rather than some code governing the circumstances and conduct of appearances as advocate. Nor is the rule always enforceable. I know of at least one case where a planner appeared as advocate, was reported to the Institute, arraigned before its president and told he must desist, but continued to appear and was subject to no perceptible sanction. He was, significantly, a county planning officer, and his county council backed him in his stand. Short of expelling him from the Institute—a futile and damaging course which the T P I sensibly eschewed—there was nothing very much it could do about it. There is arguably a strong presumption in favour of letting anyone take part in a public inquiry in whatever role he is competent to perform. There is little or no reason for supposing that (to adopt lawyers' jargon) that presumption has been rebutted in the case of the planner as advocate.

Public inquiries would indeed almost certainly benefit from the injection of a little non-legal blood into advocacy (though the planners would have to curb their weakness for jargon). There is, however, no reason to suppose that, with a little practice, they would be any more incompetent as arguers of their case and questioners of witnesses than lawyers quite frequently are in grasping planning arguments. Perhaps that is what, behind rationalisations about professional expertise, makes some lawyers so zealous to enforce another profession's rule-book.

We have already noticed a fact which must be fairly obvious on a moment's reflection : that the minister (or ministers) cannot and does not deal with every appeal decision himself. The factors which impel personal attention by a junior minister, a senior minister (especially, under the initial D O E set-up, Graham Page) or the Secretary of State for the Environment himself are therefore a matter of compelling interest to amenity groups objecting to official planning proposals and one which might repay closer study. (I am assuming here, for the moment, that objectors believe they will stand a better chance of success if the politicians are aware of a case than if it is decided by officials. It does not necessarily always hold good.)

## Challenging planning decisions

Exactly what kind of public protest, personal argument, signature collecting or demo in Whitehall persuades ministers to take a look at the papers for themselves? Petitions are a time-honoured means of displaying weight of public concern or hostility, and are certainly taken in the D O E and other departments as one indication of it. But the number of signatures is, I believe, treated with a scepticism bordering on indifference. This is because experience shows that many citizens, approached with a friendly smile and a rather one-sided explanation of what the petition is about, will sign whether or not they really care or really understand the point at issue.

To have an M P on one's side, is useful in calling for an inquiry, as he may get ministers to take note personally of the arguments and strength of feeling. But—as backbenchers themselves would usually be the first to admit—it is by no means an automatic recipe for success. The constituency M P who writes to a minister objecting to a project which originates in Whitehall tends to get replies which are, in effect, a précis of the departmental brief over the minister's signature, with a stock assurance added that he will take note of the opinions expressed. Even this, however, does indicate that civil servants have (a) been made aware that there is an active opposition, and (b) have had to reread the brief in the light of the criticisms made by the M P.

Newspaper stories, particularly in national papers, are also valuable, provided they are accurate and not too one-sided. I know of M Ps who say that their efforts to get a minister to review a decision have got nowhere until a cutting from *The Times*, the *Guardian* or the *Daily Express*'s Action Line column landed on his desk. But the power of the press should not be overrated. Two particular notes of caution should be added. A story which is not followed up may, in certain circumstances, be counter-productive; and once a project and opposition to it has been ventilated, journalists may not be keen to keep the pot boiling unless there are striking new developments or a final decision. This is particularly so in the planning and environment field, where there is no dearth of good 'protest' stories.

The second word of caution is this. Even if a journalist finds the story worth writing, it will not necessarily be helpful to those who drew his attention to it. He will usually give the other side an opportunity to comment, and sometimes that other side will look to him—and to his readers—more convincing than the viewpoint of the people who originally drew the situation to his attention. On the whole, though, newspaper stories—and those in other publications such as specialist periodicals—are a help. So is T V coverage, but again with reservations. Because of the small amount of camera time likely to be given, T V will draw attention to the issues rather than canvass them. For the same reasons, it is likely to oversimplify the issues, and editing of the film to the required length may often leave people angered and puzzled by the selectivity of extracts. Television also, although it can have a bigger impact than the press at the time, is yet more evanescent than the newspaper story. There are no cuttings to arrive on the minister's desk, nor are they on file in the cuttings libraries of other papers for journalists to refer to when the issue next bobs up.

Probably the most powerful factor of all, in forcing a public inquiry and in getting ministers to look at the arguments personally, is the letter from the individual objector. The public may be sceptical about the value of writing a letter to the minister which disappears into a large and anonymous organisation, and is then acknowledged briefly by some unknown bureaucrat whose relationship to the nominal addressee is unclear.

But again and again civil servants testify to the considerable impact that such letters have, comparable with the flurry set up by a parliamentary question, with quite senior men and women putting aside work on which they are engaged in order to look at the case and provide the minister with an answer. In the case of letters of objection designed to bring about and provide ammunition for a public inquiry, there are two kinds of letters. One is the straightforward individual note of objection which an individual interested citizen himself pens. Its facts may be suspect, its reasoning shaky, its grammar and handwriting less than faultless, but it makes its point. Here is someone who thinks what is proposed is bad and cares enough to go to the trouble of writing. The other type of letter is the carefully worked out point of objection which is duplicated and circulated by a group or society to its members for them to sign and post. It will often contain a sentence authorising the body concerned to represent the signatory at any ensuing inquiry. That is designed to make a different kind of impact: weight of numbers. Both have their place, though I suspect that one hundred individual and different letters make at least as much point as 1,000 stereotyped ones. The achievement of objectors to a proposed hotel development at the Avon Gorge in Bristol (of which more anon) in getting 2,000 letters of protest to the minister in a period of ten days in the middle of the 1971 postal strike undoubtedly influenced Peter Walker to call the case in after the city council had given provisional planning approval.

The vast majority of appeals are not, however, looked at by ministers. They are decided in the name of the Secretary of State either by the special staff of decision officers previously mentioned or, under a power given by the 1968 Town and Country Planning Act, by the inspectors themselves. This delegation to inspectors, though in quantity it accounts now for a high proportion of all appeals, is limited in practice to relatively minor developments up to, say, back-garden, in-filling developments of a couple of dozen houses. Its purpose was to reduce one of the delays in the planning process, and it should be noted that there is no appeal on the facts from the inspector's decision since he is acting in the minister's name.

There are, however, other ways of challenging the minister's decision on certain tightly circumscribed grounds, whether it was in fact his, or the decision officer's, or the inspector's. Pamela Payne in the R T P I Journal article previously referred to, notes that decision officers' work has become much more difficult and hazardous since the 1959 changes designed to ensure fairness and provide safeguards against the executive. They have not only conscientiously to seek a right and sensible decision, but have to be looking over their shoulders all the time so as to keep 'out of the Courts, away from censure by the Council on Tribunals and'—more recently—'clear of investigation by the Commissioner for Administration' (the Ombudsman).

Delay in either hearing or deciding appeals can, of course, as in other spheres, vitiate the scrupulous attention to fairness of inspectors and decision officers. In a matter of six or nine months the economics of a development may have changed or the steam gone out of it. Some classic cases occurred during the final months of the grant scheme for hotel construction provided for in the Development of Tourism Act, 1969. Grants of up to £1,000 per bedroom were available provided a start was made on site by March 30, 1971, and if refusal of planning permission or an appeal result outstanding prevented this, the grant was forfeit just as much as if the delay had been of the developer's making.

One case in point was the plan to build a new hotel on the site of No 144 Piccadilly, and adjacent houses at Hyde Park Corner, the Victorian mansions which had been invaded by hippies in the previous year. The scheme was strongly fought by the Victorian Society and other amenity groups at a public inquiry in the summer of 1970, but the minister decided to allow it (in spite of visual and traffic generation objections to Frederick Gibberd and Partners' proposed replacement). He did not, however, give this decision until May 1971, by which time a hotel of the standard originally proposed was no longer economic, and one of the promoters, B O A C, pulled out. But on that site others were prepared to back a luxury hotel with even higher tariffs, confident that it would be filled.

In other cases where little or no demolition was involved—or at any rate permission was not required to demolish—it was often possible for a developer to make some show of preparing the ground by spending a few thousand pounds on building what were, or at least passed for, foundation works. The risk that these would be rendered useless was one worth taking when this preserved the claim for £1,000 a time on, say, 150 bedrooms. The company in the Avon Gorge case, Grand Hotels (Bristol), adopted this expedient, and whatever one thought of the merits or demerits of the hotel scheme itself, it is difficult to criticise them for seeking to preserve their claim to the grant.

The source of many of the big, set-piece inquiries, mentioned under heading (b) at the start of this chapter, is local authority development plans and structure plans. It is now necessary to distinguish between these two, because the old-style detailed development plan prescribed by the 1947 Town and Country Planning Act and showing a zoning on a map for every bit of land in the county or county borough concerned, eventually came close to overwhelming the system. The quinquennial reviews required by the Act were, by the late sixties, running as much as four or five years behind. Though this did not in practice prevent decisions from being taken, departures from the existing plans had to be submitted to the minister, and this in turn added to the bottleneck on reviews.

The structure plan prescribed by the 1968 Town and Country Planning Act and now superseding the detailed development plan is 'a totally different animal'. To begin with, there is no legal requirement that it should contain a land-use map or indeed any map (which is what most people still think of when they hear references to a city or county 'plan'). In fact, it generally does have maps, but its main and essential document is a written statement of policy about broad land use and planning strategy. Its more detailed content is provided for in local plans, drawn up by the planning authority which itself, where necessary, holds an inquiry into them. Some words of the Department of the Environment's chief planner, Dr Wilfred Burns, used at the 1971 Royal Town Planning Institute Conference in Edinburgh about the whole range of plans up to regional and national, explain very clearly the intention and spirit of the structure plan. 'What is a plan?' he asked. 'I can perhaps convey my view if I say what it is not. It is not a once-for-all target for a particular year showing how each piece of land will be used, . . . (it is) a statement of social, economic and physical objectives and policies related to appropriate time scales and levels of investment . . . which must be kept under continuous review. . . .'

So planning runs the whole wide gamut from the individual proposal to build a bungalow in a back garden, through controversial housing estate proposals in green belt land and town centre redevelopments, to structure plans for large cities and counties, regional planning frameworks like Dr Burns's own team's 'Strategy for the South-east', and truly national questions like the siting of a major airport, and whether and how much development should be allowed in National Parks and on what terms. In all these it is conceded that the public, as distinct from their elected political representatives, should have a voice. But public participation obviously means very different things when applied to a bungalow in your neighbour's back garden and a structure plan for London which it takes two years to hold an inquiry into.

*Chapter Fourteen*

# PARTICIPATION

The word 'participation' conjures up oddly in some people's minds visions of up-ended pavingstones and left-wing students fighting helmeted police with water-cannons. More reasonably, in the specifically planning and environment context, they are apt to think of long-haired, untidy architectural students with 'Stuff the Covent Garden Plan' badges doing a demo in the market piazza for the apparent benefit of the television cameras. In reality, of course, this kind of happening is a protest against the real or imagined *lack* of participation. It demonstrates chiefly lack of communication or understanding on one side or both. It is in some measure an expression of failure in effective public participation, just as the fact of a long and bitterly contested public inquiry may be an expression of failure in the consultative and persuasive arts of the planner.

At this stage some of the politicians and officials whose schemes or decisions are under threat may be tempted to fall back on a basically authoritarian response. Theirs is the elected authority; councillors are elected to take decisions for the community; some time the talking has to stop; delay is costing the ratepayer money; if this or that scheme is thwarted, the alternative will be that nothing will get done. In all these arguments there is a grain of truth, but all suggest in certain circumstances that the public has been brought into the decision-making process too little and too late.

Why should elected bodies do more than debate proposals in the council chamber, looking out for reaction in the post and the papers? Why do the 'normal processes of democracy' need supplementing in this special way in the planning field? There are a number of answers to these questions—some answers of principle, others very practical ones. Perhaps the weightiest is that the physical planning process concerns us all in a very thorough-going and permanent way: it can affect the look and feel of the surroundings of each one of us and whether they work well

267

for us, very profoundly for generations ahead. Would this road cut across the daily route to shops or schools? Would that shopping centre be convenient and pleasant and able to offer competitive prices?—these are the sort of questions in which we ought as citizens to have a direct say.

Why direct? Because of the nature of the political process in most local government areas. If all councillors—or even a sizeable proportion of them—were elected on an environmental ticket after election campaigns in which planning questions played a prominent part, there might be less need for 'participation'. But for the most part they are not. In so far as local elections are decided on genuinely local issues—and their results often seem to be rather an expression of satisfaction or dissatisfaction with the government in power nationally—, even quite important planning and environmental issues rarely become major election issues. Though they have a broader impact on more people's lives, sharper political issues, often with a party edge, are more likely to affect how people vote. Environment may gain from not having in general been a party political issue, but in this respect it loses out: election time is not usually the best time to focus attention and exert pressure in planning matters.

I would mention two other linked reasons for special public participation machinery in planning. The environmentally aware view tends to be one which is ahead of public opinion and ahead of council chamber opinion—but which does become accepted later. Second, on a crudely practical level, belated awareness of what is proposed can cause more trouble from a public opinion which thinks it has been misled or kept in the dark, than explaining, listening and modifying earlier on. The explosion of wrath from a public which thinks it has been duped, and the often quite skilful and resourceful campaign of opposition it may put up in the Press and at the public inquiry which then becomes necessary, is a price less and less worth paying to avoid the initial trouble, time and expense of early, adequate, public consultation.

The spearhead of public participation has been, and increasingly will be, the amenity societies. Broadly there are two groups of these: the national bodies, such as the Society for the Protection of Ancient Buildings, the Georgian

Group, the Victorian Society and the Civic Trust. These four organisations have formed themselves into a joint committee to enable them to mobilise resources more efficiently and to make better use of their networks of local activists, who draw to their attention any threats to good environment which emerge in particular places. The S P A B, Georgians and Victorians are basically preservationist bodies, but they are selective as to the grounds on which they fight. Their double test seems to be broadly (1) Is this a building so special that it ought anyway to be saved? If not, (2) is the case for demolition and redevelopment really so strong in social or economic terms that no conservationist alternative can be put.

The Civic Trust is in purpose and constitution very different from the other three. Founded by its president, Duncan Sandys, M P, in 1957, it has no individual membership. Unlike the principal rural conservation organisation, the Council for the Protection of Rural England, it has no political structure by which branches control and elect the central body. The Civic Trust is an independent agency. Some 800 local amenity societies are registered with it, use its services for information and advice and feed information to it. But the Trust is independent of these societies, and they of it. And in a curious way I think this produces a more informal, less inhibited relationship than can exist where the central body and the local ones feel committed to and responsible for each other's policies. With its conferences to focus attention on current problems (derelict land, conservation and so on), its annual awards for good developments, its facelift schemes for drab streets (now several hundred) and its reports and publications, the Trust has been a great lever to improvement of our surroundings and creation of public interest and awareness of their importance. The Trust has four associate bodies in Scotland, Wales, the North-west and the North-east. The C P R E, which has a structure of county branches, has separate sister bodies in Wales and Scotland.

Another national voluntary body which demands mention is the Council for British Archaeology, which in 1966 listed 324 historic towns in Britain. Its short list of the fifty-one best—'so splendid and precious' that they should ultimately be regarded as a national responsibility—has itself had a considerable effect in persuading local councils to respect them, central government to build by-passes round them and give grants for buildings in them, and property owners and prospective property owners to buy, cherish and maintain them.

Also more in the spearhead of participation of late have been several professional bodies—notably the Royal Institute of British Architects and the Royal Town Planning Institute. On big issues like the third London airport these and other professional bodies climbed down off their dignified fences and lobbied ministers and harangued the Press. A logical extension of that lobbying was the formation of a Presidents' Committee of the land-based professional institutions to put their case on major environmental issues. Decentralisation of the R I B A, with a stronger regional structure recently introduced, and a weakening of the assumption that architects should be artists rather than political animals, are also strengthening this sense of involvement. A major contribution to the G L D P inquiry came from the R I B A London Region, which argued a broad policy case not only against the G L C motorways strategy but at odds with another major objector, the Town and Country Planning Association, in that, unlike the T C P A, it thought massive dispersal of population from London a recipe for bad, not good environment.

Then there are the local societies, of which the majority are affiliated to the Civic Trust, and of which altogether there must be well over 1,000. They range from (non-political) ward residents' associations concerned with no more than a neighbourhood of a few hundred households to large civic societies of several thousand members with M Ps, bishops and university professors spread portentously over their letterheads. Their purposes can vary from simply joining together to fight a specific threat—building on a nearby green belt or a road plan which severs the community—to well-rounded, intelligent and long-standing concern with good environment, including positive encouragement of good and sympathetic new architecture. The motto—'Cherish the past, adorn the present, and create for the future'—of one Civic Trust affiliated society (Faversham) is probably fairly representative of the approach of most of them. The majority exist to promote ideas and influence the action of others—some actually take tangible action, like planting trees or even restoring an old building which otherwise seems unlikely to survive. One example of this was the Faversham Society's action in painstakingly restoring an old gunpowder mill (here conservation and industrial archaeology merge) to the point of having the mill wheels turning—though with sawdust between them, not saltpetre.

This sort of activity is more often, however, carried out by local historic buildings trusts with that as their prime purpose. There are good legal, economic and political reasons for separating the argument from the bricks and mortar—though indeed there are cases where historic buildings trusts and civic societies run almost in double harness. The number and variety of amenity societies grows steadily and seems certain to continue growing. They are bound to remain the spearhead of public participation—if only because where a grievance exists and battle is joined, the objecting or disgruntled citizens are likely to form one. But it is wise to remember that, though at best they express the enlightened concern of their communities, they represent only their memberships, or sometimes only the active part of their memberships. They have their vested interests, their prejudices—which may run counter to the eventual direction of public opinion in the area. So public participation cannot be concerned just with organised groups. There must be a place in it for the individual non-joining citizen—and in many areas, if it is to be a meaningful exercise, the planners must go out and find out what their public want. Participation is a flower that grows well in some soils—middle-class suburbs or small country towns, for instance—but needs careful tending and feeding in others.

The unhappy fact that many planning authorities, far from going out of their way to encourage the uninfluential and inarticulate to understand what was intended and comment on it, were limiting consultation to the briefest public discussion of decisions already arrived at, was the main reason for the setting up in March 1968 of the Skeffington Committee on public participation in planning. Its report, in 1969, suggested forty practical ways in which participation could be increased and made more meaningful. But Skeffington consisted of recommendations which planning authorities are under no legal duty to carry out. They must under the 1968 Town and Country Planning Act give an opportunity for the public to comment on their development plans. But the way in which they do it, and whether they honour the spirit of Skeffington in matters outside development plans, is up to them.

## Bases of effective participation

Basic to meaningful public participation, it seems to me, are two essentials: (1) that it should be early enough in the planning process for the public to feel that there is a real chance of major changes if they are shown to be needed: that the council has not already made up its mind and is not just going through the motions of consultation; and (2) that the choice is a real one, not just 'Take it or leave it'. Indeed, wherever possible, draft proposals should give a reasonable number of options—though here the realist acknowledges that these will usually have to be kept fairly simple if a clear picture is to be presented which the lay public can hope to understand.

That is a broad strategy for public participation. The tactics will vary in their mix according to circumstances. Newspaper, radio and television coverage all help—at lowest by alerting individuals to the fact that changes are afoot; at best by explaining, with maps, drawings, fact and balanced debate and comment, what is proposed and what objections, if any, are being raised to it. Basic to a number of the Skeffington Committee's points was the realisation that town halls are alien territory to most citizens. If you really want to know what they think, go out and ask them. Planning exhibitions with models of city centre redevelopment are fine, but better not in town halls—rather in premises which people pass, say, in the shopping centre and which they do not associate with 'them at the council'.

The G L C, who should (and generally do) know better, made this mistake when they mounted a very clear exhibition on the G L D P. I went as a private citizen to look at it, and in the main County Hall foyer found an attractively displayed trailer with blue arrows pointing to 'Room 183' out into a corridor. Once in that corridor, the arrows falteringly pointed to a stairway and then the citizen in pursuit

of participation was confronted (if he guessed, or knew as
I did, that 183 was on the first floor) with closed glass
doors leading to what at County Hall used to be known as
'the Principal Floor'—a high-ceilinged, dark panelled place
full of imposing, closed doors with names like Chairman of
Establishments, Director of Highways, Majority Party Whips
and so on. Nine out of ten brave citizens would at that
point, I think, conclude they had lost their way—this corridor could not be intended for the humble likes of them—
and retire baffled. In fact, you were expected to follow it
past a dozen formidable doors until you hit one marked
G L D P exhibition, and go in. Here was the exhibition, and
a helpful council official who asked you after you had
looked round whether there was any extra information you
wanted, or any questions he could answer. But how many
got that far? In fact the G L C sent other similar displays
out into the boroughs. But as far as that County Hall exhibition was concerned, it was not an effective contribution
to public participation at all.

There are other circumstances in which the operation by
the planning authority of its planning powers affect a property owner or prospective property owner and he ought
to be told what is proposed—but sometimes is not. Let me
instance two examples: there have been cases in which
a prospective house purchaser has asked the planning authority if it knew of any intended development affecting the
property—a stock part of the 'search' carried out by an
intending buyer or his solicitors—and the planning authority
has said no. It has later transpired that everybody in the
planning department knew a road was planned to cut
through the back garden of the house. But the council's
answer to complaints that the answer was misleading has
been: 'We had no official knowledge of this. Therefore we
could not reply otherwise than we did.' Probably the
majority of authorities generally give sensible advice, although it is noticeable that solicitors acting for vendors
often suggest that they should visit a town or county hall
themselves and make informal inquiries to supplement the
official check.

A second circumstance in which information is not
always available as it should be occurs when the planning
authority gets an application for redevelopment affecting

nearby properties. It is the practice to write to owners and householders of neighbouring properties and invite their comment. Most authorities act by the spirit of this, but council timetables are such that the time allowed for comment is sometimes very short, and worryingly even a three-week absence on holiday can mean that a householder returns to find that the suggested deadline on comments has already run out. The manner in which requests for comment are invited also seems to be often a hit-or-miss business. Sometimes it is simply a notice pinned outside premises where neighbours might be expected to—but do not always—read it. Letters are sometimes sent to long-since departed occupiers—though there should not be too much difficulty for a local authority in tracing ratepayers—and sometimes to one householder and not to his neighbour. In areas of fluctuating multi-occupation, there are difficulties —though they do not always produce so bizarre a response as that received from the city planning officer by a Bristol barrister, Mr Paul Chadd.

Mr Chadd, who had done battle for local amenity groups against Bristol Corporation both at the public inquiry over the case of the Avon Gorge hotel project and in House of Lords committee in an effort to keep navigation rights for other craft when the city's dock system is closed to commercial traffic, owned a large Victorian house in Clifton. It was converted into flats—two of which were vacant. There were three bell-pushes, one marked Chadd, and, rather than leave the two others unnamed, he marked them flippantly 'Dr Jekyll' and 'Mr Hyde'. Then in the autumn of 1970 the Bristol city planning office sent letters to Dr Jekyll and Mr Hyde asking them for any comments on the proposed extension to a school next door (to provide a recreation room and a small laboratory). Paul Chadd found the Jekyll and Hyde letters on his doormat, but no letter addressed to him.

His solicitor, who also has a nice sense of humour, replied for him, commenting on the 'exquisite feeling for public participation in the planning of Bristol' shown by the city planning officer. 'Only this, my client feels, could have led you to sign two letters dated 1st October, one to Dr Jekyll and the other to Mr Hyde. We understand that neither of these gentlemen is likely to raise any objection to the school's proposals—indeed, to the first-mentioned a laboratory would be most welcome.' There was a formal post-card of acknowledgement.

The Avon Gorge hotel affair was an example of how not to provide for meaningful public participation in a decision of great moment both to the citizens of Bristol and a far wider public. The city council received a planning application for a 126-bedroom hotel with car parking to be built in a massive structure on the side of the Gorge very near the Clifton suspension bridge. The planning committee gave it prompt outline planning permission, arguing that the developer would lose the benefit of grants under the Development of Tourism Act if they did not, despite a quite massive wave of protest from amenity groups and individuals—who, in default of any proper models or elevations being made available, produced their own spine-chilling impressions of what the structure would do to the romantic landscape of the Gorge—plainly intended to approve the plans in detail with quite indecent haste in the minimum time feasible. At that stage the minister, very properly, called the case in for inquiry.*

At the same time, there must be limits to the participation process. Its purpose is, after all, to help the authorities responsible for taking a decision—the local authority and, in seriously contested cases, the minister and/or his officials —(a) to understand all the facts and circumstances and (b) to be aware of what the public, or groups and individuals from among the public, think, and how different interests stand to lose or gain. It is not its purpose to be a vehicle for filibuster or delay, nor a clinging dead-weight on all development, good or bad, which any group of citizens opposes.

There must be a guillotine, a cut-off to discussion, and the need for thorough ventilation of all factors and viewpoints has to be balanced against the crucial consideration that time does not stand still. The most thorough study, the most diligent and resourceful participation exercise, is useless if the planning decision process goes on so long that events have left it behind. An imperfect plan, which has been based on and moulded by a reasonable amount of public discussion and involvement, is infinitely better than the painstakingly perfected one which is never implemented

* He later refused planning permission.

because it is out-of-date. That is why participation cannot be open-ended. The reality is that the opposers of any plan will usually see delay as an ally, its promoters be aware that it is their enemy. A balance has to be struck, and it will not please everyone.

## The lesson of Covent Garden

The GLC's Covent Garden Plan was one which in 1970 and 1971 developed into almost a *cause célèbre* of participation. Though in conservationist and people-versus-roads terms, it could certainly be regarded as a test-case, the participation issue was in my view very much less clear-cut than some have tried to argue. The Covent Garden team's first plan was put out for public discussion in 1963, and by the public participation standards of the early sixties they were doing pretty well. There was an exhibition in premises in the plan area, and the project team made themselves accessible to affected parties in a very informal way in their offices in the Strand within easy reach of the area. They did not go out and canvass opinion—carry participation-seeking into the offensive, as it were—but that was not expected at that time. They had by the standards of the time a fair participatory response, but later it became clear that many of the smaller property-owners and householders had either not sought information, or not been given as clear or full replies as they might have expected, or not understood what was going on. This is a constant dilemma of planners. When the plans are at a fluid stage, public interest is often not focused on them. It is only when decisions are hardening and the plans becoming a reality that people begin to understand and object. And this is the strongest argument for Skeffington-style active participation seeking, especially in areas where no organised community or amenity body exists.

The reality of the Covent Garden story seems to me to have been this. The GLC did its consulting duty tolerably well by pre-Skeffington standards, and then just when it needed to start tying things up—with time's winged chariot in the shape of the actual market moving to Nine Elms galloping away at its back—got clobbered with post-

Skeffington standards of public participation imported to the aid of disgruntled residents by two or three planners plus a group of young outsiders whose capacity for riling the politicians frequently exceeded their talent for persuasive argument. The two did not talk the same language. The official planners were talking about Covent Garden redevelopment carried out so as to do as little violence to existing social and commercial interests and environmental capital as possible. The so-called 'Covent Garden Community' regarded the protection of these existing interests as paramount, and basically challenged the whole concept of large-scale redevelopment. Even with the best public participation in the world, these two views could never have been reconciled.

This situation suggests one of the basic dilemmas of planning with public involvement: that local opposition to proposed change obscures, and sometimes defeats, the wider community benefit. The way in which local opposition to homes for the mentally handicapped has made it difficult to find locations for them has become a scandal. They are needed—everyone recognises that—but no one wants them nearby.

There is an element of this in the Covent Garden situation. It is arguable that any central area redevelopment with hotels, conference and entertainment facilities and office space is likely to run counter to the interests and wishes of many people in the existing community—especially if they are paying low rents on stub-end leases. But if such a redeveloped area is judged necessary—leaving aside in this particular case whether it might not have been better sited on the South Bank—then the wishes of the present inhabitants will to some extent have to be overridden. Participation can then usefully be directed towards achieving the redevelopment end with the least damage to community, property and environment, and the most constructive, acceptable deal for those disturbed. The danger of a late and luxuriant flowering of active public participation such as occurred at Covent Garden is that the very notion of participation will be oversold. Presented as a panacea to all manner of discontents and fears, it may unhappily become discredited because the usefulness of its true function—to ensure that the planners know what people think of the plans and can suggest changes—is lost sight of.

The Covent Garden affair also illustrates how, the later real participation begins to work, the less fruitful it is. Attitudes harden; the official planners and the participators find they are talking different languages (in Bristol, the amenity groups came unhappily to the conclusion that their road-orientated planners did not really understand the language of conservation at all); and relations may even erupt, as in Edinburgh, into something like open war, with stalwarts like Sir Compton Mackenzie sitting down in front of corporation workmen who came to spread tarmac over the cobbles of the Georgian new town.

Civic societies should be brought into the picture early, but they have to be vigilant to see that they are and that nothing is glossed over which may later prove controversial. Councils should employ community development officers to go into those neighbourhoods where organised amenity groups do not easily flourish, and explain, listen and discuss. Here as elsewhere the best kind of community involvement will often be at a practical level: deciding how the eventual overall plan should be implemented; whether these terraces can be rehabilitated and what mix of new accommodation they can best be converted into; which roads should be blocked to cut out through traffic; whether local school children might be made guardians of newly planted trees— with street groups of residents active in what directly and practically concerns them.

Yet, with this plea for earlier, better and more detailed public involvement made, one is pushed back to the acceptance that in many cases there will be disagreement between local groups and the official planners, and a fight at a public inquiry. And this always presents acute problems of resources. An intelligent man can argue his own case against a modest or even medium-sized development which affects him, but even the strong and enterprising amenity society may find its resources in money, time and skill taxed by a development plan inquiry or the struggle to argue that a motorway should follow a different route from that proposed by the ministry's regional Road Construction Unit.

It is a David and Goliath confrontation, and to adduce the rare case where David has felled his opponent with a pebble pitched at just the right vulnerable point in his armour is not the same as saying no steps can or should be taken to make the struggle more equal. Even such national bodies as the C P R E and the joint committee of Georgians, Victorians, S P A B and Civic Trust have stated publicly and warned privately that they have no funds for further battles, and may fail to appear in test cases where major points of principle for the environment, and of some public importance fall to be decided. Surely, therefore, something needs to be done to redress the unequal balance in these contests. If it is not, then an important sanction which helps to keep public participation meaningful will have been eroded, and amenity bodies representing increasingly important sections of public opinion will often be reduced to the status of camp followers in those cases where either a dissident district council or neighbouring county or the big private objector carries the main burden of the battle. Had not the G L C's Historic Buildings Board marshalled the technical resources and forensic fire-power of County Hall at the Whitehall inquiry, then the picture would have looked very different. Though the Joint Committee briefed counsel and produced a splendid array of celebrated witnesses, it was Mr Harold Marnham, Q C, for the G L C, marshalling technical cases both for preservation and against the proposition that no viable use of Scotland Yard was possible, who made the biggest holes in the M P B W's defences.

## Participation and the future

So what answer is there to these disparities in strength between public—and particularly central government—development and the cause of amenity? I would put forward two suggestions. The first is that central government, which some years ago abolished most of the attributes of the old legal principle 'the Crown can do no wrong', should take steps to sweep away the last vestiges of Crown privilege embodied in the doctrine of Circular 100. In theory this document recommends government departments and public undertakings to submit themselves to consultation with local authorities in whose areas they plan developments even where in law they need no planning permission. In practice there is all too often a large element of double talk about this.

Even where the consultation is thorough and carried out at a stage where plans are still fluid, the planning authority often feels that there is no point in objecting too strongly since the state agency concerned has no obligation to act on its suggestions or objections. The post office, at least when it was still a department of state, built its towers in town centres sometimes in utter disregard of the town and county planners' views. And whereas a city or borough has sometimes persuaded a private developer wanting to put up a tall office block to 'do a swap' for a council-owned site in a position less damaging to the townscape, the M P B W rarely proved susceptible to such pressures. The local planners had no sanction, no lever to exert. The state, in the view of many conservationists, got away with murder.

Yet since the Secretary of State for the Environment now has the ultimate say, there is no compelling reason of political theory why his agents should not be subject to local authority planning permissions like every other developer. If dissatisfied, it should be possible for the minions of the minister to appeal and go to public inquiry. Of course, in a sense, he would still be judge and jury in his own cause. Yet in reality he would be taking an informed and considered final decision after an inspector had weighed up the publicly debated pros and cons and made a recommendation. This seems to me to be vastly preferable to a decision 'fixed' privately within the D O E or between Whitehall departments on the balance of state or civil service convenience rather than overall public advantage. I can think of three objections which will be advanced. Objection (1) is that it is politically unacceptable for the Secretary for the Environment to have the final say over developments sponsored by ministerial colleagues from other departments. There are surely ways round this. Precedents exist for the joint reference by two or more ministers to a public inquiry. There could be joint appointment of an inspector, and perhaps involvement of the developing department with the D O E in consideration of his report. And under such a system, as now in cases of other major clashes between departments, the Cabinet would sometimes be the final arbiter. But then, as we have seen, planning decisions are ultimately political decisions anyway, and properly so.

Objection (2) is that the DOE as an integrated department exists to take decisions on an overall view, and that the balancing and adjustment of competing factors and influences will have been done before a development project is ever put forward by the department. It must, by its very nature, try to set a good environmental example, and its development proposals will now increasingly reflect this. There would be no advantage, runs this argument, in superimposing on top of this process of adjustment of conflicting factors another process with the same purpose though using different means. This is an argument I reject, for two reasons. First, because unless what the public thinks about a state development is really crystallised by the planning permission/public consultation system with the ultimate sanction of refusal and public inquiry, the ministry adjudication is to some extent a private Whitehall affair, with only muted strains of public opinion getting through. Second, because the government should set the best possible example to local planning authorities in this business of submitting oneself to public scrutiny and argument, by going through all the hoops like any other developer. The DOE at least would quickly learn to do so with consummate grace.

Objection (3) is a down-to-earth practical one, and to my mind the most serious. It is that making government department developers subject to ordinary planning permission and trial by inquiry would throw a huge work load on the DOE which it could not without disruption carry. There are two answers to that. One is that it may nonetheless be judged a price worth paying; and the other that the change could be accomplished bit by bit to ease the strain.*

* Peter Walker went a very long way towards meeting this point when he issued a new circular, No 80 in November 1971 which requires government departments to submit all major developments and alterations to listed buildings to the scrutiny of local authorities, with the possibility of public inquiry in cases of disagreement. It remains to be seen, however, to what extent this will strengthen the hand of the local authorities against Whitehall in cases of what they regard as bad development.

My second suggestion to equalise the contest, and to answer the lack of cash and expertise available to objectors, is to provide a Sir Galahad organisation which will come to their rescue in cases where their cause is most worthy and their resources most hard-pressed. This would in no sense be an Ombudsman figure—the legal and administrative machine provides a whole array of opportunities for appeal against planning decisions. (It is indeed arguable that they should be fewer and better, but there seems little to be gained by adding another and further balkanising the province of the Ombudsman, one of whose great assets in Scandinavian countries is that the one official covers the whole range of public activities.) Rather would it be an independent official or organisation with funds and some technical resources which would be able to say: 'Here is a planning issue which, whatever the right ultimate answer, ought to be argued at the public inquiry. You, the local civic society (say) have raised it with us. We think it needs more thorough study and research. We will help you to pay for planning consultants, lawyers, expert witnesses so that the other side of the question can be adequately put.' Such support would not imply commitment to the case supported, but simply that there was, as the lawyers put it, 'a case to answer'.

What kind of a body would it be, this Council for Planning Aid? I see it as complementary to the existing Centre for Environmental Studies, which finances research into a whole spectrum of environmental matters. The C E S draws its funds in roughly equal proportions from government and from firms and charitable foundations. This gives it a measure of financial independence to give substance to the independence which its constitution affords in principle. The C P A might be able also to tap the local authority associations.

Cynics may say: 'You've a hope. Do you think government and local councils would really cut their throat like that by financing opposition to their plans so as to further impede decision making.' I think they could—and it is essential that they should. Law courts as representatives of the community give the accused in a serious criminal case legal aid to defend himself. A planning decision these days can sometimes have a greater effect on the life of an individual than a prison sentence—and certainly on an individual as a member of a community. We should therefore give communities and groups of individuals at least a chance of receiving planning aid to oppose authority's proposals that this or that should be changed in their environment. The argument that it would be too costly and create too much extra work for officials can be answered in two ways. First, there might be an apparent increase in the workload, but the whole participation concept causes extra work and expense. Its justification is that the quality of decision should be better if those making them are better informed, and that the easing of friction will perhaps also ease the workload elsewhere. The second answer is, quite simply, that if we are a democracy, the extra cost in money, time and trouble is worth it, in order to let people have their say.

These arguments are both good for public participation in general, and for some effective means of providing planning aid. I hope and believe that Peter Walker and the Department of the Environment will be 'big' enough to accept them.

# FURTHER READING

John Barr (ed.), *The Environmental Handbook: Action Guide for the UK*, Ballantine/Friends of the Earth, 1971.
Rather frenetic in tone but a useful reference work.

Gordon Cullen, *The Concise Townscape*, Architectural Press, 1971.
This gets to the heart of the visual environment.

Sir Frank Fraser Darling, *Wilderness and Plenty*, Ballantine/Friends of the Earth, 1970.
Fraser Darling's classic 1969 Reith lectures.

Peter Greffwell, *Environment: An Alphabetical Handbook*, John Murray, 1971.
The best factual reference book on environment in Britain.

Judy Hillman (ed.), *Planning for London*, Penguin, 1971.

John Liley, *Journey of the Swan*, Allen and Unwin, 1971.
A canal enthusiast's fighting plea for the British inland waterways.

Kenneth Mellanby, *Pesticides and Pollution*, Fontana, 1969.

Ben Whitaker and Kenneth Browne, *Parks for People*, Seeley Service and Co., 1971.
A humane plea for space for people to walk and sit.

# INDEX